Loving Olivia

Why is Liz Astor's story such compelling reading? Is it the human-interest factor: that she has dared to bare her soul by describing her family life in graphic detail? Is it the story of shock, and the struggle to cope, following the discovery of her daughter's autism? Is it the remarkable energy of a mother who has left no stone unturned in her search to find the best help for her daughter? Is it the extraordinary altruism of a woman who will climb Mount Kilimanjaro to fundraise for autism? I think it is all of these, and more.

Liz writes about her family's journey with an exact memory for events, names and places: from the day she remarried, through to becoming pregnant with Olivia, to the slow realisation that Olivia's autism was going to need her life-long support. Along the way she has had to face the fact that other relatives in her family may have had undiagnosed Asperger Syndrome. The book reads like a diary of self-education. As we turn each page, we can't help but empathise with her hopes and disappointments, lurching from offers of help from professionals, to the crises, such as the terror and despair of her child going missing.

The drama of the Astor family is one that parents of children like Olivia will readily identify with. Readers with no prior knowledge of autism will find it gripping, at times heart-breaking, yet written with an unquenchable spirit of overcoming every challenge.

Simon Baron-Cohen
Professor of Developmental Psychopathology and
Director of the Autism Research Centre, Cambridge

Liz Astor is one of the most driven, determined, and caring people I know. She devotes much of her incredible energy to campaigning for children whom life has dealt a cruel hand. This is the story of how she helped one of those children – her own daughter; learning as much as she could about her autism, and focusing on giving her a future by helping her to learn and develop. It is a book glowing with hope – hope and support for other parents as they grapple with the world of the autistic child. And, above all, hope for the children themselves.

Peter Sissons
Broadcaster and Presenter, BBC News 24

Loving Olivia

Bringing Up My Autistic Daughter

Liz Astor

RODALE

This edition first published in the UK in 2006 by
Rodale International Ltd
7–10 Chandos Street
London W1G 9AD
www.rodalebooks.co.uk

Printed and bound in the UK by CPI Bath using acid-free paper from sustainable sources.

1 3 5 7 9 8 6 4 2

A CIP record for this book is available from the British Library

ISBN-10: 1-4050-8815-X
ISBN-13: 978-1-4050-8815-2

This paperback edition distributed to the book trade by Pan Macmillan Ltd

Notice
The advice in this book is intended as a guide only. It may not be suitable in all situations or for all individuals. It is not intended as a substitute for professional medical, legal or other advice. Neither the author nor publisher shall be liable for any loss or injury arising as a result of information in this book.

Mention of specific companies, organisations or authorities in this book does not imply endorsement by the publisher, nor does mention of specific companies, organisations or authorities in the book imply that they endorse the book.

Websites and telephone numbers given in this book were accurate at the time the book went to press.

For my two beautiful daughters,
Natalya and Olivia, who have taken me
far from the beaten track and opened my eyes.
And for my beloved husband Johnnie, my rock,
who has supported me all the way.

Acknowledgements

My heart-felt thanks and deep gratitude naturally must go first to my very loving and supportive family. And then to Kay McCauley, my dynamic agent, without whom this book would never have been written, and to my dear friend Jane Posen, who was the first person to suggest that I write Olivia's story. Thanks also to Dr Lorna Wing, Dr Judith Gould and Dr Sue Shepherd, for their expertise, guidance and friendship, and also (in no order of preference) Gay Schoene, Olivia Howard-Collings, Jane May, Judy Mowschenson, Vikie le Sache, Dorothy Josem, Claire Roberts, Lance West, Françoise Percy-Davis, Mavy Burden, Denise Seely, Vanessa Boutefeu, Henrietta Spink, Clare Driver and Jacqui Ashton Smith for their love and support. Thanks also to my sensitive editor, Carol Franklin, and my PA, Gill Willis, for her endless patience and good humour. To Anne Lawrance and everyone at Rodale UK, Phil Barnett and all the staff at Broomhill Bank School, all Olivia's past nannies and helpers and my personal trainers, Sonya Clark, Samantha Lucas and Georgina Hollings, for getting me strong and fit. And to the NAS press and fundraising teams, past and present, and all those, too numerous to name here, who work so hard to raise funds for, and awareness of, autism and ADHD and work with these people. Finally, to all those who have joined me on a fundraising trek, with fond memories of a great time!

If you would like to make a donation to either the National Autistic Society (NAS) or The National Attention Deficit Disorder Information and Support Service (ADDISS), you will find their contact details in the *Useful Addresses* section, pages 239–242. You can also make donations to the NAS online at *www.nas.org.uk*.

Contents

Foreword

by Lorna Wing

This book tells what it is like to have your life shifted into a different and totally unexpected direction by the birth of a child with autism. Having personal as well as professional experience in the field of autistic spectrum disorders, I know that all parents in the same situation will recognise and empathise with Liz Astor's account of the childhood of her daughter, Olivia. Readers who have not had any personal experience will find the story deeply interesting and moving.

Olivia was born into an aristocratic family – but children and adults with autism are the same the world over regardless of ethnicity, creed, culture or class. They are alike because they all have the 'triad' of impairments of social interaction, social communication and social imagination linked to a narrow, repetitive pattern of activities and special interests. Their lack of an inbuilt social instinct makes them indifferent to the social pressures of their culture. Nevertheless, each is a unique individual. This is partly because they each have their own special personality but also because the triad can be and often is accompanied by other developmental, or physical, or psychological conditions. Any mixture of such conditions can occur, leading to a range of almost infinitely variable patterns. The level of ability can vary from severe learning disability to very high intelligence, though the profile on psychological tests is in most cases patchy, with highs in some areas and lows in others. Because the clinical pictures can vary so widely, and many do not fit the picture of typical classic autism, the term 'autistic spectrum disorder' is used to refer to the whole range.

Olivia is certainly a strong personality in her own right. She has her own special pattern of skills and disabilities comprising good expressive speech, with good grammar and a large vocabulary, but combined with poor, very literal comprehension. Because of her lack of interest in and understanding of other people's feelings, in social situations she can speak clearly but with alarming and embarrassing frankness. She has poor ability to organise complex movements so, despite being able to read surprisingly well, she has major problems with handwriting. In addition, she needs a lot of help with self-care. Unlike some children with autism, she has little or no ability in working with numbers. Like many, she is over-sensitive to sound and has some odd movements. Liz describes vividly the host of everyday problems that flow from this particular combination of high and low abilities.

Liz also writes about Natalya, her first daughter, who has Attention Deficit Hyperactivity Disorder (ADHD). After nearly five years of denial that anything could be wrong with Olivia, her second daughter, Liz accepted and faced with indomitable courage, determination and humour the challenge of being the mother of three children, one with autism and one with ADHD, and three stepchildren each with their own personalities and needs.

In addition, she has had to fight every step of the way to obtain the type of special education Olivia requires. Other parents of children with autism will certainly understand this battle. It is difficult for people who have no personal experience of autistic spectrum disorders to realise that children with these conditions are not simply delayed in their development. They have their own idiosyncratic view of the world that is very different from that of other children. In order to educate children with autistic disorders, teachers have to have wide experience of the autistic spectrum and a deep understanding of each individual child. But it is not only in lessons in the classroom that this understanding is essential. The environment of the school outside the classrooms, and most especially the playground and playtime, has to be organised appropriately. If not, a school that does not specialise in teaching children with autistic disorders can be a nightmare for such children, even if they are doing well in formal lessons. Education authorities tend not to understand, as Liz found out from her personal experience.

Yet another maze of doubt and confusion into which parents can be drawn is the ever-increasing list of methods claimed by their proponents to be cures or at least to dramatically improve autistic conditions. When she first accepted Olivia's diagnosis, Liz investigated some of these. Her clear-eyed, objective descriptions and discussions of the various methods she looked at should be read by all parents of young children with autistic spectrum disorders.

What is truly amazing is that Liz, given all that life demands of her, has found the energy to work for charities for autism and ADHD. She has organised and led highly successful fundraising expeditions to climb Mount Kilimanjaro, and to trek through Inner Mongolia and Peru. She has even run in the London Marathon. Her love for her whole family and the support she receives from them shines through all she writes. The book ends with Olivia in her thirteenth year, still autistic, still with many odd behaviours, but much improved from her early years. Liz knows the future is uncertain but faces it with confidence and her characteristic determination.

Lorna Wing, MD FRCPsych
Psychiatrist and founder member
of the National Autistic Society

Introduction

In February 1997 my youngest daughter, Olivia, who was then aged four and a half, was diagnosed with moderate/severe autism, dyspraxia (impairment of motor function) and a moderate learning disability. Nine years later, I can hardly remember the time when my life was not immersed in the complex and fascinating world of autism.

My story is, in many ways, similar to that of millions of parents and siblings who find themselves with a disabled child, brother or sister. Although Olivia's primary disability is her autism, nearly everything that I have learnt, such as how to interpret and complete the Statement of Special Needs to the long list of treatments, some mainstream, some alternative, is all part of the complicated minefield that parents of special needs children experience. When Olivia was born, I knew absolutely nothing about autism and very little about the world of disability. I was also equally ignorant about Attention Deficit Hyperactivity Disorder (ADHD), the very existence of which is so often denied in our daily press. I didn't even know where to begin to look for help and it was an exhausting process of trial and error just to get started.

What I hoped to achieve, when I set out to write my story, was primarily to hand a road map of disability to parents of newly diagnosed children, wrapped around my particular experiences. My hard ⁀ ⁀d knowledge was too precious not to be shared and I hope tha⁀ it down in a book, it might spread to many others who w⁀ reading my experiences and at least have some pra⁀ as a starting point in learning how to help thei⁀

this in mind, I have included a recommended reading list of books that helped and informed me, a list of useful addresses of where to find certain computer programs or special needs tricycles, for example, and a list of most of the therapists and practitioners to whom I took Olivia for treatment.

I also wanted to share my hopes and dreams, triumphs and failures, joy and despair so that others would know that they are not on their own, as so often I have felt deeply alone and isolated, not knowing where to turn or how to access help and advice.

But above all, I wanted to give my reader comfort, courage and hope. We all put on a brave face to the world, with the admirable, quint-essentially British attitude of 'mustn't grumble' said with a stiff upper lip, while silently carrying a lead weight in our hearts. Too brave a face can sometimes make others wonder if one is a superwoman, who can cope so well that they are left feeling even more depressed and inad-equate. Whatever our backgrounds and abilities we all love, suffer and laugh.

And now, nine years after her diagnosis, I can say with complete hon-esty that I would not have a different Olivia. She has changed my life entirely and through both my daughters it has been greatly enriched. Without Olivia's autism and Natalya's ADHD, I would never have climbed the highest mountain in Africa, run the London Marathon, or walked across the semi-arid desert of Inner Mongolia. I would not have started a programme of exercise that has become an intrinsic part of my daily life, met hundreds of truly remarkable people and been inspired daily by what other people achieve. It has filled me with the desire to live my life as fully as possible. I hope that Loving Olivia will inspire others to climb mountains, fundraise for their special charity and most of all, to celebrate our differences.

Liz Astor
March 2006

CHAPTER 1

And They Lived Happily Ever After

IT WAS 5 MAY 1990. I had celebrated, somewhat chaotically, my 40th birthday the night before and half-way through my life (there's optimism for you!) a miracle had happened. After seven long and lonely years as a divorced mother of one, out at work and having given up the fantasy of living happily ever after, I was to marry the handsome and charming Lord Astor of Hever, Johnnie.

As I walked down the aisle on the arm of my brother, Charles, I felt as if I were in a dream. It had been a whirlwind romance, carried out discreetly over the autumn, with a glorious pre-wedding honeymoon in January, in Barbados. We were getting married in the beautiful Unitarian church in Hampstead by my friend and Minister, David Usher, with the address given by my Unitarian Minister stepfather, Roger Tarbuck, whom I adored. The sun poured in through the stained-glass windows and never have I been more certain in my life than when I said, 'I do'. Johnnie's youngest daughter, Violet, and my daughter, Natalya, were our bridesmaids, in pale pink silk. I wore a Jaques Azagury pale pink silk chiffon skirt and lace top, and carried my favourite tulips, Angelique, amongst my bouquet.

I had always wanted a large family as I loved children, and in marrying Johnnie, I became stepmother to his three lovely daughters. At the time of our wedding Camilla was aged 16, Tania 12 and Violet nine. Natalya, my daughter, was nine months younger than Violet and only just nine at our wedding. Natalya and I had moved into Johnnie's

1

house just three days before the wedding. Every evening, over dinner, his daughters would delight in quizzing me on the members of the extremely extensive Astor family. Questions were flung at me in rapid succession, 'Who is the daughter of?', 'What is the maiden name of?' and so on. Inevitably, I would confuse grandfathers with sons, and babies with aunts, much to the delight and shrieks of laughter from Johnnie's girls. It was a dramatic change from living alone with Natalya, who had been my world, for so long.

In the autumn, our son Charles was born. He was a fine 7 lb 8 oz healthy baby and there was great rejoicing. After his divorce, Johnnie had bought a house in Kent, which needed a complete overhaul, and it was, of course, not ready to move into by the time Charles was born. So we moved into half of it and lived with the banging and drilling for months, until Christmas, when it was just about finished.

Our first Christmas at Frenchstreet House in Westerham was both joyful and chaotic. The Christmas holidays had seemed to be the perfect opportunity to invite everyone we knew locally to both dinner and lunch in our new home, as well as having a first family Christmas with our collective five children, plus giving Christmas lunch to Johnnie's three sisters and their families, his mother and his brother. I was up most of the night feeding baby Charles and had employed a temporary nanny to help look after him during the day and settle him at night, after feeds. On Christmas Day, I had trouble rousing her. By lunchtime she was sobbing loudly in the kitchen. She was exhausted, she said and couldn't carry on. On top of that she had just phoned her alcoholic mother who was completely drunk and in no state to cook the family's Christmas dinner. She decided she had better go home. That night, Charles was introduced to bottles, himself, for the first time.

On New Year's Eve we gave our first formal dinner party. The table looked lovely and although we hadn't yet hung a single picture nor had time to decorate the house with our belongings, the house had a naturally warm and friendly atmosphere. Just before 8 p.m., we lit the fire in the drawing room. It had been a very windy day and within seconds thick smoke billowed out and immediately set off the smoke alarms. We had to open all the windows and the freezing December air quickly chilled the room as our guests began to arrive. In order to keep them warm, we briskly served drinks and took them rather rapidly in to dinner in the warm dining room. It was the first time that we had asked the new couple we had employed to serve at table. Sean was so nervous he held a trembling plate of meat so high that the guests could only guess at what they were trying to put on their plates. As he went round the table, the angle of the serving dish sharpened dramatically and I tried in vain to catch his eye, making frantic hand gestures to him to lower the dish. Gravy trickled into a cleavage. There were profuse apologies and calls for damp cloths.

After dinner we moved back into the drawing room, which was once again warm. I served coffee and was beginning to think that it hadn't gone too badly, after all, when Ella, our black spaniel, rushed into the room and was sick all over the new Persian rug. I shot off to the kitchen for paper towels and made a mistake that I have never repeated. I threw the whole mess into the open fire. The stench that quickly filled the room emptied it of our guests with equal speed. They suddenly had to get home, and with cries of 'Golly, is that really the time?' and 'Thank you for a lovely evening, just remembered, early start and all that', we found ourselves, not much after 10.30 p.m. on New Year's Eve, deserted!

Charles grew into a butterball. He blossomed on bottles of goats' milk and had such chubby legs that we called him 'thunder thighs'. One morning, when he was around six months old, there were cries of 'Lady Astor, come quickly!' I rushed to the nursery passage to find our nanny and housekeeper doubled over with laughter. The cause was baby Charles, who was propped up in a laundry basket with a cushion to support him, in uncontrollable fits of laughter. He was bent over in delight with tears rolling down his divinely plump cheeks. What set him off, we could not imagine, but his laughter was so infectious that we all stood around him and joined in, recreating a scene from Bedlam. When I rang my mother to tell her the story, she told me I had done exactly the same thing, at the same age.

Our first summer at Frenchstreet was hot. We had a large garden of over 11 acres plus 40 acres of woods, which Johnnie had been replanting since the devastating hurricane of 1987 had flattened most of the surrounding area. We lived next to Toys Hill, which was particularly hard hit, and were on the Greensand Way, which produced wonderful beech trees which, because they are shallow rooted, were particularly vulnerable to the strong winds. It was an exciting project, rebuilding a garden that had fallen into neglect. The previous owner had attempted to look after the garden entirely alone, an impossible task, so we had to start almost from scratch. Johnnie had great vision for the bigger picture and I loved plants, so we naturally fell into our preferred roles; he was landscape and I was plants. We dug out a second large pond to complement the existing one and built a hump-backed bridge between the two. We laid York stone paths, planted trees in the valley and created a rose garden. None of this would have been possible without our two wonderful gardeners, Eric Card and Jack Friend. Eric was our head gardener and a great plantsman. His specialities were primulas, fuchsias and pelargoniums. His wife complained that he spent every evening poring through gardening books, and Johnnie and I did the same, as well as visiting many of the wonderful gardens of Kent and Surrey to gain knowledge and ideas.

The following Christmas, I discovered that I was pregnant again. I didn't tell anyone until the early spring. I was so pleased because at nearly 42, I wasn't sure if it would be possible and I wanted a playmate for Charles. When we eventually told the girls, there was a very mixed reaction. Camilla, who was 18, was appalled. 'You can *not* be serious!' she exclaimed. 'That is, … well, it is … *disgusting!*' she spluttered. 'I mean – you're so *old*! And it's *cruel,* too. That poor baby, having such ancient parents! I'll have to be its mother, that's all.'

Tania, Violet and Natalya, who were much younger, were delighted. I excused myself by explaining that Charles needed a sibling closer to him in age. We compromised. If Camilla would allow me to have the baby, I would let her bring it up! She didn't need to, of course, and she has been a wonderful, devoted sister, as have all the girls.

CHAPTER 2

Another Girl!

AT NOT QUITE THREE MONTHS PREGNANT, I went for a check-up with my gynaecologist, Mr Glyn Evans. He had seen me through my pregnancy and delivery with Charles, and had told me, when I mentioned that I wanted another child, that at my age, weeks count. I knew that after the age of 35, fertility dropped at the same alarming rate as the risk of having a disabled child increased. We discussed my having an amniocentesis, which could tell me, with almost 100 per cent accuracy, if my baby had Down's syndrome. As I was nearly 42, the risk of having a Down's baby was high, as age is a major factor. I had had an amniocentesis during my pregnancy with Charles, with no ill effects at all and decided to have one with this pregnancy. We were already blessed with five healthy children between us and I had a very full life, and had decided that if there were something wrong with this pregnancy, I would have a termination.

When I was 12 weeks pregnant I had my amniocentesis, which was done in the morning. It is a fairly simple and painless process, but while the needle is withdrawing the fluid, it is vital to remain absolutely still. A few minutes later it was all over and followed by an ultrasound scan so that the doctor and I could actually see the baby on a small black and white screen. If the baby had spina bifida, for instance, it would be visible by this stage. As I lay on the bed in the doctor's surgery surrounded by machines, I suddenly heard the thump, thump of my baby's heart. It was quite magical. I instantly connected with this minute child of mine, which I could only just make out in the snowy picture on the monitor, and there was no spina bifida.

In the afternoon I went to the hairdressers, and at 7 p.m. that evening

I met my friend Stephanie Berni at the Royal Opera House, Covent Garden, to see a ballet. I was full of happiness and confidence about the new baby and regaled Stephie with my hopes and dreams for this last, precious, child. Half-way into the first act, however, I felt a rush of liquid between my legs. Horrified, I whispered to Stephie, 'I'm flooding, I've got to get out of here!' I was also wearing a cream-coloured suit. 'Stephie, will you go behind me and tell me if I am bleeding?' I asked her. We apologised to the row of people we had to disturb to get out and I rushed to the loo. What I had lost was liquid that looked like tea. Stephie immediately took charge and said, 'Sit here, I'll get a taxi, we are going straight to the Portland Hospital.'

Gratefully, I sat on the bench in the lobby of the Royal Opera House, while a lady from St John Ambulance looked after me and told me that her daughter had only recently had a miscarriage, which had started just like this! I couldn't believe my ears and she seemed completely oblivious to her implications.

At 11 p.m. Mr Glyn Evans arrived to see me at the hospital. The last time I had been at the Portland, a private hospital in central London, was when I gave birth to Charles. The anxiety of this evening was in stark contrast to that joyful occasion. I was in bed and had sent Stephie home. Johnnie arrived at the same time, looking worried and tired, having driven up from Kent. He wasn't sure what to expect and had left in such a hurry that he loaded our three black spaniels into the car, as well. Mr Glyn Evans examined me and told me that the tiny hole made to extract the amniotic fluid had torn and that I had lost a great deal of fluid. It was almost certain that I would miscarry and, if not, I would probably get an infection in the womb, which would in itself cause a miscarriage. I was to lie very still and do nothing. He would visit me in the morning.

It was a long night. I didn't sleep much and during those dark hours, realised just how very much I wanted to have this baby. I spent most of the night making calculations. If I miscarried, would I be lucky enough to conceive as quickly again? Another pregnancy wouldn't happen for at least two months and I was already three months pregnant. That would mean I would be six months older, would it matter to the baby, would it be born with Down's? The next morning I was taken for ultrasound. It was as Mr Glyn Evans had said. There was almost no amniotic fluid and two days later I still wasn't making it up fast enough. After five days in hospital and no miscarriage, I was sent home with orders to 'Live a dressing gown existence', which meant lying around all day, taking no exercise and absolutely no sex!

The weeks went by. Every trip to the loo was full of anxiety. I refused all invitations and pottered about the house and garden with Charles. After three weeks, a call came from the laboratory to say that the results of the amniocentesis had arrived and that the baby was healthy, normal and was a girl! I was terribly relieved to still have the baby and my anxieties waned with the news. I gradually grew more confident and by May I was six months pregnant and thought that I would be able to attend the State Opening of Parliament, as I had succeeded in winning a seat in the ballot, without putting the baby at risk. As Johnnie is a hereditary peer he is entitled to attend every State Opening of Parliament, but the seating is limited in the Chamber and peers must apply for a seat for their wives if they wish to attend. Johnnie's grandfather had become a lord at almost the same time as my grandfather became a viscount, and had taken the title Lord Astor of Hever, to differentiate between himself and his nephew, who was Viscount Astor. A couple of weeks before the State Opening I had borrowed a beautiful dove-grey chiffon dress from Lady Abergavenny, an old friend of Johnnie's mother, who had many outfits to choose from as she had been lady-in-waiting to the Queen.

On the day of the State Opening, Johnnie left an hour before me in order to queue for his robes. I was to find my own way to Parliament by taxi, with a special car pass that would allow the taxi to take me right to the Peers' Entrance. The roads surrounding Westminster are closed for State occasions and only a pass will allow a taxi through. However, not long after Johnnie had left, I realised that I could not zip up my dress. Alone in our London house I had no option but to lock the door behind me and in my long dress, half unzipped at the back, wearing a diamond tiara borrowed from my stepmother, walk to Eaton Square and try to hail a cab. At 9.30 a.m., I was a curious sight and had to put up with catcalls, flashing lights and hooting cars, before I managed to flag down a taxi. Before I opened the door, I had to ask the cabby if he would mind very much zipping me up. He obliged and on the way there asked me if my husband was a lord. I said yes, he was and that was why I was in my Cinderella outfit practically at dawn, as I was to attend the State Opening of Parliament. A silence fell, and then he said 'Blimey, Miss, you don't sound very impressed!' I wonder what he expected?

I entered the Chamber of the House of Lords and was shown to my seat, finding that I was sitting next to the actress Jamie Lee Curtis. Her husband, Lord Haden-Guest, had only recently inherited his title. As it was almost certain that the position of hereditary peers in the House of Lords was to change, they had decided to fly from California, where they lived, to be able to attend a State Opening of Parliament at least once. 'Hi, I'm Jamie,' she announced as she shook my hand firmly. I felt like saying 'Yes, I know!' but gave the standard reply. 'Hi, I'm Liz. Where is your husband?'

We searched the rows of men in scarlet robes edged with ermine, sitting on the opposite side of the Chamber and in the benches facing the Throne. She pointed out her husband and I found mine, in a gang of smirking, preening men all looking eagerly in our direction. Johnnie actually nodded towards Jamie and winked at me! I decided to ignore him and we carried on a perfectly ordinary conversation about our children, until we were joined by an elderly peeress of operatic proportions, who squeezed in tightly, between us.

'Look, I think you're getting a note!' the peeress announced. Her accent was as full as her figure. I looked across the Chamber and saw Johnnie handing a small piece of paper to an elderly doorkeeper who, in full regalia of velvet navy knickerbockers and shiny patent leather shoes with rosettes, attempted to cross to the other side of the packed Chamber to deliver the note. Everyone was watching. The peeress said 'He probably wants to know what's for dinner!' It was much, much worse. The note read, 'Do you know you are sitting next to Jamie Lee Curtis?' In fairness to Johnnie, I mostly don't recognise people, but I was now in a hell of a predicament. I was surrounded by an expectant silence. 'Oh, men!' I exploded and, putting the note in my bag, turned to Jamie and asked her to tell us about her latest film.

I struggled through the rest of the summer with a very uncomfortable pregnancy. I never fully made up the lost amniotic fluid and there seemed little cushioning between the baby and me. On top of this discomfort, I had acute indigestion at night and the only cure was to eat nothing after 5 p.m. Every evening while the family ate dinner, I only ate melon. This lasted for nearly three months, but fortunately I never tired of it! At nearly eight months pregnant I went for an antenatal check-up with Mr Glyn Evans. He thought that I should have the baby as soon as possible and that I had done well to maintain the pregnancy so far, but that it would be better off born. I wanted to wait a little longer to give the baby a chance to put on weight. We compromised and decided that she would be induced at 37 weeks and, this time, I was determined to have an epidural. I had had two deliveries without one as I had left going to the hospital too late for an epidural with my other children.

On 20 August, Johnnie drove me to the Portland Hospital. By 1 p.m., I had my epidural in place and had been induced. By 11 p.m. I was still in labour, feeling terribly nauseous and shivering from the epidural, which I hated. The nurse decided it was time to call Mr Glyn Evans, who took one look at me, listened to the baby's heart beat and said that although there was no foetal distress, I had to have an emergency Caesarean. Johnnie, who is at best rather queasy, left the room. Within minutes, the delivery room was alive with nurses and my anaesthetist. I was grateful for the epidural now, as it meant the operation could take place swiftly, and after a few minutes Olivia was born. Before she was given to me Mr Glyn Evans exclaimed, 'Has anyone got a camera?' 'Johnnie has,' I told him, and a nurse was sent to bring it to the delivery room. Johnnie, when asked if Mr Glyn Evans could borrow his camera, said 'How nice of him to want to take a picture of my daughter!'

Little did we know until later, Olivia had been born with three proper knots in her cord, like tying shoelaces three times, which, after delivering over a thousand babies, Mr Glyn Evans had never seen, nor heard of, before! She must have spent the last nine months turning somersaults to achieve this but the result was that this knotted cord was now not long enough for her to have a normal delivery, and the danger of oxygen deprivation if the cord pulled too tight was huge. The pictures were later printed in *The Lancet*, the medical journal, along with an article written by Mr Glyn Evans.

Despite this drama, Olivia passed all her five APGAR tests of a new-born infant, which are for muscle tone, skin colour, respiratory effort, heart rate and response to stimuli, and after 24 hours, I decided that I was going to bottle feed her. I felt exhausted from the whole pregnancy and delivery, and I was going home to all our other children who were in the middle of their summer holidays.

Olivia quickly put on weight. She was tiny at birth, weighing only 6 lb 2 oz (2.8 kg). Johnnie's nanny, Jean Paterson, came to help. Jean had been with Johnnie's family since he was born and was now 78 years old! She said that she would love to come for a month and help me, provided there was a nanny to look after the other children, and do the washing and ironing. Jean had also been my maternity nurse when Charles was born and we all adored her. She seemed to exist on a diet of incredibly weak coffee and fresh air, and nothing flustered her. She spent hours telling me family stories, which I loved to hear, especially about Johnnie as a boy.

In September, only three weeks after Olivia was born, Natalya, aged 11, started her first term at Benenden School as a boarder. I felt extremely tearful when we dropped her off. She and I had never been parted and I wept pathetically all the way home. However, life settled into a pleasant routine, and in November Olivia was christened by my stepfather, Roger Tarbuck, in our drawing room, wearing my mother's family christening robes. As Olivia was to be our last child I had invited many friends to be godparents, so it was quite a large gathering that assembled for the ceremony.

As Roger began the service Ella, our black spaniel, ran into the room and lay panting loudly, on her back, at Johnnie's feet. Charles attempted to climb up onto the sofa, but fell off with a bang. The girls tried to control their giggles, when, to my horror, my housekeeper began to vacuum our bedroom carpet which was directly overhead. Completely unfazed, Roger took Olivia in his arms, blessed her and christened her Olivia Alexandra Elizabeth. I was filled with joy; standing by my beloved husband surrounded by my close family and friends I felt truly content. Olivia was a beautiful baby and one day, I hoped, would be married and have her wedding reception at this same house. Frenchstreet House, with its lovely drawing room and terrace facing the lawn, leant itself to just this type of family occasion.

On a glorious spring day on 8 May of the following year, we celebrated my mother's 70th birthday. She and Roger had come to stay for a few days and my sister Diana, brother Charles and his French wife Isabelle, joined us for lunch. It was warm enough to eat out on the terrace, but I was vaguely aware of my mother and sister talking anxiously together. They smiled as I came into the drawing room and asked if I could take a picture of them sitting on the fender in front of the fire with Olivia, by then eight months old, between them. 'Be careful, won't you?' I asked, 'She doesn't sit up by herself yet. You'll need to prop her up and hold her firmly round the waist.' This was exactly what they had been discussing: Olivia's rather alarmingly late development and my seemingly total lack of awareness, or perhaps denial, that there might be a problem.

My mother decided to approach the subject with great sensitivity. 'Darling, Roger and I think that Olivia doesn't seem to have quite arrived in her body yet, does she?' 'What do you mean, Mum?' I asked, perplexed. 'Well, she seems rather dreamy, almost as if her soul is halfway between heaven and her body. It is as if she hasn't fully arrived, or woken up yet …' my mother tailed off. 'She seems OK to me, Mum,' I answered. 'She is just such a sweet, easy baby, maybe it is the contrast to Natalya and Charles you're noticing. Anyway, with such a houseful I am not complaining!' I laughed, as I scooped Olivia up into my arms.

My mother and sister decided to press no further but were amazed at what they saw as my complete denial that anything could be wrong. It wasn't denial; I genuinely didn't see a problem at that stage. Olivia ate well, slept well and was no trouble at all. She would sit by herself soon enough and, at eight months old, she just wasn't ready yet.

A month later, I flew to our flat in the South of France with Charles and Olivia. Johnnie had gone ahead a day earlier as he had to attend a meeting, but before we took off Olivia started crying. By the time we landed she had a high temperature and as soon as we arrived at the flat, Johnnie called the doctor. She had an ear infection and was given antibiotics, but the next morning her poor little body was covered in angry-looking eczema. Two days later she was no better and the eczema had spread all down her arms and legs. We had had little sleep and asked the doctor to come again. After examining her, he said that she had a secondary throat infection and that was why she was in such pain. He gave further antibiotics and by the end of our week's holiday she was better, but the eczema was not.

I tried bathing her in Oilatum (a soothing skin product for very dry skins) and creaming her with gentle emollients, but nothing worked. She slept with white cotton gloves on to stop her scratching and luckily didn't seem uncomfortable or distressed by the terrible state of her skin, which must have given her intense itching. Two months later, I took her to see Dr Atherton, a paediatric skin specialist at Great Ormond Street Hospital for children in London. He rather proudly told me about his new treatment. 'I have noticed that babies never have eczema on the nappy area,' he said, 'which is always warm and wet. So I have developed a treatment for eczema which seems to have excellent results.' 'What is it?' I asked, my hopes rising. 'What do I do?' 'I'll give you a prescription for 1 per cent hydrocortisone in cetomacrogol, which is just an emollient. Night and morning, you cover the affected area with the cream. Then, with tubigrip bandages, wet half of the bandage. I will give you large tubigrips for her trunk and narrower ones for her arms and legs. Pull the wet half over her – it has to be really damp – and then take the dry second half and pull that over the top. It will take a bit of practice, but this way she is kept warm and wet with the cream on the skin. You can dress her on top of the bandages, if you want to. Do this for the next two weeks and then telephone me and let me know how you are getting on.' He gave me a quick demonstration on a teddy bear, then we shook hands, and I took Olivia straight to a chemist, where we emerged with two bulging plastic bags.

It was difficult to do at first but, after two weeks, Olivia's skin was vastly improved, and I could feel Dr Atherton beaming down the phone as I told him. 'Keep up the creaming,' he told me, 'and revert to the tubigrips if it flares up again.'

At nine months, Olivia was at last able to sit up unaided. She was still rather wobbly and we used to surround her with cushions to soften her fall, if she overbalanced. She loved books and would sit for long periods of time, surrounded by them, picking them up and turning the pages delicately with her thumbnail. She also liked to eat the paperbacks, and most of her baby books have a missing top right corner.

It is at this age that children usually become acutely aware of their mothers and are often very tearful and clingy if they are approached by anyone unfamiliar. My brother Charles and his wife Isabelle came to visit one weekend and while we were sitting drinking cups of tea in the kitchen, our talk turned to babies. 'I want to have one just like this!' said Isabelle, who had Olivia on her lap. Olivia had been passed to Isabelle and without a murmur of protest or pleasure, was sitting staring straight in front of her. 'I know, I'm very lucky,' I said. 'She's such a sweet, easy baby. She rarely cries and will stay in her cot quite happily bouncing on her bottom until I come, in the morning. The only thing that I'm worried about is the slightly hairy lump on her back. I am sure it has come from that awful dry pregnancy.' 'Why don't you ask the skin specialist what he thinks?' suggested Charles. 'Good idea, I'll ring tomorrow,' I said, which I did and was recommended 'Dr X' at another private London hospital.

Olivia was almost a year old when we went for our initial appointment. She was sitting firmly now, but had shown no attempt at crawling, let alone walking. I sat her on the examining bed, undressed her top half and showed Dr X the scaly patch.

'It is called a hairy haematoma,' Dr X told me. 'Quite benign, but unattractive. It will show in a swim suit, and think about when she is older and would like to wear a backless evening dress.' 'What could you do and how would you do it?' I asked.

'I would remove it and there would be a few stitches. She would be left with a pencil-line scar, which, in my opinion, would be infinitely preferable to what she has now.'

'Are you absolutely sure that this is the right time to do it?' I asked anxiously. 'Would she be better to wait until she is older and knows what is happening?'

'Not really,' he replied. 'As she is so young she will not be too troubled by the operation. It is either now, or waiting until she is about 18 and fully-grown. She would have to remain very still while it heals and I think that it would be harder for her to do so at that age, when young people are always on the go, than now.'

'But look at her now,' I pointed out. She spends most of her time sitting on the floor bending forwards stretching her upper body in all directions, to reach her books. Is that still enough?' 'Absolutely,' he confirmed and so I booked Olivia in for a general anaesthetic and the cosmetic surgery.

A few days before the operation, I was still in a quandary. As Olivia lay on her tummy in the bathroom after her evening bath, Elizabeth, our nanny, and I examined her back closely. 'What do you think?' I asked Elizabeth. 'If she were my daughter, I would definitely go ahead,' she replied. 'She is going to hate it when she gets older.'

A week later, the operation over, we were back in the bathroom, with a whole new problem. Olivia kept leaning forwards to reach for her books and toys. Each time she reached forwards, her wound reopened and the skin under the steristrips was raw. Her back was in such a mess and all we could do was keep her as still as possible and try to find a fresh area of skin to stick the steristrips to.

Olivia's back took weeks to heal. I felt an agony of guilt that I had inflicted this on my baby. The scar stretched upwards and healed at a width of half an inch. So much for the pencil-line scar I had been promised! It was also much longer than I had been told it would be, reaching from under her right arm all the way across her back to her spine.

I rang Dr X and made an appointment to see him. By the time I had travelled with Olivia from Kent to London, I was in a rage at the thought of finally being able to confront him. I wondered how I would keep my temper. As we entered his consulting room, he introduced me to three visiting Italian plastic surgeons. 'Good,' I thought to myself. 'An international shaming.'

'Dr X, let me show you and your colleagues the result of your work,' I snapped as, with shaking hands, I removed Olivia's vest and top. 'It seems to have healed well,' he commented, lamely. 'Tell me, Dr X, would you call this mess your usual standard of work? Is it something that you are proud of?' I hissed. 'Please do measure the scar, as you assured me that she would be left with one of pencil-line thinness.' Turning to the three rather puzzled and now rather embarrassed Italians, I explained: 'You see, gentlemen, Dr X saw my baby before the operation. I pointed out to him that she sat and reached forwards for toys and books. He was adamant that this would not affect the outcome. What do you think of his work? Not much, I suspect. I am extremely angry as you can see. What an appalling mess. What have you to say, Dr X?'

Red faced, he told me that he could redo it when she was 18! 'Do you *seriously* think I would ever let you anywhere near my daughter again?' I picked up Olivia and, shaking with anger, stormed out of the room. Poor kid, I thought. First eczema and now this, all in her first year. Little did I know that these problems would fade into insignificance as her life began to unfold.

CHAPTER 3

A Very Slow Beginning

OLIVIA CELEBRATED HER FIRST BIRTHDAY in late August. She was beautifully round and plump by now, with short dark hair that stood straight up of its own volition in a fluffy angelic halo around her head. She had green eyes, a tiny button nose and a small, full mouth with a complexion so fair that the children said that on a suntan scale, hers would be 'neon'. Olivia had begun to bottom shuffle her way across the floor, but never travelled far. She rocked in her high chair, thumping her back against the back of the chair, staring vacantly into space. I presumed that she was just a dreamy type of child, as I had been when I was young. She had bounced and rocked so hard in her cot that she had managed to break two of the wooden slats that supported the mattress. Every morning Johnnie would greet her in the kitchen, but she never responded. He found this rather disconcerting. 'She never seems pleased to see me,' he commented with a rather puzzled expression. 'All my other children used to at least look at me and smile when I wished them good morning.' I waved away his concerns. 'Not all children are alike. I really shouldn't worry.' But there were more comments about Olivia, which came in a slow drip, drip fashion.

One morning, as I walked past the kitchen on my way upstairs I heard Sandy, my housekeeper, saying to the nanny: 'If that was my child, I'd have her straight down the doctor's.' I waited, my heart beating, to hear the nanny's reply. 'Oh she's all right, just a little slow, that's all,' came the reply. Yes, I thought, nothing to worry about at all. I had a vague feeling of unease, but would have been far too embarrassed to go into the kitchen and ask Sandy exactly what she had meant. I have often been asked since whether I was in denial that there was anything wrong with Olivia during that period and it is something that I have difficulty answering, because I really am not sure. I can't think now why I didn't investigate any possible problem then, except that my life had changed so dramatically, from living with one child alone, having to earn my own living and having no one to share my problems, to a house full of people, a large garden to build and getting to know all Johnnie's relations and friends that perhaps I unconsciously baulked at having to address a major difficulty. I was also finding my new life fun, but very tiring, and I don't think I could have fitted another thing into my already busy schedule. Ask anyone who has remarried about the emotional exhaustion of melding two families and they will all, I am sure, say the same. A new family is like a delicate young plant. Its tender shoots require gentle handling and nurturing. Put it out into the border too soon and the frost can do irreparable damage. I so desperately wanted everyone to be happy, to feel treasured and valued. We were all learning about each other as we bumbled along, strangers thrown together, and to add to that a major problem with Olivia was just not an option, nor did I see one, at that stage. As well as our new family and two young children to care for, we had to run Frenchstreet with its 11 acres of garden, stables, cottages and farmland, as well as our flat in France and our house in London. I had been brought up in large family homes, but had lived in a small garden flat, with only Natalya, for years. At that time I had had to work as well as do all the gardening, cooking, cleaning and so on myself, which stood me in good stead as it meant that I was generally fairly capable. We also had five children at four different schools at that time! Was this the reason I appeared to my family and friends to have my head firmly stuck in the sand? Perhaps so. I look back, but even now, I am not sure.

I was still unconcerned about Olivia's progress when I took her to Dr Morrison, our GP, for her 18-month check-up. 'Not walking yet?' he asked, gently. 'No, but she took ages to sit and to bottom shuffle,' I said. 'She seems to have her own agenda.' 'How do you feel about the not walking?' Dr Morrison asked. 'Are you worried about it?' 'Not at all,' I replied, and at the time this was really how I felt. I was grateful that Olivia was such a placid, sweet child and having already had two children, I knew how different even children from the same family could be. Plus I never have been an over-anxious or protective type of mother nor a deeply competitive one. Until she was nine, Natalya had been to school in north London, where the children were given so many after-school and weekend activities by their parents that it was a relief to be out of that loop, living in Kent. I wanted my children to be enthused and encouraged to try new things, but also have time to daydream and learn to create their own fun. 'All right,' Dr Morrison said. 'That is why we have these check-ups. Just to see if the children are reaching their milestones. As you say, they are all different and some get there earlier than others. Let me know if you want to do anything about it,' he said sweetly, and we left.

But he had planted a seed. Four weeks later, I rang him. 'I want to do something about this non-walking child of mine,' I said. 'That's fine,' Dr Morrison replied. 'I'll get you an appointment with a physiotherapist at the Portland Hospital.' This was where Olivia was born and where her records were kept.

The same week, I had spoken to my accountant whose two girls were born with acute urinary problems. He had gone from pillar to post with no success in trying to find someone who could help them. I told him of my worries about Olivia and he recommended a paediatrician called Dr John Fysh, whom he found both sympathetic and helpful, so I asked my doctor if he would also refer me to see him.

My mother came with me and we sat quietly in Dr Fysh's consulting room as Olivia bottom shuffled on the floor around his desk. He asked me endless questions about my pregnancy, delivery and what she was currently capable of doing. Occasionally, Olivia would stop by my chair and look up at me. Otherwise, she played with the toys in a box in the corner. After some time, Dr Fysh concluded that as she looked at me, she was making a relationship and I didn't really have anything to worry about. Olivia was a late developer, but he knew of many children who didn't talk until they were five and then came out with whole sentences! I was to hear this sort of story many times, but each time, I felt comforted by it. Dr Fysh was, after all, a very experienced paediatrician who must have seen dozens of children just like Olivia during the course of his practice. Greatly relieved, my mother and I took Olivia out to lunch at Fortnum & Mason, where we ate our favourite dish on their menu of fishcakes on a bed of spinach, before we went home.

In July, just a month before her second birthday, we were downstairs in the bowels of the Portland Hospital for Olivia's first visit with a physiotherapist. She was a lovely young Asian woman who put Olivia down on her tummy on a mat while I sat on a tiny chair with my knees up against my ears. Olivia hated being on her tummy and cried loudly. Nor did she want to try to climb up on a foam square, nor support herself with her arms. Watching what she should have been able to do was shocking. I sat stunned and tearful, dying to go and pick her up, finding it almost impossible to remain seated while she cried so plaintively. 'She is still very hypotonic, unusually so, for a two year old,' the physiotherapist told me. 'What does hypotonic mean?' I asked. 'It is the extreme flexibility that babies have. After a few months, their limbs begin to straighten out, and their muscles strengthen, but Olivia's haven't. She doesn't lock her knees at all and I think that should be the first step.' She explained that she was going to order some pads, which look rather like cricket pads, to put on her legs. The idea was to prop Olivia up against a wall so that she had to stand for a few minutes twice a day. Because she was a bottom shuffler, she hadn't developed any strength in her arms and couldn't pull herself up on to her knees. She had missed the crawling stage, so we also had to try to get her to crawl on her hands and knees. The physiotherapist thought that Olivia wouldn't like it, but that these stages of development are fundamentally important. She finished by saying, 'Come back and see me again in two months.'

A few days later, the 'cricket pads' arrived in the post. Elizabeth Jeremiah, our nanny, and I had tried to get Olivia to crawl on her hands and knees, but each time, she collapsed on the floor and cried bitterly. The first time we put the pads on her legs, we propped her up in the corner of the playroom. Her face had a look of complete disbelief, which turned quickly into horror, and then out came a howl of protest. It must have hurt and I simply couldn't stand it. 'Get them off, quickly!' I shouted to Elizabeth. 'I can't bear this!' I was weeping as I tried to comfort Olivia, my hands shaking so much I could hardly hold her, but she didn't want to be held and tried to push me away.

Later in the day, Elizabeth and I conferred. She said, 'I think we have to do this. As I am not her mother, I can bear it. Why don't I sit with her while she has the pads on, as it is only for a few minutes, and you go to the other end of the garden?'

And so every day my poor child was put to torture. At first, I would run to the other end of the garden, pacing the grass, hearing her cry in my mind and agonising. Was I doing the right thing? Wouldn't she walk eventually, without this twice-daily ordeal? But by her second birthday, she was standing for a few minutes, with the pads on, and not complaining too much. I was now able to sit beside her and read to her to try to distract her, keeping one eye on the clock.

Vanessa Boutefeu and her daughter Jessica, my god-daughter, who live in Portugal, were staying with us when Olivia turned two. We had made a small birthday cake and when I put it in front of her, she reached out and touched the candles! She pulled her hand back quickly, but didn't seem to register the heat nor the pain. She had no idea how to blow out the candles. Vanessa asked how her speech was coming on. 'Not very fast,' said Johnnie. 'She can say 'book' and that's about it.' Vanessa said nothing, but looked concerned. Other friends began to check her age, and seemed surprised when I said that she was now two years old. How I didn't notice that she was still like a baby, I don't know. Everyone else did, but it didn't concern me at the time as she was beginning to make progress and it seemed that she was just a late developer. I began to hear the phrase 'some children march to a different tune, but they all end up in the same parade ground' regularly, and I took Olivia for one of those. I told myself that any child with such an avid interest in books and who also had above average periods of concentration could not have anything wrong with her brain. She would learn to walk and to talk, but in her own time. It was something that I can still not understand, not even in the deepest searching of my soul, but it was to come back and haunt me again and again a few years later.

Meanwhile, Natalya had begun her second year at Benenden. She loved the school and had made great friends, but when we had gone to the parent/teacher meeting in her first year, we had had rather a shock. The history teacher was particularly vehement in her protest. 'Frankly, she is the most disorganised child I have ever come across in 30 years of teaching,' she declared. 'Short of sticking her files to her hands, I cannot see how she will ever get her work, files and herself to class simultaneously!' The feedback from all the other subject teachers was the same. The geography teacher told me that she had not attended one class during that week, and she said that when she asked Natalya where she had been, 'She told me – can you believe this? – "I'm sorry, Miss, but I just had to get outside for a while, so I went for a walk across the fields." This is not the sort of thing that we have ever had to deal with at Benenden, Lady Astor!' The only good reports came from the sports mistress and the drama teacher, who enthused, 'She is an absolute joy to teach! Incredibly talented, but I'm sure you know that, and she has such creative ideas. In fact, I am putting her in the school play. We have never had anyone from the first or second year in a school play. It is usually only for the sixth form.'

It appeared that things hadn't improved as I spoke to her housemistress, one chilly autumn morning in Natalya's second year. 'We sometimes use Dr Etkin, who works at Ticehurst Hospital, for girls who have problems,' she told me. 'He is the psychiatrist for Benenden and is extremely experienced. It allows girls who might have something on their mind to talk privately and get things off their chest. He gives sound advice and it might help her settle down.' I felt that I had no option but to agree to an appointment with him and two weeks later drove to Benenden to collect Natalya and take her to meet Dr Etkin.

We went into his cosy room and talked openly about her difficulties at Benenden. After 40 minutes, he announced: 'She's a classic ADDer, the sort of person who will go straight to the top or, equally likely, straight to the bottom. No middle ground at all!' 'What on earth is ADD?' I asked in amazement. 'It means Attention Deficit Disorder and your daughter is a text book case. Get her on to Ritalin and she'll be fine. Lots of my patients take it, and it keeps them on track. Come back next week and we can discuss it further,' and, rising, he shook my hand. That was the end of the consultation.

I discussed the interview that night with Johnnie and our new nanny, Angela, who was Australian. Angela was a teacher and had taught for several years before deciding to come to England for a year. She was totally against Ritalin. 'The kids in my class who were on it were complete zombies,' she told us. 'It is a powerful drug and although they were quiet, they were so dopey that I couldn't get them to learn anything. I wouldn't give it to a child of mine.'

At the next meeting with Dr Etkin, I told him that I didn't want Natalya to take Ritalin. He left it at that and never enquired why, nor gave me any further information about ADD (or ADHD, Attention Deficit Hyperactivity Disorder, if the person is also hyperactive). Years later, I confronted him about it. Why had he not given me more information about ADHD? Why did he simply accept that I did not want to give her Ritalin? He said that as I had made up my mind, he thought that I had made an informed decision. I had not, but I was to learn that I must check everything that I did not understand, and ask questions again and again, and seek second opinions. Information and knowledge, using my skills as a researcher, were to become paramount. Natalya continued to visit Dr Etkin on a monthly basis for the next couple of terms, until I received a phone call from Gillian du Charme, the headmistress of Benenden. 'I'm afraid that I am going to have to suspend Natalya for a few days,' she said. 'She has been very naughty and was also found camping in the grounds last night. Can you imagine my surprise, when I opened my office door, as she had been sent to see me, to find her perfectly unconcerned, practising her cartwheels in the corridor, directly outside the room!' I took Natalya home and gave her a terrifying 'dressing down'.

In October Rene, Johnnie's mother, invited her five children and their families to spend the weekend at Hever Castle, to celebrate her 75th birthday. Johnnie's great-grandfather had bought Hever Castle and Cliveden in 1903 and Gavin, his father, had been brought up at Hever, but it was sold in 1982. Rene thought that it would be lovely to spend the weekend there so that her grandchildren could enjoy it and know it as it had been when she lived there, because most of her grandchildren had been born after the castle had been sold, and so she hired the castle and grounds from Saturday afternoon until Sunday tea time. We walked around the grounds after the castle and gardens were closed to the public for the day. It was a beautiful, balmy weekend and as we strolled through the Italian gardens, still filled with autumn colour, Johnnie, his sisters and brother told many hilarious stories of the things they got up to as children. Inside the castle in the long gallery, Louise, Johnnie's sister, remembered when a group of visiting Americans had asked if the castle were haunted. Johnnie overheard the question and ran to hide inside a cupboard from which he made moaning, sighing noises as the Americans passed, terrified. He told me how his father and two uncles had learnt to roller skate in the vast cellars underneath the castle. And how one of their uncles had been invited to spend Christmas at Hever, but when he arrived, he had parked the car so close to the moat, that upon stepping out, he fell straight into the water!

We made a very happy, noisy party of 23 at dinner in the exquisitely carved oak dining room on Saturday night. The castle had undergone considerable reconstruction between 1903 and 1906 after Johnnie's great-grandfather had bought it and the linenfold panelling, minstrels' gallery and fireplace had all been carved by one man, the sculptor Nathaniel Hitch. We drank a champagne toast to Rene, but what made the weekend really special for her was that it was this particular weekend that Olivia walked by herself, for the first time. Whenever we reminisced about her 75th birthday weekend, she always said, 'And wasn't it wonderful that Olivia chose my birthday to take her first steps!' Olivia was two years and two months old. I had been focusing so intently on her not walking, that when she finally did walk, it was as if heavy veils had fallen from my eyes and I realised that she had other, much more serious problems.

CHAPTER 4

What Is Wrong With My Child?

JUST BEFORE CHRISTMAS IN 1994, I took Olivia back to the physiother-apist at the Portland Hospital. She walked; she managed to climb a whole flight of stairs, both up and down but still refused to lie on her tummy. The physiotherapist was pleased. 'You have done very well, Olivia!' she beamed. But at the end of the session, she confessed to me that when I first brought Olivia to her, she secretly thought that she might never walk.

I felt that I had much to celebrate that Christmas, as we arrived in the snow at Tillypronie, Johnnie's brother Philip's estate in Aberdeenshire. Charles had come out in spots the night before and Camilla was just getting over a bad attack of pneumonia, but we were all together and I was not going to let a mere case of chicken pox spoil a large family Christmas.

But I found that I couldn't put off the nagging doubts at the back of my mind. What was wrong with Olivia? This was made infinitely worse by the contrast between another child of exactly the same age, two-and-a-half, who was also staying with Philip. Thomas was the complete antithesis of Olivia. He was tiny and very, very bright. The two of them sat in their high chairs side by side, Olivia not uttering a word, and still eating with her fingers, and Thomas, who watched Charles taking his medicine and asked, 'Why is that boy having med-icine? What is the matter with him?'

I decided to take her back to the paediatrician Dr Fysh, where I laid out my concerns. She wasn't talking, she hadn't a clue what to do with a potty and spent hours on the floor, not playing, but more like sorting toys into colour groups and endlessly 'reading' books. Even more odd was that she didn't seem to recognise the difference between night and day. She would spend hours at night, sitting up in her bed thumping her back against the headboard. We could hear it over the baby alarm in our bedroom, a steady, thud, thud, thud and loud 'talking' and laughing too, until we decided that as she was not going to get up in the middle of the night and wander around the house, we could unplug the alarm and try to get a good night's sleep ourselves.

'And another thing,' I added. 'Whenever my husband and I go away, for a day or even a week, Olivia doesn't seem at all pleased to see us when we return. Surely she misses us? All children miss their parents, don't they? Only she doesn't even look up when I come into the room!' 'Perhaps you should see a neurologist,' Dr Fysh suggested. 'None of those things you have just described are anything much in themselves, but it would be a good idea to see if there is anything neurologically wrong with Olivia. I am sure she will catch up; she's walking now, isn't she? But if it will put your mind at rest, I'll arrange for you to see Dr Marion Crouchman in Denmark Hill.'

Johnnie was more concerned, in some ways, about Olivia's lack of communication, than I was. He mentioned it to his secretary, Kathleen Winch. Kathleen's mother had worked as a teacher of special needs children in a Rudolf Steiner school for over 30 years, and Kathleen had often helped her there. At lunch one day, Johnnie told me that in discussion with Kathleen, she had suggested that perhaps Olivia could be autistic. This was the first time that I had come across this proposal and I was incensed! 'That is absolutely ridiculous!' I practically shouted. 'What does she know? How DARE she make such assumptions? Autism is a very serious condition, and Olivia is nothing like that at all. Look at *Rain Man* (a film about an autistic adult, which I had seen once, long ago). Do you see anything in Olivia that reminds you of that man? Of course not!' I continued to rant for some time, until I calmed down, but I was very angry with Kathleen. My fears about and general conception of autism at that time were fairly typical of the average person. The sum total of my knowledge of the disorder was what I had gleaned from the film *Rain Man*, whose central character was both severely autistic and also an 'autistic savant', which occurs in only 1 per cent of autistic people. The 'savant' has a genius for a particular skill. In *Rain Man* it was for numbers, but it can be for drawing a highly complex building from memory, or working out dates, for example. I also had no idea that there was a spectrum of disability within autism and that some people with autism are so able that they have never been diagnosed and some are so severe that they remain non-verbal and necessarily institutionalised all their lives.

On an unusually cold, windy day in July, I struggled with an increasingly heavy Olivia who was nearly three, in her buggy on several trains from Kent to get her to her appointment with Dr Crouchman, the head neurologist of King's College Hospital in Denmark Hill, south London. I had received a letter in which I was told that Olivia would have an MRI scan, which would mean a light anaesthetic and then once she was fully awake, an EEG. I was to bring food, toys and nappies, as it might be quite a long session. The MRI (magnetic resonance imaging) would check for any breaks, blockages, damage or malformation to the neural pathways of her head and body, and the EEG (electroencephalogram) would do the same specifically for her brain, also looking for any abnormality.

I felt extremely emotional as I stood beside the MRI scanner and watched her little floppy body, deathly pale, enter into the metal tube. I was asked to leave the room while the scanning took place, wondering what on earth I was doing putting her through all this. I felt tired and frightened and terribly alone. I should have asked a friend to come with me but I hadn't realised how distressing the day would be. After an hour and some food, we were taken into Dr Crouchman's consulting rooms. 'I will take an EEG, now,' she said. 'It could be quite tricky, so if you could hold Olivia on your lap and make sure that she doesn't pull off the electrodes, it shouldn't take too long.' That was easier said than done, but eventually, holding on to Olivia's tiny hands, we succeeded in covering her head with the small metal discs that would take a reading of her brain.

Once that was over and the electrodes removed, we returned to the consulting room. Dr Crouchman said, 'I will send you the results shortly, but in the meantime, it does seem that Olivia has special needs and so I will let your local authority know about her and they will get in touch with you.'

Too dumbfounded to think, and totally exhausted, I put Olivia back in her buggy and we began the long, difficult journey home. It was the first time someone had used the term 'special needs' and I wasn't at all sure what it meant. Surely she couldn't have meant that Olivia was disabled, I thought to myself on the way home. No, absolutely not, just a slow developer. What did special needs mean? I remembered that when I was 20, I had worked in a school in Newcastle upon Tyne for children with physical disabilities. They had spina bifida, near blindness, legs in calipers, but none of them remotely resembled my daughter. I didn't understand what had been said to me and was too tired to talk much about it when I finally opened my front door in the early evening.

Over the course of the summer of 1995, I found a new preoccupation: potty training. Olivia would be three at the end of August and it was time to get her ready for nursery school, in September. Charles was at Combe Bank Nursery School, which had been a great success, as it had for Natalya, who went to the main school for two years before moving on to Benenden. I rang Combe Bank and explained the potty-training problem. They were expecting Olivia as I had booked her a place when Charles began. Would they be willing to take her if I hadn't managed to potty train her by September? 'I'm afraid not,' came the reply. 'We have a fixed policy on potty training and never take children unless they are reliably dry.' 'But I am sure it will only be a matter of weeks, at the very most,' I begged.

Combe Bank was resolute. I was furious and without a nursery place. Then someone told me about a nursery called Winnies in Westerham, our small town, which is less than two miles from home, which took children from babies to school age, so I rang and explained my problem. 'Why don't you bring Olivia and come and see us?' said a very sweet voice down the telephone. We made a date and as I liked what I saw,

I booked Olivia in to start in early September, but I still hoped that she would be potty trained before then.

I began a campaign. Angela, our nanny, was given instructions that potty training was paramount, since we hadn't much time. But I had other distractions. Natalya was in big trouble again at school. Gillian du Charme rang me and said: 'Natalya is such a lovely, bright, energetic girl, with a huge personality and an equally huge smile. However, we have tried very hard to accommodate her here, but she simply isn't Benenden material. It is extremely serious to expel someone, so I wonder if you could take her somewhere more suitable, as soon as possible, too,' she added.

Natalya had been suspended again and I was at a loss to know what to do. I fell with a thud on to the sofa in our sitting room, holding my head in my hands. Natalya was only 13 and still had years of education ahead of her, but I was in shock and it took some time to take in the terrible telephone call before I was able to think clearly. In my mind, I ran through all the possible schools in the south-east of England. With Johnnie's three girls, we had been round most of them and had had daughters in several. I couldn't see that any of them would welcome her, or that a move to something similar would be appropriate or indeed successful. Then I remembered the Arts Educational School in Tring. This school was dance and drama based, and much more the type of school that Natalya would benefit from. I rang the headmistress and within a week Johnnie and I were being interviewed in her study.

'Of course, she will have to pass an audition,' Mrs Billing said. 'What does she need to prepare?' I asked. 'One speech of no more than three minutes,' she told us. 'Something modern, but you don't have much time, the last auditions for the autumn intake are in three weeks. I'll put her name down, good luck!'

When I rang Gillian du Charme she was delighted and very helpful. 'I'll get the drama teacher on to it straight away,' she said. 'Tring is a brilliant idea, and I am sure she will thrive there. We will give her all the help we can with her audition pieces.' Natalya passed her audition and won a place at the Arts Educational School for September.

We weren't so lucky with Olivia. She was still not potty trained, and it was driving poor Angela round the bend. We were visiting my friend Stephanie Berni at her house in Jersey. Angela followed Olivia around with a mop and bucket as I waited anxiously for the results of her scan and the EEG. Eventually, Stephie said, 'Why don't you ring the hospital and find out today, instead of waiting in agony?' I thanked her and rushed to the phone. Dr Crouchman apologised for the delay in giving me the results. 'I've been so busy,' she said. 'And I have been on holiday, too.' I felt like telling her that I had been in agony, waiting, while she had been on holiday, but managed to ask for the results and keep my caustic comments to myself.

'The MRI scan was normal,' she said, 'and the EEG showed a slight immaturity, but nothing to worry about. There is certainly no petit mal, a mild form of epilepsy, which I know you were worried about, as you had described how Olivia seemed to blank out sometimes. I am afraid that this leaves us without a definite cause for Olivia's delay, but I feel quite hopeful she will make some 'catch up' as her brain matures. I'll put the papers in the post.' I thanked her and hung up. 'It's good news, Stephie,' I called. 'There was nothing wrong!' I was overjoyed with relief and threw my arms round Stephie and hugged her, before picking up Olivia from the play pen and holding her high in the air, kissing her tiny pink toes. 'There, I told you so,' Stephie said. 'She's fine. She'll catch up, you'll see.'

At the end of the long summer holidays, Charles started at The New Beacon prep school, in Sevenoaks, Natalya went to The Arts Educational School in Tring and I took Olivia, who had just turned three, to Winnies Day Nursery in Westerham, where she was to begin with three mornings a week. There were continuous comments at the nursery, mostly very subtle, about Olivia's development. Phrases such as 'Don't worry, they all get there in their own time' and 'I think that having Olivia's nanny here would help: she does seem to need one-to-one attention, doesn't she?' Or, 'How is Olivia at home? Does she ever play with her brother?' were all said with a concerned expression and a furrowed brow. Friends continued to check her age and, when I told them, said nothing. My mother and sister always asked how she was progressing, whenever they called. The word 'autism' had been bandied about, but I continued to be angry that it should be applied to Olivia. I was still living in complete ignorance about autism and therefore, as far as I was concerned, it just wasn't worth considering in her case. In September, I received a letter from Pembury Child Development Centre, in Tunbridge Wells, inviting me to visit them as they had a letter of referral from Dr Crouchman that said that Olivia had 'special needs'.

Dr Wendy Holmes was approaching retirement and had soft grey hair, glasses and a very kind manner. She greeted me in the waiting room and led Olivia and me into one of the consulting rooms. It was a large room with child-sized tables and chairs, boxes of toys, books and mats on the floor for physical exercises. Olivia immediately went to the toy box and began to take every item out, one by one, and line them up in a neat row.

'I have a letter from Dr Crouchman,' she began. 'I gather you took Olivia to see her in July.' 'Yes, that's right,' I replied. 'Olivia had an MRI scan and an EEG, both of which were normal. She suggested that I come and see you, as she thinks Olivia has special needs.' 'What do you think might be the matter?' Dr Holmes asked me. 'I just don't know,' I replied. 'She is a late developer, but speaks quite a bit now, and after a long time, can walk. One or two people have suggested that she might be autistic, but I think that's ridiculous! I most certainly don't want her diagnosis to be autism, because even if you think she is, it can only be very slight and having that diagnosis might make it very difficult to get her into school. I have already had problems finding a nursery school, because she isn't potty trained yet.'

Dr Holmes looked at me curiously over the top of her glasses, as if assessing me and my judgement, and then said, 'OK, let's see what she can do.' Olivia was taken over to a table where Dr Holmes had several small wooden bricks. She built a tower of four bricks and then asked Olivia to copy what she had done. I sat beside Olivia who didn't seem to know how to begin. She managed to put one brick on top of the other after considerable prompting by Dr Holmes and clearly couldn't wait to get back to her books. Similar tests were carried out and Dr Holmes asked about her development and what she could do at home.

After 40 minutes, she said, 'I think that Olivia has a social and communication disorder, with a moderate learning disability. She would benefit from speech therapy and Portage. She has special needs and will need quite a lot of help at school and so I will contact the preschool adviser. I will let those people know and they will contact you directly.' I thanked her and, although I felt I was no better off as I hadn't a clear diagnosis, we went home. And thus began an 18-month search for a diagnosis. I had to find out what was the matter with Olivia. How could I help her if I didn't know what was wrong?

Only a week later, the phone rang. 'Hello, I'm Liz Critchlow, your Portage teacher,' a cheerful voice announced. 'Let me tell you about Portage and what I shall be doing with Olivia.' Liz explained to me that the Portage method had been developed in Portage, Wisconsin, in the USA. It was a way of breaking down tasks into tiny steps, so that the child could learn a task at their own pace with almost guaranteed success. This method worked for all children who had any kind of learning disability and Liz would visit me every week and spend an hour or so with us both. I was able to tell her of any problems that I might be having in total confidence and she would do her best to help me.

And so the wonderful Liz Critchlow entered our lives for the next two years. Every Wednesday afternoon she arrived with a box full of goodies, which included puzzles, books, games and soft toys. Olivia quickly settled into a routine and Liz would show me how to approach a new task, such as getting Olivia to feed herself, in a far simpler way. She also listened to my fears and concerns, sometimes devoting most of the session to me. During the first session, Liz asked me what I felt was the paramount task I would like Olivia to learn. 'Potty training!' I said immediately. Liz laughed. 'It is almost always that,' she said. 'I find that most parents are desperate to train their children, but in my experience, it happens eventually and will be in the child's own time. It seems that nothing you can do will force these delightful children to become potty trained any faster. I try to comfort parents by asking them how many adults they know who are still in nappies! Have you been very anxious about it?' I confessed I had and told Liz that Olivia wasn't even aware of when her nappy needed changing.

Wednesday afternoons with Liz Critchlow were something we all enjoyed. Liz was comforting, practical and full of positive thoughts. She used to tell me that she had taught children like Olivia before who had ended up at university!

Around the same time, we had a visit from Sue Brown, a speech and language therapist sent from Kent local education authority. Sue observed Olivia and told me that she was typically 'echolalic'. I asked her what that meant. 'It means that rather than respond to conversation, a child will repeat what the adult has just said.' Sue went on to explain to me that as Olivia had trouble processing language, if offered a choice of toys, she would probably choose the last one, as she couldn't remember the list, nor had the ability yet to hold on to the information while making a choice. 'I would start off with only giving her a choice of two things,' Sue recommended. 'Give her plenty of time to answer and encourage her to ask for a drink, rather than taking your hand and pulling you to the fridge door.' Olivia did this all the time. If she wanted anything, she would toddle over to me, take my hand and pull me towards the desired object. She would then either point, or say one word, such as 'drink' or 'book'. It might be a book that was on a shelf she couldn't reach or a video she wanted to watch. I was so used to this method of communication that I hadn't thought it odd, only rather sweet.

Olivia babbled to herself, but never made conversation with anyone and she only spoke to us if she needed something. Sue suggested that to get Olivia to engage with me, I should try sitting quietly in the room with her and describe out loud what she was doing. 'Like this,' Sue said, and began to talk. 'Olivia, I see that you are playing with the farm animals. You have taken a brown horse and are putting it in the stable. Now you have taken a pink pig and have put it under the tractor.' To my amazement, Olivia looked up at Sue, at first puzzled, then she said, very quietly, 'Yes, that where he lives.' Sue was able to respond, 'Very good, yes, a horse does live in the stable.' It was tremendously exciting. We have found a way in, I thought, thrilled. I didn't want to overdo it, but encompassed this little trick into our everyday life. Olivia did respond, but only under these special circumstances. She did not suddenly start to communicate, but I felt that I was able to help her, which made me feel less helpless and inadequate, and little by little we saw improvement.

Sue visited us twice more, but was unable to come on a regular basis. Being part of the Kent Health team, she had an enormous workload and so we decided to look for a private speech and language therapist and soon engaged Mary Hampton for a weekly lesson.

We were beginning to talk to our friends of our concerns about Olivia. Many had had problems themselves with their own children and happily gave us advice and recommendations. For example, it was on the recommendation of one friend, Bella Campbell, that I took Olivia to see Mrs Mary Lobascher, Principal Clinical Psychologist at Great Ormond Street Hospital. Bella explained that Mrs Lobascher was highly experienced and had helped enormously with Bella's two dyslexic sons. She said that Mrs Lobascher had seen everything and would be bound to be able to give a diagnosis for Olivia and some sound advice too.

Back in Great Ormond Street Hospital again, Olivia sat beside Mrs Lobascher's bookcase and began to take out her books, one by one. I ran through her history to date and laid out my concerns. 'She is rather inattentive,' I explained. 'She also rarely turns around if we call her and quite often seems to switch off completely, almost as if the light has been turned off inside, leaving her face quite vacant. When she plays, it is mainly container play, or sitting with books for long periods of time, just like now!' I pointed to Olivia on the floor beside the bookcase. Mrs Lobascher carried out a variety of tests, including a picture memory test, which is rather like the game of matching pairs and the Revised Stanford Binet Intelligence Scale form L-M. All the tests were to check her IQ and also her basic understanding of language and the world around her. Olivia accurately named the picture completion, saying which part of the picture was missing, but couldn't relate to block building or copying a circle with a pencil and paper.

At the end of November a letter arrived from Mrs Lobascher detailing the tests and giving her conclusion. She wrote that Olivia 'certainly did not present as a small girl who would have serious learning disabilities in the future'. She went on to note, however, that Olivia was still very young and 'the degree, if any, of specific learning disability is unknown' but that Olivia had a most unusual 'absorbed play' and 'devoted interest in books', for this age! Mrs Lobascher recommended occupational therapy and physiotherapy to help Olivia with her gross and fine motor skills. Gross motor skills, I had learnt, meant big movements, such as swimming and running, and fine motor skills meant small movements, such as feeding, pencil skills and doing up buttons. 'Good,' I thought. 'No major problem, but no diagnosis either.' Once again, my emotional roller-coaster flew to the top of the track where the sky was clear, except for a black cloud of doubt in the distance. What was the matter with Olivia if all Mary Lobascher was recommending was occupational therapy?

Another friend, Carola Law, telephoned me one morning. Johnnie and Carola's husband, Victor, had been in The Life Guards together and had recently met for lunch. Johnnie had told Victor about our concerns with Olivia and he recommended that I speak to Carola. Their daughter, Nina, who was five years older than Olivia, had oral dyspraxia, which meant that the brain's messages to her muscles got scrambled. It's like trying to watch cable TV stations, Victor explained, without the right descrambler. There's nothing wrong with the TV station and nothing wrong with your set. It's just that your set can't read the signal that the station is sending out. She was at a local school for children with a moderate learning disability. Carola had found that cranial osteopathy had helped Nina a great deal and also something called 'brushing'. I took down the details and began to make appointments.

Stuart Korth's paediatric osteopath practice in Tunbridge Wells was in a large 1930s family home that had been converted into an airy reception area and a series of small rooms, just large enough for an examination bed and one armchair. Once I had heard about this treatment I discovered many proclamations from parents of babies who had cried all day and all night, but after one treatment by Stuart Korth or one of his colleagues had emerged from his practice blissfully asleep with a contented smile on their lips. Osteopathy for children uses gentle pressure and manipulation on the body to ensure the correct functioning of all the different body systems – the nervous system, digestive system, muscular system, skeletal system, circulatory system and immune system – because if they are working effectively, the body can function at optimum level, easing muscular tension for example or ensuring the smooth flow of the lymphatic system. With children, whose bodies are so responsive, treatment can be highly effective for all sorts of problems from colic to cerebral palsy, autism to asthma, glue ear to gastric reflux, epilepsy to eczema. I had heard that osteopaths work at a gentle fundamental level and there are often quite profound results, as many parents testify.

Stuart had a team of earnest young people working for him, who obviously treated him with great respect and devotion. We were shown into one of the small rooms and Olivia played on the floor while I gave Stuart Korth her medical history. 'We see a lot of babies and late developers,' he said. 'Let me look at her and then I can tell you after a treatment what I can do.' He then began the treatment, which was bizarre to watch, the first time. Olivia lay on the bed on her back fully clothed, except for her shoes and socks. I sat beside her and tried to occupy her by reading stories while Stuart, sitting at the head of the bed, behind Olivia, pressed his fingers on her head. His eyes were closed in deep concentration and I wondered if my reading out loud would put him off. Every so often he would emit a huge grunt and a large exhalation of breath, before moving his hands to another part of her head. Once or twice during the treatment, he moved round to the long side of the bed and placed one hand under her spine. There must have been something going on, as Olivia often tried to pull his hands away as if she were being made very uncomfortable.

At the end of the session Stuart said, 'I think that I will be able to help Olivia. I suggest that you bring her to me once a week for three months and then I will review her progress.' Olivia's afternoons were beginning to fill up. She already had Portage and speech and language therapy, and now cranial osteopathy was to be added to her list.

Next, we looked into 'brushing', pioneered at the Centre for Developmental Learning Difficulties, which was set up by Steve Clarke in 1990. I had been sent the brochure, which made interesting reading.

The three main aims of the centre were:

- To treat children with problems which fall into the diagnostic category of developmental learning difficulties.
- To research the developmental processes which cause the problems inherent in developmental learning difficulties.
- To educate. We give talks and lectures around the country in order to offer our experience of the causes of many psychological, behavioural and educational difficulties. We feel it is crucial to increase public awareness of the difficulties developmental anomalies can cause.

It sounded interesting, although rather wide in its claim to treat 'all developmental learning difficulties'. However, Carola had said that it had made a difference to Nina and so I rang Steve Clarke, the director. 'I don't work in Kent, any more,' he told me. 'But I can put you in touch with Paul Burnett, who works at the Helios Clinic in Tunbridge Wells. The essence of the brushing technique is that late developing children, in our experience, have late developing nerves. We try to mature the nervous system by stimulating the nerve endings with gentle brush stroke using a real hair paintbrush. We have had wonderful results.' Encouraged, I rang Paul Burnett, who sent forms for me to complete before we made our first visit to the clinic. He also wrote that he had a large file of letters at the clinic from delighted parents 'for my perusal', as well as the testimonials he had enclosed. I hoped it wasn't going to be too evangelical.

Tunbridge Wells is a curious town. It is renowned for the retired 'Colonel Blimp' type of character who writes frequent letters of protest against almost every aspect of the modern world to the BBC and the broadsheets, but I was to discover that the town also had an extremely active alternative side. Almost anything that could interest one in the field of alternative medicine, séances, healing with crystals, readings with mediums, yoga and so on was available. The Helios Clinic, being just this sort of establishment, was at the top of an excruciatingly steep set of stairs, with the door into the clinic on the top step. Negotiating Olivia and the buggy up them was a task of gross motor difficulty that

I was unsure we would manage. It never ceases to amaze me that these clinics for ill or disabled people are so frequently accessed by impossible stairs and escalators, or lifts that are too small or simply don't work.

Once inside, we were met by Paul Burnett. I found it hard to suppress my amusement at his overly deferential behaviour. This reminded me of the first time I had experienced 'Title awe'. I was 14 when my grandfather died on Boxing Day and my father inherited the viscountcy. Returning to school after the Christmas holidays, my housemistress, a stern, stout tug of a woman whose corset was as rigid and inflexible as her brain, emerged from her room, which opened onto the hall, and accosted me. With a sycophantic smile and rubbing her fingers together she said, 'Ah Elizabeth, I don't have to call you The Honourable now, do I?' which she completed with an attempt at ribald laughter. I fled. Back at the Helios Clinic, I sat Olivia on the once cream, shag-pile carpet that had been so popular in the early 1980s, and we discussed the brushing technique. Paul observed Olivia and her movements (or lack of) and prescribed the following: we were to use a fine paintbrush and brush with 20 strokes under each eye socket from her nose to the side of her face. Then we were to use the non-brush end of the brush and run the tip 20 times from her buttocks up to the top of the spine, ¼ of an inch to the side of her spine, on both sides. This was to be carried out morning and evening. We had a practice run there and then. Olivia did not like it and wriggled. She tried to get hold of the brush. She moved out of the way and would not keep still. It didn't look good, but Paul promised that she would get used to it in a few days. I wasn't quite so optimistic, but it seemed a benign enough treatment and possibly worth the effort.

It seemed that each and every treatment we tried claimed that it was their method alone that resulted in any progress Olivia made, but in all honesty I can't say that any treatment worked better than any other, if indeed they had any effect at all. Apart from speech and language therapy, Portage and, later, physiotherapy, all the rest, including brushing, were interesting, non-invasive and probably of only slight benefit to Olivia. It is almost impossible to make a qualified judgement about which treatment really makes a difference, unless there are obvious, very real, results. One has to consider the normal development of the child that would be taking place naturally, without any extra help and then try to tease out any extra improvements. If one is running several treatments together, then the task becomes more difficult still. Most parents are prepared to try alternative treatments that they think will benefit their child. My only criteria were that they should all be non-invasive.

At the end of September 1995, I had another crisis. Mrs Billing, the headmistress of The Arts Educational School in Tring, telephoned. 'I am afraid I have to suspend Natalya for a week,' she announced through clenched teeth. 'Please come and pick her up as soon as you can. Her behaviour is appalling and we have caught her smoking, not for the first time, either. She walks around arm in arm with a boy, and I don't feel either of them are a good influence on each other.' I mumbled a hurried apology and said that I would be there as soon as I could.

Natalya, at 14½, was bursting with indignation and fury when I collected her. She told me that she couldn't stand the stupid rules and that the teachers were incredibly strict. There was too much dance and the students who were mainly interested in drama were few, and not taken much notice of, in her opinion. 'They go mad if you have one hair out of place in class!' she exploded. 'I must put my hair into this ridiculous tight little bun, and if one hair comes loose, they send me out of the class!' I was only very slightly sympathetic. We drove home in silence, me wondering what I was supposed to do with her for a week when I already had such a heavy daily programme with Olivia. It is all very well to suspend a student for bad behaviour, but does it actually help that child? I can see the benefit for the rest of the class and the teacher, but what if the parents are working and cannot be at home to look after their child?

During the course of that ghastly autumn, Natalya was suspended again. When she was returned the second time, Mrs Billing decided on a new tack, which she hoped would give her a chance to excel. She was given the main part in the school production of *Bugsy Malone* and this, it was hoped, would turn her round. Johnnie and I went to Tring to watch the play. Natalya played Bugsy with a perfect American accent and was so relaxed on stage that her performance, in every way, out-shone all the others. I was bursting with pride and felt sure that this wonderful idea of Mrs Billing's would make Natalya settle at Tring. My joy and relief lasted two weeks. Then came the final phone call. 'It is impossible to keep her here any longer,' declared Mrs Billing. 'If you can take her away tomorrow, I will simply say she has moved schools. If she keeps getting expelled, you will find that you are in an impos-sible situation, as no one else will touch her. Shall we agree that I will have Natalya and all her belongings ready at 2 p.m. tomorrow? I don't want a scene in the school and think it will be better if she leaves qui-etly, during classes.'

Panic set in. What on earth was I to do? I hardly dared tell Johnnie, but I had to face it. I couldn't think of another school that would be suitable. All the lovely girls' public schools in the South-East were like Benenden – full of bright, academic girls from good families who worked hard and had fun, but were not relaxed, open minded and arty enough for Natalya. Then I remembered Bedales! I rang immediately, explained the situation in rather vague terms and asked for a brochure and an interview. Bedales was just the sort of school that I should have sent Natalya to in the first place. My father had been one of its first pupils when the school opened and it was a hot favourite with artistic parents whose children had inherited their artistic ability and temperament.

One week later, I was catching up on my mail in the beautiful oak barn that housed the Bedales school library. Natalya was taking a three-hour assessment and, so far, we had loved what we saw. The pupils walking around the school wore their own clothes and appeared to be allowed to wear more or less what they wanted. They looked very relaxed with a variety of mad hairstyles. This was it! Home at last, I thought to myself as I bent over the large library table, wishing that I had sent her here when she was 11.

We had to wait a week for the results of the assessment and inter-view. I opened the letter with great anticipation and, to my horror, read that she had not been accepted. I couldn't think why, unless even Bedales thought that Natalya would be too much to handle. There were still six weeks before the end of the school term and Natalya had no school and I had no idea where to look next. I spent the morning drinking endless cups of tea and making fruitless phone calls. In the afternoon I went to a local antiques shop to discuss a piece of furniture that was being restored. In conversation with the owner, David told me that he had had a similar problem with his son. He had taken him to James Stephenson, an educational psychologist in London, who had given them very good advice.

Natalya and I went to see James Stephenson within the week. His office was in a lovely mews house off Eaton Square and I was sent 'out to have coffee' for two hours, while Natalya was interviewed and took various psychological, IQ and personality tests. Back in his office, James went through the results of the tests. 'Natalya has a perfectly good brain and a great personality, but I can't honestly say that any school apart from possibly, Gordonstoun, would be at all suitable. She needs to be far away from temptation and with a lot of sports to wear her out!' I didn't like the idea of Gordonstoun for Natalya and said so. I had hated my boarding school and from what I had heard about the strict regime at Gordonstoun, the cold showers and early morning runs, I couldn't image that Natalya would tolerate such harsh conditions and unnecessary discipline for more than a week. This time I had to find something that suited her, so that she had every chance to succeed. 'Well, there is one more alternative, if you are brave enough to consider it,' he said. 'I have been working for some years with a school in Canada, not far from Montreal. Beryl Puddifer, the headmistress, takes children like Natalya and gives them another chance to do their GCSEs and A levels.' He explained that there were about 40 students, mostly British, all of whom had a similar story to that of Natalya. They learnt French, skied all winter and sat English exams. If they wanted to smoke, they had to go outside to do it and as it was minus 30 in the winter, it was not very tempting. He asked me what I thought.

I was amazed to be even contemplating such a school. Natalya looked horrified. We discussed the whole idea in detail and, after an hour or so, it was agreed that James would phone Beryl immediately to find out whether she would take Natalya in January. Beryl was anxious about her age, given that most students started at 16 and Natalya was only 14, and the fact that the other students were allowed to go to town and into the bars. How did I feel about her drinking beer? I wasn't crazy about it, but I certainly wasn't going to miss what might be her only chance of another school for the sake of a few beers. In any case she would be under age and so it would probably never be an issue. It was agreed. Natalya would start at the Laurentian International College in St Agathe, Canada on 6 January 1996. James also found a college that would take her for the interim period, in Gloucester Road, in London and so she would have to commute from Kent every day. We returned home, exhausted, excited and relieved. Natalya now had a future and somewhere to go until January.

CHAPTER 5

No Stone Unturned: Alternative Therapies

As the automatic doors opened at Montreal airport, Natalya and I emerged into the starry Canadian night and were almost knocked over by the intensity of the freezing January air. In my warmest English clothes, I felt as if I were standing completely naked. The wind whipped through my layers and froze the air in my lungs. I had never experienced cold like it. We ran to a taxi and drove to the small town of Saint Agathe, which was to become home for Natalya for the next 18 months during term time. I had gone with her for a few days before the beginning of term, so that we could explore the town and the surrounding area and buy the necessary skiwear, thermals and other items vital to keep one from getting frostbite in this frozen winter wonderland. I had heard about the 'wind chill factor', but these temperatures made the inside of my freezer feel like the Sahara.

Natalya and I spent three days together in Saint Agathe. We marvelled at the ice palace, which was beautifully lit at night and went skating on the thickly frozen lake that nestled beside the town. We tried several of the local restaurants and I booked myself into a clapboard house for bed and breakfast for the half-term in six weeks' time. I enjoyed having these few days alone with her. We had had a very rocky time since she had had to leave the Arts Educational School and it was good to be able to make our peace and look forward to a brighter future. When I asked her why she thought that Bedales had rejected her, she told me that it might have been because she had said yes when they asked her if she smoked! I also badly needed a few days' break myself, after a difficult autumn and a hectic Christmas. When I left Natalya, I had high hopes that this school of highly energetic teenagers, many of whom had ADHD and dyslexia, might be the right place for her, at last. She was to ski every afternoon, learn French and continue with her frequently interrupted GCSE course work. Saint Agathe seemed a safe place to leave my daughter, with no evidence of threatening behaviour, drugs or nightclubs. It was to prove to be a great experience for Natalya, but it turned out that what she learned was about life and nothing much academic.

We had had a big family Christmas at Frenchstreet. Johnnie is the eldest of five and we had invited all his siblings, with their husbands and children, to stay. Together we made a family party of 25, some of whom stayed with us and the rest with Johnnie's mother, whose house was at the top of our drive. On that Christmas morning as we opened our presents in the drawing room, there was much noisy laughter and squeals of delight. Olivia was sitting next to her pile of presents surrounded by hastily torn wrapping paper and loud, laughing relatives. She began to look increasingly distressed and then she covered her ears and started to cry. I was terribly upset, what could be the matter? This was such a surprising reaction to the delights of Christmas morning that I quickly picked her up and took her into the library and shut the door. She sat on my lap sobbing, not saying a word and very slowly she began to calm down. 'Was it too noisy for you, darling?' I asked her, gently stroking her back and holding her close to me. She managed a muffled, 'Yes, Mummy' and so I decided that she would open her presents in that room, quietly, and with only me there. Inevitably, everyone came into the library to enquire what was wrong and soon it was almost as full and noisy as the drawing room had been. No sooner had I explained that Olivia couldn't seem to cope with the noise and would they please leave us to open her presents quietly, than someone else would come in to ask what the matter was!

It was on that Christmas morning that I realised Olivia found large crowds and noise extremely difficult. She was only three-and-a-half and I did not realise for another year or two how she suffered with sensory overload. Loud noise, a high pitch or even a blowing sound, sounds that I would never consider a problem, caused her terrible distress, and I remembered with horror all the pantomimes and shows I had taken her to, which must have been tantamount to torture for her. And that was only auditory sensory overload. I was to learn years later that Olivia had the same sensory difficulties with touch and hated to get her fingers sticky or walk on sand, for example. If one sense was heavily loaded, the others appeared to go into shutdown, so that if she were required to look at something that required concentration, she was unable to take in any auditory information simultaneously. Too much visual input made her auditory system effectively collapse and too much noise made her unable to 'see' while she focused entirely on trying to unscramble and process the sounds and chatter surrounding her. The same occurred with an overload of touch or taste. I had noticed that at mealtimes, unless it were only the two of us, she 'switched off'. Her face took on a completely blank expression as if she were there only in body, but not in mind. Her expression was, frankly, rather frightening, because it was not the expression of someone who is deep in thought, it was empty. It was almost eerie to look at her, but once the meal was over and she was back in the playroom on her own, she seemed all right again. I later learned how difficult and stressful it was for her to try to follow cross-conversation and constant interruptions. She still can't. Olivia is now 13 and she gives me only two goes at understanding what she is trying to tell me. *Two chances, no more.* If I fail to understand her mumbled speech, softly and rapidly spoken, and the usually completely random or out of context subject matter, she will become very angry and frustrated and walk away shouting at me: 'No Mummy! Don't ask me that again!' I am left feeling both extremely bereft and a failure, and have long since had to cope with the sadness of all too often not being able to understand my own child.

Olivia needs my complete attention, a very quiet room and my not doing anything else, such as making a cup of tea or even sewing. It is not that I cannot hear her unless I am still, but my movements distract her and she finds it so much harder. As I am a naturally energetic person and a typical woman who feels able to do several things at once, I find it hard to down tools and just listen. It has added a whole new dimension to the 'art of listening' for me. I have learned the value of complete attention and I notice how much I appreciate those who really listen to me, rather than just hear what I am saying. One is done with the heart, while the other is just an acceptance of incoming material. Most people do not listen; they are just waiting, often impatiently, for the speaker to finish so that they can speak themselves. Olivia needed the whole person to listen to her if she were to be able to tell them something that was important to her. Was I always in so much of a hurry that I couldn't stop? I had heard at a conference on speech and language the value of looking at the person who was speaking. Olivia's eye contact was always fleeting and she only really looked at one when she was speaking. When she was spoken to, or even had her name called, she seldom looked at the speaker. The speech and language therapist who was addressing the conference told us that she often said to her husband: 'Did you hear what I just said? Please look at me, as it will help you to listen and process!' I found this phrase 'to listen and process' wonderful. It was hilarious, in that she had had to use it on her own husband, as I strongly suspected all wives could, but it was a phrase that summed up Olivia's enormous difficulties with speech and conversation in general.

Occasionally, Johnnie collected Olivia from Winnies, the nursery in Westerham. Mary, who was mainly in charge of looking after Olivia, had commented to him that perhaps she might be autistic. Once more I railed at the term. 'We do not know what is the matter with her', I said, again. 'It is completely out of order for people to make such suggestions, when they know far less than we do. I am trying so hard to get a diagnosis and these sorts of comments are very unhelpful.' Poor Johnnie had just passed on a remark, but how I hated to hear the 'A' word, as I saw it, used in connection with Olivia. After all, I had taken her to see one of the foremost neurologists in the country as well as specialist paediatricians and none of them had suggested that she might be autistic. Surely they were far better informed and equipped to make such a suggestion than a nursery school assistant? She already had a full programme of speech and language therapy, paediatric osteopathy and now we were 'brushing' as well. Olivia did eventually get used to it and so we brushed up her nerve endings as prescribed, night and morning, creamed her body to keep the eczema at bay and had weekly Portage sessions. By the spring, at nearly four she was practically potty trained and typically, once she was completely potty trained, unlike all other children, she never, ever, had an accident. Not only that, she never once wet her bed at night and even went to the other extreme of holding on for so long that we had to set a small kitchen alarm to remind us to take her to the loo. It was wonderful to finally get rid of those nappies. Olivia had learnt to go to the loo and we were very pleased and grateful, but I was amazed to discover that the loo was the only place she would go. If we were out for a walk, there was never any question of her going behind a bush, but she would at least use toilets that were new to her. I was beginning to count my blessings, to see how much she had learnt in the past year and not think too much about the progressively widening gap between her and her peers.

Mary Hampton, who gave Olivia speech and language lessons every week, suggested that I join Afasic, the UK charity representing children and young adults with communication impairments, which works for their inclusion in society and supports their parents and carers. They hold meetings for parents whose children have language difficulties. The first meeting I attended was in the YMCA in Tunbridge Wells. One of the women there, Carol, ran a charity called Action Support for the Special Needs Child and offered her help when I mentioned that I was trying to work my way through the minefield of a Statement of Special Needs. This invaluable document is a child's only passport to gain the help and therapies that he or she so desperately needs. It carries a brief description of the child's current ability and, without it, the child is entitled to no extra help in school, no individual education plan, no occupational therapy, no speech and language therapy, no physical therapy, nor extra time on a computer, the list is endless. Olivia's statement described her as functioning at a two-and-a-half to three-year old's level, when she was nearly five years old. It said that she frequently had a tantrum when her needs were not met and that she rarely interacted with her peers. Her gross and fine motor skills were immature and she was unaware of danger, among her many other difficulties. There followed a whole page of objectives and strategies within her educational provision aimed at meeting her needs. These included a social/emotional/behavioural section, a speech, language and communication section and a general section, ending in a plan to monitor her progress with short-term targets, which needed to be checked at a review each term in the school and a renewed statement each year. It had been put together by an educational psychiatrist with a vast amount of input from me as I described her current abilities and difficulties.

I was further terrified when Carol told me that unless I had the wording in exactly the right place, then there was no legal requirement for the local authority to provide any of the therapies Olivia needed. This meant that, in Olivia's case, unless the need for speech and language was written into Section 3 and the hours each week were specified, in all likelihood, the speech and language therapy would never happen. This vital piece of information was passed on to me by chance. What would have happened if I hadn't met Carol? There is nothing in the Statement that makes this clear. I felt that it was a case of withholding information and it almost seemed like a deliberate trap to catch unwitting parents. I was to learn that each and every form pertaining to Olivia had to be gone over with a fine-tooth comb and, better still, given to an expert who was fully au fait with the lack of information in each document. I went home with Carol's phone number and said that I would send her the draft copy.

Afasic sent me their membership form in due course and along with it came a list of glossary sheets, which described various learning difficulties. I ordered some of the sheets, such as Glossary Sheet 18 on Dyspraxia/apraxia and Glossary Sheet 22 on Comprehension or Receptive Language Difficulties. Also, there were papers on Alternative/Augmentative Communication, Articulation, Cocktail Party Syndrome, Developmental Language Delay/Developmental

Language Disorder, Aphasia/Dysphasia and so on. It was a steep learning curve for me. I had to learn what half the words I read meant and most of them were technical so were not always in the dictionary. Then I had to understand their meaning and how that applied to Olivia, then, finally, what I could do to help her, in other words, how I would apply my new knowledge and in what appropriate form. I was lucky in that we had Mary Hampton whom I could ring for help if I couldn't wait until the next speech and language session. It was also Mary who spotted that Olivia had learnt whole phrases without understanding their meaning. Even more confusingly, she would use them in context. This was called 'expressive language' and I learned not to be lulled into thinking that her language skills were improving when she was, in effect, speaking 'parrot'.

One of the Afasic Glossary Sheets I ordered was on Autism and another on something called Fragile X Syndrome. I decided to order them both. On a hot summer day at the hairdressers, I read the sheet on autism. It said 'that some children fit the description of any particular term quite well, while many others appear on the borderlines'. Further down the sheet I read 'the specific characteristics of each child's difficulties still need to be identified and addressed as children vary greatly'. There we are, I thought, vindicated! Olivia might be borderline autistic, but that was not the cause of her difficulties. What was fascinating and made my hands shake with excitement as I read on, was the glossary on Fragile X. Almost every point of description of this disorder applied to Olivia! I read and re-read the paper, becoming more and more convinced each time I went through the list of characteristics of Fragile X that this was the root cause of all her problems. The paper described these children in the following way:

- Inattentive
- Distractible
- Shyness and social withdrawal are striking features in girls
- Poor eye contact
- Difficulty in relating to other people
- Anxiety in social situations often leading to tantrums

- Insistence on familiar routines
- Hypotonia (low muscle tone)
- Delay in the development of speech and language
- And, lastly, a very common physical feature is flat feet! Olivia's feet are as flat as pancakes!

This was it! Olivia had each characteristic; I had discovered what her problem was! I could now DO something about it. I cannot describe the feeling of joy, intense relief and excitement I felt as I sat having my wretched hair blow-dried. All I wanted to do was rush to Johnnie and our family, and tell them the good news. We could make a plan, move on and have a sense of direction, instead of my years of searching, groping in the dark all alone and grasping at straws.

That evening we were to go to drinks in the Cholmondeley Room, one of the many rooms let out for entertaining in the House of Lords. This particular room led on to the terrace, which overlooked the Thames, and it was lovely to watch the boats cruise up and down the river in the summer. In winter, the terrace was covered with a large heated marquee, and lost all its magic. When I got home from the hairdresser the words poured out in a jumbled rush as I told an astonished Johnnie that I had found the cause of all Olivia's problems. Not only that, all it required was a blood test and that would clarify, absolutely, that she had this Fragile X syndrome. I ran to the phone and called my mother and then Natalya, who was home for the Easter holidays from Canada. I could hardly wait until the following morning to phone Dr Morrison, our GP, and ask for a blood test. I was slightly surprised when he said that he actually didn't think that Olivia had Fragile X, but if I really wanted to, he would take a blood sample and send it off to the laboratory. I really did want to; he had no idea just how much I wanted to know why Olivia was such a late developer!

We had to wait a couple of weeks for the results. It was my birthday in May and we decided it would be fun to visit Beaulieu in Hampshire for the Bank Holiday weekend. We took Violet, Charles and Olivia and on a lovely sunny spring day drove from Kent to Lymington in Hampshire, where we stayed in a romantic old hotel near the New Forest.

Beaulieu is the stately home belonging to Lord Montagu of Beaulieu, who has a superb collection of vintage cars, which he houses in the National Motor Museum, next to Beaulieu Palace, and set in wonderful grounds. This year was the 'Spring Classic Car Show' including 'Pride of Ownership', where owners of vintage cars were invited to bring them to Beaulieu for the admiration of all who came to the show. We spent the evening strolling through Buckler's Hard, a charming 18th-century shipbuilding village near Beaulieu before having a delicious birthday dinner and falling happily into bed.

The next day we went straight to the car show. Charles had taken after his father and adored cars, so Johnnie took him around hand in hand and they discovered old Bugattis and very early motorcars. Edward Montagu, who is a friend of ours, invited Olivia and me to ride around in the oldest and certainly the slowest car in the country! I enjoyed it but Olivia just sat beside me staring straight ahead as I tried to interest her in this ancient machine. Lunch was laid out buffet style in two large marquees and when we thought that the children needed a rest, we headed for the main marquee. Johnnie took our drinks order and went up to the bar. Olivia had asked for an orange juice and was obviously either very thirsty or impatient. Johnnie became caught up in conversation and took ages to bring us the drinks. On the table next to us, the people were already eating. A beautifully dressed lady in a large hat sat opposite us and, to my amazement, Olivia slid off her seat and before I could stop her, took the lady's orange juice and, right in front of the astonished woman, drained her glass. Just at this moment, Johnnie turned round from the bar with his hands full and saw Olivia standing by the lady and also saw her expression of utter bewilderment. He was overcome with embarrassment and I, with amusement. I took the full glass of orange juice from Johnnie and gave it to the lady with abject apologies. Whatever made Olivia do that, we wondered? Didn't she realise how socially unacceptable such an act was? Also, at nearly four, wasn't she rather old to be doing such odd, babyish things?

The following week Dr Morrison rang me with the results of the blood test. 'It is as I suspected,' he said. 'Olivia does not have Fragile X.' I couldn't believe my ears. I was so certain; all the factors hung together. As high as I had risen on first reading about Fragile X, I now fell correspondingly low. It was a heavy blow. I began to wonder if I had the energy to carry on trying to find out what her problem was. It had even been suggested that she could be PDDNOS (Pervasive Developmental Disorder, Not Otherwise Specified), but that was too vague for me. The world, it seems to me, is divided into two specific groups, the 'knowers' and the 'deniers', and I was 100 per cent in the knowers camp. Some people cannot cope with the reality of cancer or Alzheimer's, and can only bear to continue living if they have hope held together in a thick mist of ignorance. I don't know how doctors decide who needs information and who needs as little as possible; it must be a very difficult and delicate choice. But I needed to know. Strength, for me, is in knowledge. It gave me a sense of being in control (even if I were not) and a feeling that I could effectively do something. The more information I had, the better. Yet here I was, thrown right back to the beginning again. We still had no diagnosis. I could hardly bear it.

I was also beginning to notice and to read articles in newspapers and magazines about parents whose children had learning difficulties. One of these articles was about Henrietta and Michael Spink, whose two boys had normal brains, but could not talk or walk. Henrietta had gathered an extensive bank of hard-earned information on a wide variety of alternative therapies, all non-invasive, which she had discovered, just as I had, on her long search for helpful treatments for her sons. She wanted to be able to share this information with other parents who were in the same situation, and was setting up a website and a charity in the name of her elder son, Henry. She sounded just my type of woman and I wrote to her immediately. Thus began a new friendship, and a year later Henrietta invited me to become a patron of her charity, the Henry Spink Foundation, and to attend the launch at St James's Palace. It was wonderful to have a friend who was in a similar position. I had often felt deeply isolated with the enormous difficulties of trying to help Olivia without really knowing how. Henrietta had tried vitamin supplements among many other treatments and recommended I explore that avenue with Olivia. I decided to take Olivia to Biolab, in Weymouth Street, London, on the advice of my sister-in-law, Claire Mackintosh, who told me to ask for John McLaren Howard, who had been very helpful to her when she had been left feeling run-down after a virus.

John McLaren Howard was a gentle middle-aged man, who took us into his consulting room and asked me to tell him Olivia's history. I was becoming adept at delivering a short medical history as I had done it so many times in the past two years. He cut a small piece of her hair to analyse and also took a sweat sample, by attaching a piece of blotting paper to Olivia's back for an hour. These were sent off to the lab, and in a week the results came back, which showed that Olivia was low in both zinc and magnesium. We were sent tiny sugary pills and drops to put in her drink, both of which were easy for Olivia to take. She did this for over two years, but I couldn't see any visible improvement in any area of her behaviour, skin condition, alertness, muscle tone, speech or any other physical or mental manifestation.

I had also read about the possible very beneficial effects of taking large doses of vitamin B6 and tried to get hold of a supplement called 'Super Nu-Thera with P5P' from a firm in North America. Kirkman, the producers, claimed that its benefits would include:

- Increased communicative skills
- Reduce restlessness
- Less irritability
- Reduced repetitive self stimulation (this is something autistic children do, such as rocking, hand flapping, head banging or container play)
- Better eye contact

The P5P stood for Pyridoxal-5-Phosphate. When the Super Nu-Thera finally came, it was in pills so large that a horse would have trouble swallowing them, so I rang Kirkman and asked if they produced it in a more child-friendly form. Eventually a tub of powder arrived, which we then had to disguise with liberal quantities of Ribena, as the taste was sweet and quite strong, in an artificially fruity way. I wondered if all the added sugar would negate any efficacy the supplement might give, but we had no choice. If Olivia saw me add anything to her drink, she would refuse to drink it and there was nothing I could do to persuade her. It was the same with food. No amount of cajoling would encourage her to eat. She was adamant and I quickly learnt not to worry.

While we were working our way down the vitamin route, I thought it worth while also to investigate any possible allergies Olivia might have. She had had eczema, but that only flared up when she was ill or the weather turned cold and it was something that we could keep under control. She certainly suffered from hay fever and occasionally had red eyes, but that, too, was seasonal except when we went to our stables, where she would have an instant allergic reaction to the horses and began sneezing within minutes. Her skin was extremely dry, and when I took her to a new paediatric skin specialist, he told me that she had ichthyosis, which was a chronic dry skin condition that she had been born with. He suggested that we bath her in Oilatum and cream her face and body top to toe every day, which we were already doing. Her nasty scar on her back suffered in the cold weather. It was now an inch wide and the scar tissue often split and cracked. How I hated the skin specialist who did such a bad job on Olivia, every time I looked at her back.

The allergist who worked with Biolab in London was Dr Damian Downing. I had made an appointment and was warned that he would have to take blood samples and that would not be pleasant for Olivia. There seemed to be no choice, but my kind and helpful GP, Dr Morrison, gave me a small quantity of an anaesthetic cream, which he recommended I put on the top of her arm, where the needle would enter, and cover it with cling film to allow the cream the best chance to penetrate the skin. I was to do this on the morning of the visit to anaesthetise the area. Olivia howled as the blood sample was taken and I felt a real heel. The look of complete astonishment on her face as she registered the pain made me more convinced than ever that I would not try any therapy that was more invasive than an injection. It simply wasn't worth it, unless, of course, it guaranteed a cure for whatever mystery disorder she might have. After a fairly long discussion about

Olivia's difficulties, which included her diet, sleeping patterns and skin condition, Dr Downing recommended that, once he and I had discussed the results of the blood test, I should visit a nutritionist. As it was part of the allergies package, I agreed. The tests taken that morning were a cytotoxic test for allergies and essential fatty acids and amino acids. The results showed that Olivia was low in DHA, which is docohexaenoic fatty acid in the omega-3-series, and Efamol, a mixture of omega 3 and omega 6, was recommended to raise her levels.

The nutritionist was Dr Keith Eaton whom we also saw at Biolab. The consultation took over an hour as he wanted to know Olivia's history. As we were currently engaged in a variety of other treatments, this took some time. Dr Eaton was also an allergist, and he had the results of the allergy tests taken by Dr Damian Downing.

Olivia was allergic to eggs, green beans, chocolate, berries and citrus fruit, and we were advised to rotate cows' milk with sheep and goats' milk and also rotate whole wheat with oats and rice. Dr Downing had already sent me a list of foods that Olivia could eat and what she must avoid. I had read it with dismay. However, it was nothing in comparison to Dr Eaton's list of foods to avoid, which included all dairy, eggs, chicken, fish and shellfish, pork, ham, bacon, yeast and wheat in any form, as well as all sugars including honey. Olivia was nearly four and had the usual diet that most four year olds enjoy. She ate cereal at breakfast with cows' milk, and liked cheese, ham, eggs, chicken, ice cream and sandwiches. She was not particularly easy to feed, as if she didn't want to eat something, nothing in the world could make her. I seemed to be left with spinach and venison and I didn't think that she would take to soya milk.

Having just been on a wheat- and dairy-free diet myself, I found that it wasn't as difficult as I had envisaged. However, for my not quite four year old, who was a picky eater in the first place, I came to the conclusion that this was a mountain too high to climb. I took it all with a pinch of salt and decided to cut down as much as possible in the wheat and dairy area, while trying to give her a balanced diet that she would actually eat.

The Statement of Special Needs said that Olivia needed occupational therapy. During the summer, a lovely young therapist called Terry arrived from the local authority. She watched Olivia and asked me what I thought was Olivia's area of greatest need. 'Eating,' I replied. 'She can only use a spoon or a fork at the moment, but still prefers to use her fingers.' Terry suggested that I buy a set of baby cutlery that had a special place at the top of the handle to stop the fingers from sliding down. We decided that it would be a good idea for Terry to see how Olivia ate, and so it was arranged that Terry's next appointment would be at lunchtime.

Two weeks later, Terry arrived at 12.45 p.m. I had bought the special cutlery and Terry helped Olivia to hold it correctly. She then held her hands over Olivia's and showed her how to cut her food, saying, 'Now saw, saw, saw, Olivia!' Terry also recommended that we have a smaller, lighter cup for Olivia and that she practise pouring, by playing in the bath, or outside, as it was summer. Terry was fun, a real inspiration, and I was looking forward to starting a full occupational therapy programme with her in the autumn.

However, the autumn came and went, but we heard no further word from Terry. When I finally chased down someone in the local education authority who was responsible for occupational therapy, not an easy task in itself, I was told that Terry was pregnant and would not be coming back to work for at least a year. Not only that, but there were no more occupational therapists available! Fortunately for us, we could afford all these extra treatments and therapies, and I rang around to find a local occupational therapist who would take Olivia privately. How others manage on a limited budget, and maybe speaking English as a second language, makes me shudder to think. First, you had to know what your child needed. That required the right person to advise you. Second, you had to know how to access that treatment, or how to fight for it if it were refused. Third, you needed the time and knowledge to know how to practise at home, take your child to the therapist and afford any necessary equipment. It was easy for me. To begin with, having a title meant that, generally, people either answered your call or returned it. Being articulate meant that you could express any concerns that might arise, and not having any financial worries was perhaps the most important of all. The treatments and therapies we tried were all costly. Some were much more expensive than others, but I never had to consider the telephone bill, for example, or the cost of recommended equipment. It was for these reasons that Henrietta Spink of the Henry Spink Foundation wanted to share her hard-won knowledge. Otherwise we were all chasing the same information, which was a long, expensive and heartbreaking process.

I found Jill Christmas, a paediatric occupational therapist, who ran her own clinic called the Christmas Children's Clinic, from her home near Tunbridge Wells. Jill had built a therapy room, which was full of wonderful equipment, toys and games. On our first visit, I went through the now well-rehearsed history of Olivia's development, her current therapies and her most obvious difficulties.

Jill was about my age, tall, blonde and had an utterly lovely nature. She was so obviously deeply interested in and knowledgeable about her subject that I began to learn more myself. Once more, it was a steep learning curve. There were so many technical terms that I had to constantly stop Jill to ask her what she meant. Jill immediately spotted that Olivia never crossed her 'mid line', which meant that if she were colouring, for example, she would switch the crayon from her right hand to her left, rather than take her hand across her body to the other side of the page. Jill also told me of the importance of crawling. I soon learnt that each stage of development was crucial. If one stage of development was missing, a child could not continue learning. Humans, I learnt, had a predetermined learning pattern that went from A to Z. If stage C had been missed, it presented enormous difficulties, as a child could not jump over a missed part. A child could not go from A to G having missed out stage D, whatever that stage might represent. It was not an insurmountable problem, but there would always be gaps that would make each next stage of development more difficult.

We began a weekly visit to Jill's clinic. Jill often lent me her books to read and also loaned me equipment. Olivia loved her toys, which were used as a bribe to get her through the more difficult exercises that would help Olivia's stability. Hand–eye co-ordination was a major problem for Olivia and so Jill devised different approaches to teach her to write. This is called a 'multi-sensory approach' to learning. Many children like Olivia are visual learners, and some learn predominantly through sound or touch. Jill incorporated all Olivia's senses in order to help her learn and to train her muscle memory. She used sand in a small tray in which Olivia formed letters, and chalk on a large blackboard, among other methods. Olivia had to take a thick paintbrush and dip it into water and then paint over the letters or word that Jill had chalked on the blackboard. Each week Jill had something new for Olivia to do, as well as the old favourites and so our visits to her clinic were both pleasant and informative, although quite tiring for Olivia, who had to come straight from nursery. On the occupational therapy days, we didn't get home until 6 p.m., which was late, as Olivia had left the house at 8.15 in the morning. I considered it worth it and so we fell into a programme of a different therapy outside school hours every other day.

In the New Year of 1997, during a speech and language session with Mary Hampton, Mary suggested that I get in touch with Claire Roberts, whose son Marc was autistic. Claire had fought to get Marc into a mainstream school and, after a long and difficult battle, succeeded. I was in the process of deciding which school to send Olivia to that September and Mary thought that I would find it helpful to talk to Claire about how to get a child with a Statement of Special Needs into a mainstream LEA school. Mary had given speech and language lessons to Marc, who had made a remarkable developmental leap after he had had a treatment called Auditory Intervention Training (AIT). The essence of this treatment is to lower noise sensitivity by jumbling up sound and playing the new mix over headphones for one hour a day, for ten consecutive days. He was only four when he went by train every day for ten days to the Hale Clinic in London for AIT and the first most visible sign of improvement was when he put his own hands under the hand dryer in the bathroom. Marc had always found the sound of hairdryers and hand dryers excruciating and seeing him voluntarily dry his hands under the dryer was the first miracle for his family. The second was when he leant forward towards a man sitting opposite him on the train and, looking directly at him, asked 'What is it?' Claire asked Marc if he wanted to know the man's name, and he said yes, so the man obligingly told Marc after Claire asked him if he would mind doing so. These examples were little miracles for Marc's family and the AIT therapist they visited told them that the AIT had opened the door, but he advised them also to give Marc intensive speech therapy, which they did on a weekly basis with Mary Hampton for the next five years. He also retained all the benefits he had gained from AIT. Mary wasn't sure if AIT would help Olivia, who was also four at the time, but it seemed worth looking into. I agreed, and found a book called *The Sound of a Miracle, A Child's Triumph Over Autism*, by Annabel Stehli. Annabel's daughter, Georgie, was autistic and had severe difficulties dealing with sound. Not necessarily loud sounds, as one would immediately imagine, but covering a huge range, that could be low, hissing or almost inaudible to the normal ear. After travelling to Switzerland to see Dr Guy Bernard, the inventor of AIT, Georgie had had the treatment, and completely recovered from her autism! However, I re-read the last couple of chapters of the book a few years later after a discussion about it with Dr Judy Gould of the National Autistic Society, who pointed out to me that after Georgie had returned to the USA, her mother spent months teaching her appropriate behaviour, such as how to enter a room or welcome guests, which are part of the social difficulties and lack of social awareness that come with autism. It was an extremely inspiring read at the time and a treatment that I immediately wanted to carry out on Olivia. Although I was still convinced that autism was not the central reason for Olivia's difficulties, if she were a little autistic, then clearly, it could be cured with the right treatment! Full of hope and enthusiasm, I rang Tracy Alderman, who was my local AIT practitioner.

CHAPTER 6

Diagnosis and Devastation

ON A FREEZING COLD, DARK, JANUARY AFTERNOON, Tracy Alderman arrived with her Auditory Intervention Training (AIT) equipment. We had already spoken at length over the phone and I had told her how concerned I was that Olivia might not like the headphones at all. She hated anything on her head and couldn't bear to wear hats or hairbands. Tracy assured me that she always came prepared with bags of new toys and would massage Olivia's feet, if that would relax her. She also suggested that as Charles had had grommets fitted, due to 'glue ear' when he was three, he might benefit from AIT too. We agreed to give them both the treatment and Tracy would start with Charles, which we hoped would encourage Olivia and make her less fearful.

I took Tracy to our guest bedroom. I had decided that it was the perfect room in the house to carry out AIT as it had few distractions. Tracy also wanted to leave her listening equipment with us for the ten days of the treatment as it was heavy and cumbersome and it would be safe here from curious little fingers. With her large brown eyes and dimpled smile, Tracy exuded warmth and I felt instantly at ease. She began to open her bags and, like Mary Poppins, pulled out one toy after another, to Olivia's delight. Charles, who was six, had decided that he would read or build with Lego during his hour.

'Are you ready to do some listening?' Tracy asked Charles. He put on the earphones and began his hour of listening to jumbled up sound while playing with Lego bricks. Olivia had already begun to 'sort'

Tracy's toys. She had taken a tub of Teddy Links and was busy putting them in the same colour groups. The object of this toy was to make a string of teddies as each one could be joined to another through a small break in the head. I had tried many times to teach Olivia how to do this, as we had the same toy, but she wasn't interested. Once that toy was colour grouped, she began to do the same with another toy. Tracy looked on and asked me: 'When was Olivia diagnosed with autism?' I was astonished by the question. 'Oh, she's not autistic!' I rapidly replied. 'Whatever made you say that?' 'It is just that my son Josh is autistic and he does the same sorting that Olivia is doing. What *is* her diagnosis?' Tracy asked me gently. 'She has a social and communication disorder with a moderate learning disability,' I replied. I told Tracy about my fruitless three-year search for a full diagnosis and some of the treatments we had tried. Tracy talked about Josh, who was born autistic. She had recognised it very quickly as she had worked with autistic children for many years. He had been a screamer, and had cried and screamed from morning until night for the first two years of his life. It had been extremely hard to live with and in fact Tracy's husband had found it impossible and had left her and their two children. She had had to manage alone. Josh was, by this time, aged seven and went to Cage Green, which was an autistic unit attached to a mainstream school, and was getting on very well. It was the first time that I heard that some autistic children screamed all the time and once again felt extremely grateful that Olivia was such an easy child.

We had quite a struggle cajoling Olivia to wear the headphones. As soon as we put them on, she pulled them off. It took at least ten minutes of trying a variety of strategies and distractions before she submitted to them. Tracy turned the sound down very low to begin with and I sat beside her on the big armchair and we looked at books together. By the time we were half-way through the treatment, Olivia was obviously feeling much more confident about wearing the headphones. Tracy's cheerful: 'Hello! Are you ready for some listening?' greeted us every afternoon, although Charles was rather grumpy about having to sit still for an hour every day.

On the third session, Tracy brought me a leaflet from the National

Autistic Society, called 'What is Autism?' 'I thought that you might like to read this,' she said, 'because you were interested in hearing about Josh.' That evening I read the leaflet. Across the bottom of the sheet were 14 drawings of pin people doing a variety of odd behaviours. Underneath were written the descriptions: Displays indifference; Joins in only if an adult insists and assists; Indicates needs by using an adult's hand; One-sided interaction; Does not play with other children; Echolalic – copies words like a parrot; Talks incessantly about one topic; Bizarre behaviour; Handles or spins objects; Lack of creative pretend play; Variety is not the spice of life; No eye contact; Inappropriate laughing or giggling; But some can do some things very well, very quickly but *not* tasks involving social understanding. Beside the pin people were the words, 'If your child has four or more of these behaviours, then he may be autistic.' Olivia had ten.

Even with this information, I didn't leap to any conclusion. It seems odd to me now, but there was no immediate loud ringing of alarm bells, just a persistent nagging in the back of my mind that I would certainly have to look quite seriously at the possibility of autism, among her other very apparent difficulties. Charles and Olivia finished the AIT treatment and arrangements were made for Tracy to return in a month and check their hearing again and report any changes or improvements. (Tracy thought that Charles had some definite improvement, but sadly neither she nor I could find any change in Olivia's hearing or behaviour.) I didn't mention the leaflet, but after a few days of mulling, I decided to call Dr Wendy Holmes, who had seen Olivia 18 months earlier, at the Pembury Child Development Centre. 'I wanted to ask you if you could come and see Olivia again, and disregarding any other difficulty that she may have, tell me if you think she might be autistic', I said. Then came the bombshell. '*I have always thought that she was autistic, as you know,*' Dr Holmes replied. 'I never knew that!' I protested. 'You never said she was autistic!' 'But everyone knows that a "social and communication disorder" means autism,' she replied. 'Who is everyone?' I asked. 'I didn't know that, how was I expected to know that is what that means?' My request for Olivia not to be labelled as autistic had doubtless played a part in the rather euphemistic diagnosis and subsequent misunderstanding.

Still not unduly perturbed, a few days later Dr Holmes and I went through the CARS test together. This is the Childhood Autism Rating Scale, which has 15 sections with four questions in each. One has to answer one of the four questions and add up a total score at the end. I decided to be brutally honest and the result showed that Olivia was exactly on the dividing line between moderate and severe autism.

It was 27 February 1997 and my search for a diagnosis was at an end. Also, my life, as I knew it. Certainly every hope or dream I had had for Olivia was wiped out with one single word: autism. This monster had crept stealthily and undetected into her very being, filling every pore of her body, stealing her mind and her personality. It had taken her hostage, there would be no plea-bargaining and we were left helpless innocents, locked forever outside the prison walls. Completely numb, I carried on as normal for a further 24 hours until, like a great oak struck by lightening, I cracked.

Like identical twins, grief and loss took me to their solitary planet and abandoned me there. I was inconsolable. Nothing had changed, and yet *everything* had changed. I wanted to rip the autism out of Olivia with my bare hands. I needed a fight. I would be the autism slayer. Without knowing it, I had taken the first step of the seven stages of grief: denial, followed by anger, fear, loss, despair, hope and finally acceptance. St Paul was wrong when he said that charity, or love, was greater than faith or hope. Hope wins hands down every time. It is hope that sustains us in our blackest hour. It was to be many years before I reached acceptance.

I called my mother, sobbing, and told her that now we knew, it was confirmed that Olivia was autistic. 'But why are you so surprised, darling?' she asked me tenderly. 'We knew that this was the problem all along, didn't we? So often we have talked about the possibility and that she probably had mild autism.' 'There is knowing and *knowing*', was all I could reply.

Grief is a lonely place. It is individual and cannot be completely shared or understood. I didn't know what to do, nor did I know which way to turn. I was utterly devastated. What was especially hard was that Olivia looked perfectly normal. Like most autistic people there is no outward sign of the inward confusion. It was not life threatening and she would have a normal life expectancy. That I had to be grateful for, but autism had stolen her mind. What are we without our minds? Where does one's personality begin? The body is nothing without the mind. The essence of man is inside his head but autism spoke and understood a different language. It saw the world in a unique way that I would never, in a million years, be even able to guess at. I would fight to protect her, fight to reach her, fight to make her love me. I would love her unconditionally, for she did not know how to love me back.

Ten days after the diagnosis, I flew to Canada to visit Natalya. It was the winter half term and I was to meet her at Mont Tremblant, where the school were having a skiing week. I cried all the way over on the plane and arrived looking a ghastly sight. I picked up a hire car and drove to meet Natalya and her friends. It was just what I needed. Natalya was so loving and compassionate, and her friends were often hilariously funny and bursting with youthful energy. The complete change brought me to my senses. I began to stabilise and wondered what on earth I should do. Clearly, I couldn't carry on crying day after day. What I needed was information. I realised then that I knew absolutely nothing about autism at all. The sum total of my knowledge was the film *Rain Man* and the only recently read National Autistic Society's leaflet. I felt as if I had been dumped on Mars and told to find my own way home without so much as a map. With horror, I remembered how angry I had been when Kathleen Winch, Johnnie's secretary, had first proposed that Olivia might be autistic several years before. I replayed in my mind, a thousand times, the first time I met Dr Wendy Holmes and said with confidence that I didn't want Olivia diagnosed as autistic. I hadn't a clue what autism was, so how could I have done such a thing? And why hadn't she disabused me? I had probably appeared to be knowledgeable and this had cost me, and Olivia, the last 18 months. It was not until a whole year-and-a-half later that we had a diagnosis and all that time I could have been helping her. I tortured myself with guilt and shame.

As soon as I returned home, Johnnie and I discussed my buying a computer so that I could access the Internet. Buying the computer was the easy part; learning how to use it was a much slower process. I began computer classes and research into autism at the same time. I bought every book on autism that I heard about, read voraciously and joined the National Autistic Society as a life member. I shelved almost everything else in my life, for a long time.

Gradually I became familiar with some of the names of leading professionals who specialised in autism, whose research and books were published, and who were mentioned or quoted with regularity. One of the foremost was Dr Lorna Wing, who, together with Dr Judith Gould, had carried out extensive research into autism in the late 1960s and early 1970s. Lorna Wing's book, *The Autistic Spectrum*, became my bible. Lorna had an autistic child herself, and was a founder member of the National Autistic Society. It was Lorna Wing who, together with Uta Frith, had translated the early papers of Hans Asperger and had made the connections with autism. In 1981, Lorna Wing had written the definitive paper about Asperger syndrome, a term that she alone had coined, and had brought world attention and recognition to the condition and its essential differences from autism, for which she received a well-deserved OBE in recognition of her outstanding work in this field. I learnt that autism is on a spectrum; that an autistic child can be completely non-verbal, forever institutionalised at the most severe end of the spectrum, to the opposite end, where the person is highly capable academically, but has all the social and communication disorders of autism.

Olivia fell into both the 'passive' and the 'aloof' groups, as categorised by Lorna Wing. The aloof group she describes as 'probably the single, most common type of social impairment in young children, who behave as if other people do not exist. They do not come when they are called, may pull away if you touch them, their faces may be empty of expression except when they experience the extremes of anger, distress or joy. They look through you or past you and if they want something they cannot reach, they grab you by the back of your hand or arm, not placing their hand inside yours or looking up at you, and pull you along to use your hand as a tool to reach the desired object, or open a door. They show no interest or sympathy if you are in pain or distress and seem cut off in a world of their own, completely absorbed in their own aimless activities. However, as children, most of them do respond to rough-and-tumble play.' The passive group, she writes, 'is the least common type of social impairment. These children or adults accept social approaches but do not initiate social interaction. They may have poor eye contact, like the aloof group, but are more likely to meet other people's gaze when reminded to do so. Because, during childhood, they are amenable and willing to do as they are told, other children are often happy to play with them as a passive child makes an ideal baby in the game of mothers and fathers, or a patient in a pretend hospital. The problem is, when the game changes, the passive child may be left behind because there is no suitable role for them. In general, children and adults of this kind have the fewest behaviour problems of any with autistic disorders. However, some change markedly in adolescence and become disturbed in behaviour.' I read that autism is thought to be genetic, and can be triggered by being an 'elderly' mother (me), having a difficult pregnancy (me, again) and a difficult birth (me, once more), if there is already a predisposition towards autism in the family's gene pool. I began to take a long, slow look at Johnnie's and my family.

Scratch the surface of many a family and one is bound to find someone whom Lorna Wing describes in her 'active but odd' group. Autism is found in 1 in 200 people, so in a family tree, there is almost bound to be someone who would fit on the spectrum. These are the family members whom I put into the 'Mad Uncle Albert' slot. They tend to have an over-enthusiasm bordering on obsession for bizarre interests, such as knowing the whole of the South Eastern Railway timetable off by heart, or making endless tapestries of the BBC's Test Card. They are completely unaware of their listeners' rapid loss of interest in their favourite subject, but do have jobs, live independently, and sometimes marry and have children. They probably all have Asperger syndrome, or high functioning autism. I began by looking at the men in our families, as autism, as well as ADHD, which Natalya has, is a predominately male disorder. In 1997, I was told that the ratio of girls to boys was 1:7. In 2005 it is 1:4, largely due to better diagnosis. It was very odd that both my daughters had a predominantly male disorder.

I remembered a story that I had heard about my grandfather, Harold Mackintosh, a brilliant businessman from Yorkshire, who had inherited the family confectionery firm and built it up to an internationally renowned company known most famously for products such as Quality Street and Rolo. He had also been chairman of National Savings, started up Premium Bonds during the Second World War, been a major figure in the British Empire Cancer Campaign and the Halifax Building Society. As a devout Methodist he became president of the World Sunday School Association and was also the first chancellor of the new University of East Anglia and had been the second youngest person ever to receive a knighthood at the age of 31 (after Sir John Alcock, the Atlantic aviator). He received a viscountcy in 1958 in acknowledgement of all these and his many other achievements. But before he agreed to marry my grandmother, he had insisted on shipping off one of her two 'odd' brothers to Australia, for good! I rang my father's cousin, Dennis Turner, and asked him if he knew the full story. It turned out to be far more revealing than I had imagined.

Dennis told me that Cyril Stoneham, his uncle, had impregnated a woman who worked in Woolworths in Halifax in 1937. Considered shocking at that time, he was banished by my grandfather to Dunedin in New Zealand, where he spent the rest of his life living alone and stacking boxes in the Mackintosh chocolate depot. In 1995 Dennis visited New Zealand and found a man who had worked with Cyril for many years. This man described Cyril as a loner. He told Dennis that Cyril liked to keep himself to himself, and had found it very difficult to make relationships. He had lived alone for 25 or 30 years and died in hospital in 1964. Cyril knew that Dennis, who was his nephew, loved to collect stamps. Every Christmas he sent Dennis some stamps and every Christmas his message on the card was the same, word for word. It read: 'Dear Dennis, I hope you are well. Love Uncle Cyril.' No doubts at all about Cyril being on the spectrum!

Cyril had a brother called Harold, who left home to live in Washington State in the USA, but no one knows why. He returned during the First World War in 1917 with the American army as a despatch rider. After the war he returned to Washington State, where he had a series of odd jobs, including working in an orchard. He was a complete loner and there was never any mention of his having a relationship with anyone. He died aged about 70. Another one on the spectrum!

Another family member had more information. On my father's side of the family there were four further men who showed all the traits of Asperger syndrome! I was intrigued. Also, on my mother's side of the family, there is a man with Asperger syndrome, who is the son of her first cousin, although we didn't discover this for years. There are, and have been, relatives of Johnnie's with traits indicative of being on the autistic spectrum. Looking at our families, I most certainly did have a predisposition towards autism, only I didn't know it until Olivia was five years old.

One of the first books I read on the subject was called *Let Me Hear Your Voice, A Family's Triumph Over Autism* by Catherine Maurice. Catherine writes about two of her three children who were autistic and how she recovered them from autism using a therapy called Intensive Behavioural Intervention. The therapy had been devised by O. Ivar Lovaas, who ran a clinic at the University of California, in Los Angeles. It was a powerful and very emotional read. I took a highlighting pen and underlined everything that I found pertinent to Olivia. There was a great deal, and as I read on I was filled with hope, too. I had had no idea that one could have more than one autistic child, but here was another story of children cured of autism! If Catherine Maurice could do it, so could I! I ordered Catherine Maurice's training manual and also *Teaching Developmentally Disabled Children: The ME Book*, by Ivar Lovaas.

I asked Johnnie to read *Let Me Hear Your Voice* as quickly as possible, as I wanted to begin the Intensive Behavioural Intervention straight away and needed to be able to talk about it with him. Once he had finished the book, we discussed the method at length; it was not something to be taken on lightly. The Lovaas programme was a method of teaching children with a reward system, rather like dog training, I thought. The child had a one-to-one tutor whose first 'lesson', called drills, was to get the child to sit at a small table opposite him. Each drill lasted no more than a few minutes. Once the child had sat down, or completed the task he was asked to do, he was instantly rewarded with something he loved, which could be a chocolate raisin or holding a favourite toy, but only for a few moments. The second drill was to get the child to look at the tutor. 'Look at me, Tom,' he would say. If Tom did manage to look at the tutor, he would be told 'Good boy! Good looking!' and given a reward. After a short period of ten minutes, the child was allowed to get down from the table and play with whatever he chose for only a few minutes, before being called back to the table to start another drill. Every drill was monitored and recorded in four sections. The first section was the instruction, or question, followed by the response, the date the question was intro- duced and the date it was mastered. The programme was to be car- ried out for eight hours a day, five days a week, for at least two years. So, this would mean giving Olivia 40 hours of teaching a week and carrying the work through at the weekends, too. It was an enormous undertaking. With his typical kindness, Johnnie told me that if I thought that this programme would really help Olivia, then he would support me all the way. But he had very real concerns. Had I thought about the impact it would have on my life, he wondered? And on him, too, and all our other children? I had, of course, but Catherine Maurice's children were cured of their autism. I felt that I didn't have a choice, if I were to defeat this monster. I must do the Intensive Behavioural Intervention and I must do it now.

We spoke to our girls and explained what I was about to embark upon. They knew by now that Olivia was autistic and were as ignorant of the condition as we were. They all offered their help and support, and told me that they realised that for the next two years I would be completely involved in the Lovaas programme and would have almost no time for anything else. Because this was what it would amount to.

I had also read that the sooner one began, the better the result. I was thrown into a state of panic. Olivia had lost so much time already, for which I felt entirely to blame, and there wasn't a moment to lose. She was about to begin school in September and it was already May. If we were to do the Lovaas programme, maybe school should be shelved for two years? There was much I had to learn and discuss with people who knew about Intensive Behavioural Intervention and I didn't even know where to find those people. But just before I embarked on looking for tutors, I rang the National Autistic Society (NAS) to ask whether they thought that Behavioural Intervention was a good and successful programme. To my amazement, I was told that they couldn't offer an opinion on any alternative therapy and that all they could do was advise me to speak to other parents who had tried the treatment. I was furious! What was the point of the NAS if it couldn't advise me? I didn't know a single other child with autism, I was entirely alone and needed their help. I slammed down the phone and it was to be a long time before I understood why the NAS had to take that approach.

Now came the problem of how to find tutors to help me carry out the Intensive Behavioural Intervention. I asked Mary Hampton and Liz Critchlow where I should look. Mary suggested that I put advertisements in the *Speech and Language* magazine and Liz said that she would ask if she could put an advertisement in the Pembury Child Development Centre. I rang the Central School for Speech and Drama and was told that I could put an advertisement in the student coffee bar. I also placed an advert in the local paper. We waited for the phone to ring.

The results were disappointing. Few people called and most of them were not the right type. I needed someone intelligent, with a good sense of humour and an avid interest in autism. This person had to be committed to Behavioural Intervention and learn quickly. I would have to teach them by learning myself, from the manual, which I was already doing. The weeks flew by, but at the end of June I had found two suitable candidates; one was a speech and language graduate and the other was a geography graduate called Christie Miller. I continued to look for others to work with us; otherwise we would burn out in a matter of months.

During the course of my reading everything I could lay my hands on about autism, I came across PEACH, which was short for Parents for the Early Intervention of Autism in Children, a new charity set up to help families carry out the Lovaas programme. I read that it was now known as ABA, which stood for Applied Behaviour Analysis, and was softer than the original Lovaas programme, as ABA did not use aversives such as smacking, as Lovaas had originally done. I rang PEACH and asked them if they could recommend an ABA tutor who could come and teach us how to carry out the programme and they gave me the phone number of Duncan Fennimore. We made a date for Duncan to come to Frenchstreet and go through the programme.

I was beginning to feel a little more in control, now that I had a date with Duncan, but it was all blown away with a single phone call. My close friend Jane Posen rang me one morning and said: 'Liz, I have something to tell you. I have thought long and hard about this and feel that I must tell you what I learnt at a dinner last night. I know how hard you have been working for the past few months trying to set up the ABA programme, and last night I met a psychiatrist from California. She was sitting opposite me and we got talking. She works with autistic children and I told her that my friend had a recently diagnosed daughter with autism, who was about to embark on the Lovaas treatment. She was amazed, because she said that they haven't used that in years, at her institute. They had found that it didn't have any lasting effect and that the children and parents quickly became exhausted. I really think that before you start, it might be a good idea to speak to some professionals to get their opinion. I am sorry to tell you this, but I felt that you should know what she said.'

I was floored. I had spent so much time and energy trying to set it up, but I certainly didn't want to embark on something that might prove not to be worth while. I thanked Jane and told her that I had learnt a heavy lesson by not listening to people in the past who had thought that Olivia was autistic, and knew that I must check everything. I wasn't going to make that mistake again, if I could avoid it. The most essential thing was to keep an open mind and, if it meant starting all over again, so be it. But where and how? I returned to my computer and in a few days had come up with some new names. One was Dr Judith Gould, who worked with the National Autistic Society in Bromley. It was close to Westerham and, with a trembling hand, I phoned her: 'Hello, you don't know me, but I have an autistic daughter and was about to start the Lovaas programme with her. I have just had a call from a close friend, who told me that she met a psychiatrist from California who does not think that the Lovaas programme is viable. What do you think?' Judy Gould and I talked at length over the phone. I told her that I had read Lorna Wing's book and that I was in desperate need of advice. With great tact and kindness, Judy gave me her opinion, which was, in essence, that she agreed with the Californian psychiatrist. Judy and Lorna were about to launch a diagnostic interview, which they had been researching and writing for years. It was to be called the DISCO, which stood for the Diagnostic Interview for Social and Communication Disorders. Specialists, such as doctors and psychiatrists, would be trained to use the diagnostic interview as these would be among the first professionals most likely to come across an autistic child and need to be able to accurately diagnose these children. It was agreed that I would visit Elliot House (the Centre for Social Communication Disorders linked to the National Autistic Society) with Olivia in mid-September.

Alongside all these upheavals, the summer holidays had begun and Charles was only seven and needed his mummy. Natalya needed me too. She was just 16 and had returned from Canada at the beginning of July where her school, Laurentian International College, had been falling apart during the past year. As well as the failure of the school, her ADHD made studying very difficult for her and A levels were not an option. She needed my attention and guidance to help her decide what to do next. And summer time is always busy in the UK. There is a hectic social scene as everyone tries to pack as much as possible into the two or three months of pleasant weather we sometimes have and always hope for, by holding open-air operas, garden parties and so on. I wanted to do as much as I could with Johnnie; he was entitled to have his wife by his side. But I found trying to keep everyone happy and give them all quality time increasingly difficult. The pressure was mounting, I wasn't sleeping much and I was still dealing with my grief over Olivia's diagnosis. So many extremely important decisions had to be made, including which school to send Olivia to in September.

Despite all these anxieties, as I had spent so much time and energy on setting up the ABA programme, I thought it worth while to continue with the meeting with Duncan Fennimore. All of the people who had been working with Olivia were fascinated by ABA and wanted to come along to the meeting and so it was a large party that assembled around my dining room table in August. Liz Critchlow, who had been giving Olivia Portage once a week for the past two years, was particularly interested. We had talked about the programme and were concerned that Olivia would be asked to go over old ground, which she would find both pointless and boring. Mary Hampton felt the same and so they both came to hear what the ABA expert had to say. Natalya joined us to take notes and perhaps become a tutor, as well as Karen Wilcox, the children's nanny who had joined us four months earlier. Also attending were the two tutors I had found earlier. If I were not going to do ABA, then they needed to know as soon as possible as they would need to look for other jobs.

Duncan Fennimore had told me over the phone that I did not need to worry about Olivia repeating baseline work, such as naming objects and colours, but it was a different story when he arrived. The atmosphere quickly became charged with tightly controlled anger. We all questioned his reasoning. Why make Olivia start at the beginning, just so that he could fill in the paper work? I thought it was madness and a complete waste of time. Mary and Liz both told Duncan that they had been working with Olivia for two years, and she could easily sit and attend for periods of up to 45 minutes! To go back to 'Olivia, touch nose' and 'Olivia, what is this?', showing her a car, was ridiculous. We also didn't like the very short playtime between the lessons. It seemed to us that a child with autism would find the constant change from lesson to playtime very distressing. The playtime was a reward after a few short lessons. The child could choose a toy to play with, but only for a few minutes. Even if they were deeply engrossed, they had to leave that toy or unfinished puzzle and come back to the table for more work. We argued that Olivia was already compliant and we would like to start the ABA much further into the programme. Duncan Fennimore was adamant. After two hours of heated debate he left. I told him that I would ring him in a few days with my decision. It was a big decision as I had been recommended by Alison MacDonald, an educational psychiatrist, to visit Chevening County Primary School before the end of the summer term. She had spoken to the headmistress who had had one other child with similar behaviour to Olivia in the past, and this had been a great success. If I wanted to keep Olivia's place, I needed to move fast. Was Olivia to stay at home and do ABA, or go to school with 30 hours a week of support from Christie Miller?

I agonised for a couple of weeks, then to everyone's relief, particularly Johnnie's, I decided to send her to a local mainstream primary school.

CHAPTER 7

Olivia's First School Year

WE STILL HAD A FEW WEEKS LEFT of the summer holidays and it was time to enjoy the garden and turn my attention to the rest of the family. The autumn term at Chevening County Primary would start in early September and it had been agreed that Christie Miller would work with Olivia one-to-one as her learning support assistant (LSA) for a full 30 hours a week. With a huge sigh of relief, both mental and emotional, I wondered down to the swimming pool on a hot, sunny afternoon.

As I dozed, basking in the sun by the pool, I listened to the birds and soft low buzzing of fat honey bees. I adored being outside in the fresh air and spent as much time outside as I possibly could. The garden looked lovely; the hardy perennials that I had spent many long winter hours choosing, planning colour and planting schemes, were in full bloom. Olivia sat beside me on a towel chatting to herself and endlessly sorting toys. She didn't like being outside, preferring the still quiet of her playroom or bedroom and needed considerable cajoling to get her out of doors. I had asked her why she preferred to be inside and she replied: 'It's too noisy outside!' I was surprised, but she was right. There is always the constant buzz of insects, birds sing and swoop across the sky and even a gentle breeze causes the trees and plants to rustle. I knew that she was noise sensitive, but what to me were the sweet sounds of nature, grated on her delicate hearing.

After a perfect afternoon of resting, reading and playing in the pool with all the children, we wandered slowly back to the house to get changed, as we had all been invited to Grannie's for drinks as she had friends staying with her for the weekend. Johnnie's mother lived in a charming stone house at the top of our drive with a lovely view across the valley and our stables. I called to Olivia to go up to the bathroom and that I would join her as soon as I had put the swimming towels in the washing machine. I was no more than five minutes, but when I went to the bathroom, Olivia was not there. 'Naughty girl,' I thought, as I went to the playroom, convinced that she was there, lining up some other toys. But she was not in the playroom either. 'Anyone seen Olivia?' I called out to the girls and Charles. No one had. I began a search of the house, but I still couldn't find her. I started to run, calling out 'Olivia, where are you?' I had taught her to say 'Here I am Mummy,' but she had such a quiet voice, that when she did reply, which was not often, I couldn't hear her anyway, even if I were in the same room. But it was worth calling and, before I knew it, Natalya and Camilla were calling her too. My heart began to pound and trying to keep the panic out of my voice I told the children to search the house again, while I ran back to the pool. I tore down the garden path. Maybe she had slipped back without us noticing? She was nearly five, but couldn't swim a single stroke and hated being in the water. If she fell in, she would panic and drown.

As I ran around the pool, my imagination ran riot. All I could see in my mind was her little face staring up at me from the bottom, or floating, quite still, face down. She wasn't there, so I ran to the pond. We have two ponds and they are both surrounded with bulrushes, irises and thick ornamental grasses. Suddenly everyone was outside shouting 'Olivia! Olivia!' Tania ran to look in the stables, Violet ran back to check the pool house and Camilla, Natalya and I checked the ponds and the swimming pool for the second time, bashing down the ornamental grasses. She was nowhere to be seen. We dashed back to the house and Johnnie came out looking white with anxiety. 'Where have you looked?' he asked. 'Everywhere,' I replied, 'I just don't know where on earth she could be'. I broke off in a choking sob. 'I'll get in the car and drive around,' Johnnie said. 'But she's only been gone 20 minutes; she can't have gone that far!' I cried. As Johnnie ran to grab his car keys, an unknown Land Rover came slowly down the drive. In the back, I saw the small, shining dark head of my precious girl, looking bemused.

I tore the car door open and pulled her out crying and laughing with relief. I hugged her and smothered her with kisses. After a few moments, I turned to thank the people who had brought her home. Mark and Julie Slade had only recently moved into a nearby farm. They had found Olivia walking past their farm, in the middle of the road. They stopped and asked her where her Mummy and Daddy were, but she didn't answer and didn't even look at them as she carried on walking. They quickly realised that this little girl had some kind of learning difficulty and asked her what her name was. She only replied 'Olivia', but couldn't tell them the rest of her name nor where she lived. Without the slightest qualm, Olivia got into the car with them and pointed in the direction of home.

We thanked Mark and Julie profusely and explained that Olivia was autistic and that it was the first time she had walked away from the house. We simply couldn't believe how much ground she had covered in such a short space of time! For someone who had taken two-and-a-half years to learn to walk, it was surprising how fast she could move with her wonky, odd gait when she wanted to. She was also only wearing a T-shirt and sandals and was carrying a bright yellow watering can in the shape of an elephant, its trunk being the spout. I was horrified to realise that she had no concept of danger *at all* and had quite willingly got into a stranger's car. This made her incredibly vulnerable.

We were all very grateful for a glass of wine, once we reached Grannie's house that evening, rather later than intended. I knew that the next, most important, lesson was to teach Olivia her full name and address, followed by 'Stranger/danger', our phone number and the Highway Code. Learning her name wasn't too difficult, and I knew once she started school, it would be used frequently, so that would reinforce the lesson. I decided that our phone number was next on the list, but this proved more difficult to learn, until I hit on the idea of singing it to a beat, which the whole family learned and sang with her. Like so many things Olivia learnt, as it had no real meaning for her, she forgot it with equal speed, but I didn't understand this problem or about her autistic way of learning for years. I had to teach her in ways that she could understand, with real meaning for her; otherwise it was just a frustrating waste of time for us both and left us with an awful sense of failure.

September came and, with it, Olivia's first day at school. The general consensus was to start her off slowly with only three mornings a week, working up to a full day by half term, in six weeks' time. The other children had begun the week before and were all primed that a new girl with autism was coming to their school. She looked adorable in her blue and white gingham dress, white ankle socks and navy Startrite shoes. Her hair, which had been a dark mouse colour when she was born, had become a lovely, very dark chestnut, which she wore with the proverbial fringe in a bob. It framed her heart-shaped face and the fringe hung loosely over her sea-green eyes. She had kept her dimple on her right cheek, which I simply loved and had thought might disappear with babyhood, which it never has.

I had been in touch with Judy Gould at Elliot House and had arranged to be interviewed using the Diagnostic Interview for Social and Communication Disorders (DISCO) in order to fully diagnose Olivia once the summer holidays were over and Olivia had settled in at school. It was with a certain amount of trepidation and excitement that I drove Olivia to Bromley in late September. I didn't know what to expect and I certainly didn't feel that I could cope with any more bad news. Both Judy Gould and Lorna Wing, the authors of this diagnostic interview were there, and it was agreed that Olivia should take part in research on the effects of different methods purported to help children with autism. This would involve a yearly review of her progress.

Olivia was sent upstairs to a playroom on the top floor of this 1930s house that had been converted into offices and consulting rooms. The playroom was cosy and welcoming, full of toys, and had a large squashy sofa and a couple of armchairs around a low pine coffee table. There was a large one-way mirror from this room to the recording room next door, where parents could see and hear the process, without disturbing their child. Olivia was to spend about three hours with an educational psychologist called Jo Douglas who would assess her, and the session would be videoed. Jo would check Olivia's speech and language ability, which would include her understanding of semantic and pragmatic language, her ability to communicate, her imaginative play skills and so on. Meanwhile, I would be interviewed by Judy and Lorna and answer questions about Olivia's health and ability, from conception to her current age of five years.

I settled at the kitchen table downstairs with a hot cup of coffee with Judy and Lorna who interviewed me using the DISCO. We began with my pregnancy and I told them of the near miscarriage and the difficult following months, followed by a long labour. When we started the section on her early development I was asked questions that seemed so odd, such as: 'Did Olivia point to objects when she was very young?' I had to think about it, but actually, no, she never did point. 'Did she point and draw my attention to something happening that interested her, such as a dog running to catch a stick or a child licking a lollipop?' Again, no, Olivia never did. 'Did she take my hand to open doors, reach for toys, put on a video?' Yes, she did. The questions ran on and on; some were hard to answer as they were so subtle and others caused me to dig deep into my memory to find an accurate answer. It was an extremely revealing morning and after three hours of more of these types of questions and several cups of coffee, we finished. Lorna and Judy needed to confer and also to speak to Jo Douglas who had been assessing Olivia all morning. We broke for lunch, and sat around the kitchen table eating the sandwiches that I had brought with me.

When we had finished, Olivia was taken upstairs and told that she could play, while I spoke to Judy, Lorna and Jo. The result was not a surprise. Olivia was autistic and had been autistic from birth. The DISCO was so thorough and I felt privileged to have been able to go through it. But this method made me realise how many experts had missed the diagnosis earlier. I talked for some time to these three wise and wonderful women about the numerous professionals I had taken Olivia to see and the fact that not one of them had even mentioned the word autism, although I could now see that she was extremely autistic from birth. Everything she had done, from the lining up of toys, to not pointing, with very slow language development, were all part of the autistic spectrum. 'This is exactly why we have developed the DISCO,' Lorna Wing explained. 'Most professionals need to be educated to be able to diagnose autism in order that children can then be given the right educational provision and adults given the appropriate support.' Up until the introduction of the DISCO it was a difficult task for professionals to diagnose many cases of autism, particularly in girls. It was heaven to be in safe hands, at last.

Lorna asked me if I knew that there was to be a biannual international conference in London in November given by the National Autistic Society (NAS) and also that Ivar Lovaas was coming to London to give a one-day seminar on his behavioural modification programme. I didn't know, but immediately booked for both. Judy and Jo were going to hear Ivar Lovaas because they were as curious as I was to hear what he had to say.

At the NAS conference I met Jacqui Ashton Smith who is headmistress of the Helen Allison School in Meopham in Kent. It is one of the six schools run by the NAS. Jacqui, a South African, is tall, blonde and dynamic. She exuded warmth and sympathy, and I found myself telling her all about Olivia and the long road to diagnosis. I asked Jacqui if I could visit her school and we made a plan for the New Year. It was my first experience of being with other parents of autistic children and, although I didn't know a soul, just seeing all these people who were in the same boat was extremely comforting. Over half the delegates were professionals who were there to listen to eminent speakers from all over the world, giving papers on their latest research. It was fascinating but completely exhausting. I began to realise just how much I had to learn and that, however much I read, autism affected each individual in a completely different way. I could read a whole library of books on the subject, but, even with all that knowledge I then had to study Olivia minutely to see how autism affected her. Autism was a spectrum, but if the Triad of Impairments, a phrase coined by Lorna Wing, which were of social interaction, communication and imagination, is present, then an autistic disorder should be diagnosed regardless of any other co-existing condition.

The one-day seminar given by Ivar Lovaas, the creator of behaviour intervention, was quite different. As we filed into the large auditorium, I noticed that the audience was mostly made up of young, middle-class parents of recently diagnosed autistic children, the majority of whom had already heard about ABA or Applied Behavioural Analysis and who wanted to hear the great man speak. The atmosphere, filled with pain and hope, was thick as smoke. It was going to be a day of highly charged emotion as couples sat tightly next to each other and gripped each other's hands. For many parents this was the only method that was thought to have real beneficial effects for their autistic children and so the stakes were high. Conversation buzzed around the room and, as I sat next to Johnnie, who was also curious to hear Ivar Lovaas, I could see introductions being made and phone numbers exchanged.

Ivar Lovaas's research was written in the early 1970s, but in November 1997 he was still quoting from the same results, which, he said, showed that of the 17 children who had undergone his ABA programme, 45 per cent of them had *completely recovered from autism*. Although I had decided not to use ABA on Olivia, I was fully aware that if she had been non-verbal, or much more difficult to handle, I would certainly have tried it with her. I was also very anxious that by the end of the day, I might feel that I had made a terrible mistake in not going through with ABA.

The day began with a presentation from a mother who had used ABA for the past two years with her son, who was now six. She told the audience that before she began the programme, he had not spoken and had been unable to settle to anything like normal play for more than a few seconds. With great difficulty, she had found tutors willing to come to her home and help her give ABA to her son for 40 hours a week. He was now attending mainstream school, which he had started very slowly, just an hour a day with his tutor for the first few weeks, but had built up his time so that he was there all morning. The next stage would be to increase his hours to full time and very gradually reduce his support. We watched this mother's video of her son's progress, which was indeed remarkable, then watched her son, closely prompted by an adult, playing a board game with a little girl in a separate room in the building, via a hidden camera.

Other mothers spoke of their children's progress using ABA and all talked of the enormous difficulty of finding suitable tutors and having

the energy to carry out the programme. It was physically and emotionally exhausting, these parents admitted, but worth it. The com-
mitment was huge and took a heavy toll on the rest of the family as
well as being financially crippling. What about the poor child who has
to be at the receiving end of 40 hours of therapy a week, I thought.
Imagine learning Ancient Greek and having dyslexia, for 40 hours a
week!

After a coffee break, Ivar Lovaas took the floor as the main speaker
of the day. A tall man in late middle age, he had wispy grey hair and
such an odd manner that one immediately had a picture in mind of
the stereotypical mad professor. He began by discussing the general
differences in behaviour of men and women with a few risqué jokes
that were not at all funny. I waited for the serious content of his lec-
ture with increasing impatience and listened in disbelief as he trotted
out the same old research, which was, by now, 20 years old. There
was no mention of those 17 children now, how they had developed
or what kind of lives they were living now. Was I the only one to find
this curious? Alas, the room was full of evangelical devotees and as
far as I could see he could be speaking gibberish and the audience
would have cried for an encore. I chastised myself for my mean-
spiritedness. Desperate parents needed to hear good news; I was one
of them after all. After an hour-and-a-half of disappointment during
which I had learnt nothing new, or even useful, we broke for lunch.
I went to find Judy and Jo. 'Well, do you feel better now?' Judy asked
me with a twinkle. She knew of my anxiety that I might regret having
sent Olivia to mainstream school instead of doing ABA at home. Judy
and Jo pointed out subtleties that, with my small germ of knowledge,
I had not noticed. The boy in the first film was playing with a girl
who was a year older, as well as being very gentle and patient. Girls
are much more willing to be tolerant to others, allowing their maternal
instincts to come foremost. If it had been a boy the same age, who
would make no concessions for his autism, they would probably not
have played nearly so well together. Also, did I notice how much
prompting the autistic boy needed? It was a huge amount, without
which he would probably have not been able to play the board game

at all. I listened in fascination to these two highly experienced specialists discussing the morning, confirming that my decision to send Olivia to school had been the right one.

In the afternoon session the emotional fireworks started. There were open discussions on how to set up home programmes, how and where to advertise for tutors, how much they should be paid and how many hours were really necessary to practise ABA. Emotions ran high and arguments broke out. Many people found it hard to speak through their tears as they told story after story of their children's autism. Some of the parents talked about their children having been perfectly normal for the first 18 months to two years, and how they watched their children slip away, losing language and skills, into an unreachable world of their own. For the first time I heard parents question whether the MMR, the measles, mumps and rubella injection, was the cause of the loss of their children to autism, and I heard the phrase 'late onset autism' for the first time. Years later, after I had been flooded with conflicting information like the rest of the population, mainly in the press, but also on the radio and on television, I did come to my own conclusion. Alternative therapies were discussed and I made notes to investigate Neurolinguistic Programming (NLP), Kirlian glasses and the Boston Higashi Method of Daily Living. I heard about Bears Kauffman, whose son was autistic and how he had joined him in his autism through play and had set up the Son Rise Programme. I learnt that many autistic children benefit from jumping on a trampoline and made a note to buy one for Olivia. It would certainly help strengthen her weak legs and might be fun for the whole family.

By 5 p.m., when the seminar was over, I walked out of the hall, my head ringing with an overload of information and my body shaking with exhaustion and spent emotion. It had been a harrowing day. I didn't know whether to feel happy that Olivia had been born with autism, rather than have it descend upon her at the age of two, or whether I really could rejoice that she was not as severely affected as many of the children I had heard about that day. Judy and Jo said that they would be willing to come to Chevening School to talk to the headmistress and

Olivia's class teacher to try to inform them a little about autism and how they could teach Olivia. I was deeply grateful for their help and advice and considered that, in retrospect, it was a blessing the day my friend Jane Posen rang to tell me to rethink doing the Lovaas behaviour modification programme. If Jane had not rung me, I might never have met Dr Lorna Wing and Dr Judy Gould.

Olivia had settled into school quite well, although at break time she played all alone in the corner of the playground, talking to herself and turning in endless circles, flicking her fingers. She had to be watched like a hawk; otherwise she would wonder off the school grounds and down the busy road, which was just outside the school gates. Christie Miller, who was working as Olivia's learning support assistant (LSA), had begun a 12-week course on autism at Kent University in Canterbury each Thursday, but by half term Olivia was still only at school three mornings a week. I rang the headmistress and asked if we could meet. She agreed and was willing, although not enthusiastic, to meet Judy Gould and Jo Douglas to discuss how her school could learn about autism, which would not only benefit Olivia, but all the children in the school and certainly those who might have slight social or communication difficulties.

However, the meeting did not go well. The headmistress was offered courses for her staff to attend and books to read. The answer to all this free help and advice was a shrug of the shoulders and a reply that the allocated training days had been taken up and that there wasn't any time for her staff to go on any training programmes, nor read any of the literature that was offered. We finished the meeting by agreeing that Olivia could go to school full time after half term, but there were no other concessions. Judy and Jo were aghast. They had been willing to give free advice and their valuable time to the school and I felt embarrassed and angry.

Poor Christie was not faring much better either. She was getting little support from the other staff and was expected to teach Olivia one-to-one all day as well as look after her during playtime. Christie had a degree, but no teaching training or experience and as an LSA was supposed to be guided by the school SENCO, or special educational needs co-ordinator. There are quite clear guidelines on how to set a programme of achievable goals for every special needs child. As each child has a right to access the National Curriculum, this is the way it works: the SENCO is responsible for the IEP, or Individual Education Plan, for every special needs child in the school. Her job is to meet with the child's parents and class teacher to work out a set of targets for the following term, which is written in the child's IEP. The targets might be to learn to write more clearly, or to sit and listen without calling out, or to learn to add numbers up to ten. The National Curriculum is adapted to suit the ability of each child, so that he is able to follow the class course work in a way that is appropriate to his specific learning difficulty. The class teacher then has to instruct and supervise the LSA responsible for the special needs child. Good in theory, but like Chinese Whispers, the essence of the IEP is frequently diluted, if not lost, en route. Most LSAs are kind, hard-working people, who have only the best interests of the child at heart. However, they are not required to hold any qualifications and are paid a minimum wage, often earning less than one could earn at a supermarket checkout. When Olivia was eight, she had had an LSA who worked with her for six months. At Christmas she gave Olivia a card on which she wrote 'Happy Christmas Olivior'. This LSA had been teaching Olivia reading and writing that term. There is also no structure for training, and no possibility for promotion. Once an LSA, always an LSA. Consequently, the quality of teaching is hugely variable. It seems to me to be a tragedy of wasted resources, which could otherwise make a major dif-ference in mainstream schools. This is particularly apt, in view of the fact that, to date, over 90 excellent special needs schools have closed under the Labour Government. Pupils have been forced into main-stream education, where, in general, they are miserable and they fail. This policy also pays no regard to the poor teacher, who, with a class of over 30, is expected to be proficient in teaching a wide variety of special needs children with hardly any training.

We struggled on, Christie and I meeting every day at the school gates to discuss the day's progress and current difficulties. Olivia had tantrums that I nicknamed 'Hairy Marys' and these had to be controlled in the classroom. At home she would scream and yell, but I found that I could calm her down quite quickly and sort out the reason for the tantrum. None of the other members of our family were able to calm her and certainly telling her to 'be quiet' or 'calm down' only exacerbated her temper and made her anxiety levels rocket. Olivia's tantrums were almost always because she could not make herself or her wishes understood. Consequently Olivia spent quite a lot of her day outside the classroom in a small, dark room used for one-to-one teaching. When she *was* in the classroom she was at a separate table with Christie – and this is called 'inclusive' education!

We decided that we would battle on and give the school a chance, but by the end of that autumn I was so exhausted, I could hardy see straight. I was still taking Olivia once a month to Stuart Korth, the paedatric osteopath, who felt that he could really make a difference. He had told me, after Olivia had been going to him for about six months, that when he first treated her, he thought that she was beyond his help as she had such severe difficulties. But each time we saw him, he felt more and more hopeful that his treatments would show great improvement in her general ability. She also was still having speech and language therapy every week and occupational therapy, and when we were not taking classes she had exercises to do. She couldn't write at all, nor read, and I was trying to find different ways to reach her, to teach her. I realised that I simply would not make it to Christmas without a nervous breakdown if I carried on at this pace and so, with Johnnie's blessing, I took myself to a health farm, for the first and only time in my life.

I spent three days at Grayshott Hall in Hampshire, sleeping and having as many treatments, like reflexology and massage, as I could fit in. It was bliss to have a few hours to myself, eat when I wanted and sleep during the day, if I felt like it. My dear friend Olivia Howard-Collings, one of Olivia's godmothers, came to have dinner with me one evening. She had been so sweet to me when I told her, not many months before, that I finally knew what the matter was with Olivia. She didn't say a word; she just put her hand over mine and held it, looking at me, her large blue eyes deep with sympathy and compassion. After some time, all she said was 'I am so very sorry, Liz'. I will never forget that moment. I had had other friends who had taken the news entirely differently. Some had even told me to not to worry, that there was so much that could be done for autistic children these days, even that it wasn't that bad! Not that bad? Not to worry? This was an incurable, deeply complex, life-long disability and I was often completely flabbergasted at people's reaction to the news. I still felt so raw; it had only been eight months since the diagnosis and I still couldn't say 'I have a daughter with autism', without crying. The problem was compounded in that, however well-meaning friends and family were, no one knew what autism was, or understood what it meant to be autistic. The few who had even heard of it asked 'What is it, exactly?' and most of their awareness came from the heavy press coverage over the question of the connection with the MMR injection or, like me, my friends and my family, from the film *Rain Man*. Consequently many people supposed that Olivia therefore had some wonderful gift. I was often asked what special gift she had, but the gifted ones are known as 'autistic savants' and they make up a mere 1 per cent of the autistic population. It was extremely tiring trying to explain how autism affected Olivia, as I knew so little myself at that stage.

There were also daily problems with Olivia, who could not be left alone for a minute; otherwise she would do all sorts of odd things. At five years old, she somehow managed to get through a roll of toilet paper each time she went to the loo, which often resulted in the loo flooding. One day, she tried her best to flush a hand towel down the loo in the downstairs cloakroom. I hadn't noticed, but while I was saying goodbye to Violet and her friends who had been staying with us for the weekend, one of the girls pointed out that we were standing in an inch of water on the hall carpet. My antennae were acutely tuned to her whereabouts, but even with her nanny, Karen Wilcox, she could slip away to do such things as shampoo the carpet with a mixture of toothpaste and soap. My sense of humour was often stretched to the limit, and I was occasionally bowled over with sadness.

Charles was at a local prep school and I tried very hard to make sure that I spent time with him alone, listening to his happy chatter about school and his friends. He is 22 months older than Olivia, and at age seven, was still white blonde, with green eyes and a chubby body. He had a natural innate sensitivity, which for such a young child was occasionally quite uncanny. He adored Olivia and was, and still is, fiercely protective of her. Every evening we practised reading from his school reading book and did his homework together. Towards Christmas, on a black dark night, Charles sat on my lap in the kitchen doing his reading homework. I tried to keep cheerful around him, but that night I could not stop tears rolling down my face. Charles felt the hot, wet tears on his neck and turned to me, concerned. 'Mummy, Mummy, what's the matter?' he asked anxiously as he put his small, sticky hand to my face. 'It's just Liv,' I replied. 'So sorry to cry darling, sometimes I feel very sad that she is autistic and can't love us as we love her. I'll just have a good cry, as I know that I will feel better afterwards. You carry on reading and ignore me, I'll be fine.' At that poignant moment, Olivia came into the kitchen, saw me crying and grabbing a paper hanky from the box, pointed at me and laughing, said 'Oh, you're crying! Look, I'm sad and I'm crying too!' And with a huge grin on her face she dabbed at her non-existent tears. It was such typical autistic behaviour, only to grasp the fact, without any empathy whatsoever, that Charles and I fell into uncontrolled laughter, which banished my sadness for the rest of the evening.

In many ways the hardest aspect of autism to deal with is the lack of empathy. Most parents can cope with a child's disability, as they know that their child loves them unconditionally and can show their affection with hugs and kisses. An autistic child simply does not need you. Not only that, they do not even *like* your affection and often hate to be touched. It makes it hard to comfort them if they should fall and hurt themselves, and it is extremely painful for loving parents to be so utterly discounted and disregarded. Autistic children have no interest at all in their parents' or siblings' lives and hobbies, unless they share a common interest. Olivia, as a typically autistic child, does not notice people, to the extent that she will walk between two people talking, or simply climb over a person, if they happen to be in her path, with no social awareness at all. Not having any empathy also means that they cannot share in the normal joys and sorrows of family life and do not understand them in the first place. Can you imagine what it must be like not to be able to understand that each one of us has an independent mind? The autistic person cannot grasp the concept that others do not know what is going on inside their heads. Olivia will come to me already half-way through a sentence, which often ends in a question. I will have to think quickly what she might have just been watching on television, or what book she might have been looking at, or what is her most recent interest, to guess at the content of her question. She does not understand that I do not know what she is thinking. Professor Simon Baron-Cohen calls this state 'Mind Blindness' and has written a book with the same title on the subject. Olivia will still, at age 13, ask me if her foot hurts or if she has a headache. My standard reply is 'Do you know if I have a tummy ache? You do not, because you can't feel what I feel inside my body. So I can't feel if you hurt. Does your foot hurt?' Even more heart rending, she still muddles up her sisters.

This apparent self-absorption, or lack of awareness of others, makes simple classroom instructions complex. An autistic child will not realise that when the teacher addresses a class, that those instructions include her. 'Now Class 5, open your reading books at page 3, please,' would have no effect on Olivia. She would not understand that that this instruction included her, too, and so each instruction had to be given to her directly and using her name. Olivia might focus on a particular part of a drawing in the reading book, or not want that book at all, because it was a different copy from the book she had yesterday. She also has no concept of time, no ability to read any but the most basic facial expressions and body language, and like all autistic children understands language literally. I have had to learn not to use idiomatic language, if I can remember and stop myself in time. Phrases such as 'It was raining cats and dogs' or 'I nearly split my sides, laughing' would have her rushing to the window to see these cats and dogs falling out of the sky and checking my body for rips. There are two excellent books that explain idiom. One is called *What Did You Say? What Do You Mean?* by Jude Welton. The other is *An Asperger Dictionary of Everyday Expressions*, by Ian Stuart-Hamilton. English is rich in idiom and, for a concrete thinker, one who understands language entirely literally, it becomes a minefield of misunderstanding and sheer terror.

With a foundation of slowly increased knowledge, I passed on what I had learnt to Olivia's teacher and Christie Miller. Once I paid attention, I noticed that there appeared to be almost a cure a week for autism. The newspapers were full of sensational articles about the success or otherwise of treatments such as secretin injections, made from the enzyme secretin. For example, I read about an American autistic boy who was treated with secretin injections to help a bowel disorder and, as a side-effect, his autism markedly improved. Donna Williams, an Australian adult with autism who has written several excellent books on her own experiences, is a great advocate of the 'leaky gut' theory, which condition the American autistic boy had. As is Andrew Wakefield who has had much first positive, then adverse, publicity about his so-far unproven research into leaky guts caused by the MMR (measles, mumps and rubella) vaccine, which, according to him and many parents, has also brought on autism in their hitherto perfectly normal children. The 'leaky gut' theory is that autistic children and adults often suffer profoundly from flatulence, distended stomach, dark shadows under their eyes and agonising abdominal pain, as their digestive systems cannot break down wheat and dairy products. Particles of undigested protein, or peptides, pass through the leaky gut and travel around the body in the form of caseomorphine and gluteomorphine, which, when it reaches the brain, causes sleepiness and erratic behaviour. Many people claim that a gluten/casein free diet has remarkably beneficial effects, but as Olivia ate quite well and slept well and did not have any of the above symptoms, I did not see the point of putting her on this diet, nor giving her secretin injections, particularly as no one knew what their long-term effects might be. I had already given Olivia her MMR injection without a qualm, as I had no idea at the time that I had a predisposition towards having an autistic child and, as she was born autistic, in her case it could only have been beneficial in protecting her from the risk of these terrible, life-threatening diseases.

Much has been written about the MMR vaccine and it remains, at the point of writing, extremely controversial. How do I feel about it? If I had known that Olivia was genetically susceptible towards autism, I would certainly have taken the precaution of giving her the single vaccines, as I had already had a very difficult pregnancy and birth and was over 42 when she was born. Research has shown that these three factors are significant in themselves in mothers of autistic children and, given my genetic background, I would also have given them to her later; the MMR is being given to children at an increasingly younger age. However, in 1986 in Yokohama, Japan, the MMR vaccine was withdrawn and replaced with single vaccines for a ten-year period. The incidences of autism in Japan continued to rise, thus proving conclusively, it would seem, that the MMR vaccine does not, in any way, cause autism.

But there is another issue to the MMR dilemma and that is something commonly called 'late onset autism'. Not all children appear to be born autistic; many would seem to develop perfectly normally until, quite inexplicably, usually between 18 months to three years, they regress and become autistic. This is particularly hard for parents to bear, to have a normal, happy, healthy child and watch them slowly disintegrate into non-verbal, hand-biting autistic people. This late onset autism most frequently starts around the time when the child is given the MMR vaccine. Naturally, parents put two and two together and blame the MMR for their child's autism. So what about the parents of children who swear that it caused autism in their children? My heart goes out to them as a parent of an autistic child. These parents should be taken seriously and not dismissed as cranks or just wanting to blame something or someone for their child's regression. In my view the only answer is to research these cases, otherwise we will never know how or why this happened. However, experts in autism do not think that is there is such a thing as late onset autism *at all*. In fact, they find this expression extremely unhelpful and it is not a phrase that any clinician or professional would ever use. In a recent study of 100 autistic children, 75 per cent were born autistic and the rest were divided into two groups, one-half regressed in their language skills and the other in their social skills. It appears that in the latter group, there may be a genetic component and also there is a strong possibility that the parents were not asked the right questions about their child's development in early infancy at the time of diagnosis, which would have teased out problems in the more subtle cases that the parents had not been aware of at the time, which in turn would make them think that their child was developing normally. In the eight years since I have known Dr Lorna Wing and Dr Judith Gould, they have almost ceased diagnosing young children because with greater knowledge and awareness about autism, these children are now being picked up at an early stage in their development. Most clinicians believe that this is the main reason for the rapid rise in autism over the past 10 years. Simply better and earlier diagnosis. When Olivia was diagnosed in 1997, the ratio of boys to girls with autism was 7:1. In 2006, it is 4:1. Girls, being naturally more socially adept, had been passing through the limited diagnostic screening. I also hold the view that strong-arm tactics from the Government only exacerbate the problem. Most people who have concerns about giving the MMR vaccine to their children have, in their opinion, a valid reason for these concerns. Such parents are more than likely to be diligent enough to make sure that their child does have all the individual vaccines. Certainly there will be a few who will not, just as there will always be a few who will refuse the MMR in any form. But attempting to coerce parents into giving the MMR vaccine to their children using fear as an emotional sledgehammer and refusing them the right to give single vaccines only makes parents dig their heels in even harder, resulting in precisely the possibility of an epidemic of childhood diseases that the Government is trying so hard to avoid. Parents have a right to choose what they think is the best for their child and should be allowed the freedom to do so.

One newspaper article that particularly grabbed my attention was about an American woman called Temple Grandin, who has Asperger syndrome and who was now an expert in designing cattle-calming shutes that cows walk through on their way to the slaughter house. Temple had built herself what she termed a 'squeeze machine' with the aid of her superb science teacher, when she was still at school. Temple hated to be touched, but needed to be held tightly when she felt stressed. Like the cattle she had observed on her aunt's farm, she found it calming to be held firmly. She could regulate the pressure in her 'squeeze machine' through a control handle and stop whenever she had had enough. Temple had always loved 'rough and tumble' type of play, but only on her own terms. Her book *Thinking in Pictures* was a fascinating read, and I decided to try 'rough and tumble' with Olivia to get her to relate to me.

Much to my distress, Olivia never seemed to care if I went away for the day or even for a week on holiday. Nor did she ever run to greet me when she came home from school. I had to seek her out to say hello and ask her about her day. After reading *Thinking in Pictures* and remembering that in Lorna Wing's book she had written that most of the aloof group, to which Olivia belonged, responded to 'rough and tumble play', I decided that I would scoop her up in my arms and cuddle her tightly every day when she came home from school. We would then fall to the floor in the playroom and I would roll around on the carpet with her, gently tickling her and saying, 'Hi my darling! I've missed you when you were at school today! How are you? Look at me and give me a kiss! Say Hello Mummy! Did you miss me too? I love you very much. Do you love me too?' and so on. Within minutes, Olivia would be laughing, engaging with me and making full eye contact. I was thrilled with the success, which seemed to break down her natural barriers, and she continued to be more 'with me' for the rest of the day. This mad activity became a daily event, sometimes starting with a chase around the house to 'catch' her first. I often wondered what on earth people would think if they could see Lady Astor rolling around the floor, swinging her daughter up in the air and running around the house like someone possessed. Having an autistic child is not for the faint hearted. You have to develop a skin like a rhinoceros and simply not care a fig what other people might think. Tracy Alderman's autistic son had a T-shirt that read: 'I'm autistic, what's your problem?' I thought it was so funny, but never managed to find one myself.

Charles and the dogs joined in running around the house, the dogs barking with excitement. We pretty quickly had to ban the dogs from taking part, as Olivia found their barking and running next to her very distressing. The Astor family are dog mad, certainly my husband and his sisters. They grew up with several dogs each and Johnnie's mother always had at least two, as well as other animals and birds. Johnnie was dismayed to learn that Olivia, once she could express it, didn't like dogs at all. They crashed into her playroom, knocking over her carefully lined up animals and scattering them across the floor. They jumped up on her with wet paws and were entirely unpredictable. It was very sad for Johnnie who would have loved to have given her a pet and been able to share his love of animals with her. Dogs had always given him so much pleasure and he had hoped that it would be a good point of contact between them. But it was not meant to be. Olivia didn't like any pets and preferred her animals to be either plastic or the stuffed toy variety.

By the time we were half-way through the summer term, both Christie Miller and I were thoroughly despondent with Olivia's school. Even with every good intention to give Olivia the best resources they had, autism was something so far from their experience that they floundered. What capped it was when I heard that Olivia had been conveniently kept out of the classroom during an Ofsted inspection, ostensibly having a one-to-one speech and language lesson, although there was none scheduled that day. It was the last straw as far as I was concerned, and I rang Ofsted to complain. Ofsted is the Office for Standards in Education and visits every school in the country every five years. 'May I ask who is speaking?' enquired a kindly voice. 'A parent,' I replied. 'Point taken,' came the rapid response. I didn't know if my complaint would have any effect, until I received a letter from a Special Education Services Manager in mid July, who wrote to me saying that she would be investigating the situation.

Within days of Olivia's exclusion during the Ofsted inspection, I was at the Helen Allison School, weeping in headmistress Jacqui Ashton Smith's office. I had spoken to Judy Gould, who advised me to look for another school for Olivia. 'Olivia does not have the time to train a whole school, Liz,' said Judy. 'Give up and move on' was her advice.

Pat Smith, who also worked at the Helen Allison School and whom I had met some time ago, told me when I visited that day that she had heard very good reports about Otford County Primary School and suggested that I telephone the headmistress. 'They appear to have an open door policy,' Pat said, 'this means they take any child regardless of ability. For that reason they have several statemented children with a variety of learning disabilities such as dyslexia or dyspraxia and I think you will find them much more open and flexible in their attitude.'

When I visited Otford, a small school just outside Sevenoaks, this certainly seemed to be the case. The headmistress, Rowena Linn, welcomed me into her tiny, cramped office and offered me tea. I briefly explained the difficulties I had had at Chevening School and we discussed how to move forward without repeating the same mistakes. To my delight, Rowena offered to take Olivia in the coming school year and, after the necessary police checks, would also take Christie Miller to continue to be Olivia's learning support assistant.

Grasping the Nettle

FRENCHSTREET HOUSE IN SUMMERTIME is without doubt my favourite place to be. We are fortunate in living in a wonderful position, in a valley surrounded by National Trust farmland and woodland, near the small, lively town of Westerham. I didn't know Kent at all before Johnnie and I married, and it took a few years to find my way round the narrow lanes banked with hedges and filled with wild flowers. I had been brought up near Newcastle upon Tyne and in a village just outside Norwich, and had only come to Kent on day trips from London with my friend Stephanie Berni to visit the gardens and castles of Hever, Sissinghurst and Leeds. Little did I imagine on my visit to Hever Castle that one day I would become a member of the Astor family.

By the early summer of 1998, I thought that I had regained some happiness. I was slowly coming to terms with Olivia's autism; it had been a little over a year since her diagnosis and I was now able to say that I had an autistic daughter without crying. Olivia had just had her sixth birthday and we thought that we had resolved her school situation. But happiness is a fickle friend. If you search for it, it eludes you. If you don't look for it, it will creep up behind you and overwhelm you both suddenly and fleetingly. It is unfaithful, ephemeral and is often most keenly felt as a memory. I had learnt that to gain the most out of life it is important to try to be fully aware of the good and happy moments while in the middle of them. As we used to say in the 1960s, Be Here Now! Joy should be lived in the very breath of life, through the conscious mind, rather than in a sleepy haze of memory. I didn't want to live my life half awake, but happiness was about to desert me once more.

Now 17, Natalya had been suffering from a series of what we thought were panic attacks. She was working in London as a runner, which is a glorified 'go-for', for a film company, but she often could not make it to the next job. I have never experienced a panic attack, but I understand that they are totally overwhelming and debilitating. One feels as if one is suffocating and cannot get enough breath. The sufferer consequently hyperventilates, breaking out into a sweat, and is gripped by irrational fear, which feels completely real to them.

At home one weekend during the summer, Natalya told me that she had had a particularly bad week suffering from panic attacks. It felt to her as if her heart would race, then, most terrifyingly, almost stop. Her next-door neighbour, who had heart problems, had offered her a beta-blocker, which blocks the effect of adrenaline on the heart. To Natalya's amazement, this had worked and she had felt much better. 'But my neighbour suggested that as it worked, maybe I should have my heart checked Mum?' she questioned, as we sat around the kitchen table drinking milky morning coffee. I just couldn't imagine that there was anything wrong with her heart. She had always had good health and was naturally athletic. However, after my long period of denial of Olivia's autism, I had learnt a hard lesson. Never would I overlook or discount a health problem again. When I mentioned to my mother that no one had ever told me of their concerns about Olivia, my mother replied that both she and my sister had tried, but I appeared not to be interested in their views at all. With hindsight, they had probably been far too sensitive, too subtle in their approach. I had been so preoccupied with Olivia at this stage that I put all Natalya's heart problems down to the strain that she suffered through her whacky behaviour at that time. I begged my mother to throw away any delicacy if she saw other problems. 'Shout it loud, Mum,' I said. 'Make absolutely sure that I have got the message and paid attention.' And so I called my friend Jemma Bellerose, who had been working for a top London gynaecologist for the past 30 years, during which time she had learnt who was at the top of their field in every medical discipline, and asked her to recommend me a cardiologist.

Cardiologist Dr Malcolm Walker's office was down in the depths of University College Hospital in London. Hot and dusty, with chipped paint everywhere, it was a sad reflection of the current state of our NHS hospitals. Johnnie and I were to go out to dinner that June evening to the exquisite house of an elderly friend, Ambrose Congreve, in St James's, who did not welcome his guests arriving late. It was, as usual with Ambrose, a black-tie dinner, and I had strict instructions from Johnnie to arrive on time, as I am notoriously late for appointments. Natalya's appointment was at 6.00 p.m. and so I arrived already dressed in my evening suit, carrying my jewellery in my handbag. I was quite sure that there was nothing wrong with Natalya's heart: she was a healthy 17 year old, what could possibly be wrong with the heart of someone her age? I was also confident that the cardiologist would agree and put our minds at rest within half-an-hour and therefore I would easily make my dinner engagement in time.

Natalya is very articulate and was able to give a clear description of her arrhythmia, the term for any deviation from the normal rhythm of the heart, to Dr Walker. He took notes and details of her medical history and suggested that she have an EEG, or electrocardiogram, there and then. 'Most probably, you have a slight arrhythmia, which can be cured by taking tablets for about three months, just to retrain the heart to beat normally,' he said. 'But let's take an EEG and see if we find anything.' As Natalya lay on the bed, I was sure that was all that could be the matter and was quite shaken when Dr Walker said that there did seem to be something wrong. 'I think I had better take an ultrasound,' he told us as he took Natalya to the ultrasound room. Very quickly he found the problem. 'Natalya has a 2-centimetre hole in her heart, I'm afraid,' he said gently but firmly. We sat opposite him, staring vacantly, like rabbits caught in the headlights of a car. 'A what?' was all I could ask. 'She has quite a large hole in her heart and it will need surgery to repair it,' Dr Walker explained.

He turned to Natalya and asked if she had experienced anything other than arrhythmia that he should know about. Natalya remembered one particularly frightening evening a month previously, when she was on the bus coming home from work and her left eye slowly lost its sight. By the time she had to leave the bus, she couldn't see anything at all from this eye and, terrified, called her boyfriend and asked him to come and help her home. After a couple of hours, her sight gradually returned. 'I forgot to tell you about that Mum,' she added. 'Natalya, you are a very lucky girl,' concluded Dr Walker. 'That was a blood clot passing behind your eye. If it had continued to your brain, you would not be with us today. You must take an aspirin a day until you have the operation to close the hole.'

We left the hospital in a daze and headed straight for the pub. I ordered two large gin and tonics, something I never drink, and rang Johnnie to explain what had happened and to make my apologies to Ambrose. I was not going to leave my daughter to go out to dinner after she had received such a shock. Ollie Hargreaves, Natalya's boyfriend at the time, came and joined us as we sat sipping our drinks, stupefied by the news. I simply could not believe what was happening. I felt completely shattered and wondered how I was going to muster the strength to get her through the summer, keeping up her morale, and being cheerful and optimistic. In fact, it was Natalya who showed enormous courage and, until the night before the operation, only occasionally needed reassurance.

Nonetheless, the sword of Damocles hung over us, all that summer. Within two weeks of visiting Dr Walker, we had been to the Wimpole Street consulting rooms of Mr Charles Pattison, the surgeon, who explained the operation to us and booked Natalya into the Harley Street Clinic for mid-September. She had three months to wait, and although it felt like an impossibly long time, we felt very lucky to have private health insurance and not have to wait in a long queue for a National Health slot.

Our summer plans had already been made and as Natalya's heart surgeon had explained that she was not in any immediate danger, so long as she took her daily aspirin in order to avoid another blood clot, we decided to continue with them. This meant that we would simply have to get through the next three months before she had open-heart surgery with as little anxiety as we could. We had planned to take Violet, Natalya, Charles and Olivia to visit friends of Johnnie's who had a wonderful holiday house near Lake Constantine, in southern Germany, which they were refurbishing. Mausi is an interior decorator and we were looking forward to seeing her 'work in progress', both in the house and also the garden they were creating. Johnnie had met Mausi Douglas when she lived near Edenbridge in Kent many years before, but now she and her husband Tito, and their five children, lived in Frankfurt.

On the long journey through Belgium and northern Germany we drove in convoy, with me following Johnnie, who drove like Schumacher on the superb German autobahns. After one night in a hotel, our next stop was to visit Walldorf, a small town near Heidelberg, where the most famous member of the Astor family, the first John Jacob, had lived, before he left for America and made his fortune. It was the 100th anniversary of the unveiling of the statue of John Jacob Astor, Johnnie's great, great, great, great, great grandfather, and the whole town came out to greet us. Inside the town hall, with much ceremony and long speeches in German that none of us, to our shame, could understand, we were welcomed and shown the exhibits in the Astor museum. After the bowing and hand shaking were over, we were offered coffee and delicious cakes by buxom ladies with rosy cheeks, wearing dirndl skirts and broderie anglaise blouses. Charles was told firmly not to look bored, and Violet and Natalya, who were 18 and 17 respectively, were instructed not to laugh. Olivia hung on to her toy rabbit for dear life and can be seen scowling angrily in every photo.

We then began a tour of the town, which was utterly charming with old, oak-beamed houses with long, moss-covered red roofs and pretty gardens filled with roses and hollyhocks. The streets were wide and quiet, and I wondered how much the first John Jacob Astor must have missed his serene hometown and its friendly, courteous inhabitants when he lived in the wilds of the American West. There is a magnificent trading post 125 feet high, called the Astoria Column, built in his honour in an Oregon town called Astoria, as his trading company was the first to reach the Pacific coast and open up the American West to other settlers and traders. Many books have been written about this great man who made his fortune from the fur trade and then invested his fortune buying swampland near the Atlantic ocean in an area that we now call Manhattan!

The Astor name is well known in Germany and the Germans claim the family for their own. As a result of German interest we had been invited, a year previously, on to a chat show with the famous host, Thomas Gottschalk, the Oprah Winfrey of the German-speaking world. I had never been to Germany before that time and was delighted with the chance to visit Munich, a beautiful medieval city in Bavaria. Our tickets and hotel bills had been paid for by the television company and we were collected from the airport and driven to the studio in the most up-to-date Mercedes. Johnnie, who adores cars, was already smiling before we met model Claudia Schiffer's sister and French actor Jean-Paul Belmondo's son, who were also guests on the show that night. We were given earphones and strict instructions not to use idiomatic language, as it is very difficult to translate into German. We were to speak in English and be translated immediately to the live audience. What had seemed like a good idea when we accepted the invitation in Kent, turned into a nightmare of stage fright for me, just before we were due to go on. Johnnie is so used to public speaking that he was as calm as a cucumber. I paced up and down outside the large silver doors that were to be opened dramatically for us to make our entrance. I just wanted the earth to open up and swallow me whole. At the point when I would have sold my soul to the devil, in order to be let off this terrifying ordeal, I unconsciously found myself saying, 'I want my Mummy!' To my horror, a male voice replied down my earpiece: 'Don't worry, Mummy's here!' Apparently, my translator was all ready and waiting.

But the nightmare continued. On stage, Thomas cheerfully announced that every afternoon at 4 o'clock the aristocracy in England drink tea served by their butlers, and he had a butler and the tea ready for me to demonstrate just how it should be prepared and served. Almost sick with nerves, I had to pick up a delicate china cup and a huge, heavy, silver teapot in my shaking hands and pour the wretched tea. It was true that Johnnie's family had in the past employed the services of a butler. The first time that the river Eden burst its banks was in 1958 after it had been diverted by Johnnie's great grandfather, who had built a Tudor-style village adjoining Hever Castle on the reclaimed land, in order to house his staff. The castle and village flooded after 3 inches of rain fell in 12 hours and the following morning Johnnie's grandfather was collected from his first-floor bedroom in the castle by his butler in a rowing boat, to be escorted to breakfast. The butler was immaculately dressed as always, in a crisp white shirt, jacket and tie – and swimming trunks! My grandfather, Harold Mackintosh, had also had a butler with the curious surname of Mycock. He used to relish annoying my rather prim grandmother by enquiring loudly, as he descended the sweeping staircase for breakfast: 'Has anyone seen Mycock today?'

After the dreadful English tea ceremony, came the question: what would we do if one of our five daughters wanted to marry a German? Johnnie paused to collect his thoughts, trying to work out a charming reply. I was amazed that, in 1998, there was still such a powerful feeling of shame from the Second World War to necessitate such a question. Immediately, I replied that so long as he was a good, kind and honest man, it simply couldn't matter less what race or religion he was, which thankfully brought a huge round of applause.

After leaving Walldorf, we made our way to the Douglas's house, a beautiful old farmhouse with stone barns and formal gardens, surrounded by hundreds of acres of immaculate woodland, set beside a large lake. It was still in the process of being renovated, but we each had a lovely bedroom filled with antiques and magnificent views of the surrounding countryside. From the Douglas's house we drove to Sienna in Tuscany, where we celebrated Violet's A-level results. She achieved 2 A's and 1 B, which was an excellent result but, for a dyslexic, was particularly satisfying. However, Violet didn't believe it until she checked with the school. All of my three stepdaughters are dyslexics. Dyslexia is in the same gene pool as autism, ADHD and dyspraxia, although at the time of writing the reason for this is as yet undiscovered, although the connection is generally recognised by professionals. When Charles was young, he felt quite left out, with no disability to claim his own, until we discovered he was colour blind, which made him feel more part of the family!

We left Sienna and took the twisting coast road through scores of tunnels carved through the mountains to Cannes in the south of

France. Olivia had not gone to the loo for ten days and was eating very little. This was the first holiday where she didn't 'go' for such a long time and Johnnie was very worried and thought we should take her to a doctor. As I was aware that Olivia's bowels often went into 'shutdown' when we were not at home, I had not been unduly concerned. It is typical of autistic children not to use unfamiliar toilets. I had heard about a boy at a National Autistic Society school who never went to the toilet at school and saved it up for Friday night, as soon as he returned home and to his familiar toilet. But ten days was Olivia's record, and I was about to agree with Johnnie and call a doctor when Natalya telephoned from her bathroom in the next-door hotel room to tell us that Olivia had 'been'. This habit of holding on for days at a time has gradually lessened as she grows up, but she has developed other toilet troubles. When she was ten she would have to be persuaded to go, otherwise she would hold on with a full bladder all day. This, again typically with an autistic child, was corrected, but the pendulum swung too far in the opposite direction. Olivia is now convinced that after one drink, she must immediately go to the loo. I have explained the physiology of digestion, but relearning the feeling of a full bladder is very hard for her, so we let her go to the loo using a clock, or meal breaks, as a timer. This works fairly well at the moment, as she can understand when the next toilet trip will be allowed.

After our return from the summer holiday, and within days of Olivia starting Otford County Primary School, Natalya and I drove to London for her operation. To my relief, Olivia had settled in quite quickly, undoubtedly having Christie Miller continue as her LSA helped the transition enormously. The uniform was almost the same too as her previous school, with the ubiquitous navy trousers and a white shirt from Marks and Spencer; the only difference being the logo on her sweatshirt. Olivia had spent a couple of days at Otford during the summer term, so she could familiarise herself with it a little, and during the holidays, I had talked to her about the move and told her what to expect. Preparation is vital to any change, which autistic people find difficult, and knowing the plan and what to expect alleviates a great deal of anxiety they would otherwise feel.

My darling mother came down to the hospital from Newcastle on Tyne, where she lived, to hold my hand and be with her precious granddaughter Natalya. Although we had had the operation explained and had put our trust entirely in the surgeon, we were terrified. The night before the operation Natalya was taken out to dinner by her friends, who had all rallied around her, and wrote her poems. At midnight, I had to ask them to leave the hospital room as she was to be woken at 6 a.m. and operated on at 8 a.m. I was allowed to walk with her as far as the ante-room, just outside the operating theatre, and kissed her good luck, and then I returned to our room to sit and wait, with my mother. The hours ticked by and we made desultory conversation. A nurse knocked on the door and asked us if we would like to visit the intensive care unit, where Natalya would go for at least 24 hours after the operation. It was such a good idea to help prepare us, because as we walked into the unit, I saw bed after bed with young people and children, faces white as sheets, with tubes coming out of their chests, arms hands and noses. It was my first experience of an intensive care unit, and before my tears of shock started to flow, I was handed a box of paper tissues. The staff were wonderful, kind, supportive and experienced. After four hours on the operating table, Natalya was wheeled into the intensive care unit and I took turns with her father and grandmother in sitting beside her bed. She was in intensive care for nearly two days and as I sat beside her sleeping, post-operative body, her face deathly pale, I remembered what my mother said when Jenny, my step-sister, died of cervical cancer at only 43. 'Liz, may you never see your daughter leave her house in a body bag.' These words kept swirling around my head as I watched the nurse with increasing admiration as every ten minutes she checked Natalya's pulse and all the tubes and drips to which she was connected.

In order to sew up the hole, her chest had to be broken open and then repaired with eight large metal staples. The surgeon Mr Pattison was good with his sewing needle and told Natalya to wear her scar with pride! As I sat beside her I wondered how I would have coped if she had died. In the bed next to her lay a beautiful boy of 19. His Greek grandmother, dressed entirely in black, sat on a chair beside him, saying her rosary. I had heard that this was his fifth operation and his life was in danger. We all assume that with modern medicine we can defeat death and are not prepared for what 90 per cent of the rest of the world has to live with every day. Although her operation was a complete success, it took several years before Natalya was convinced that she was healed. She still occasionally has mild arrhythmia, but without that operation she would have died of congenital heart disease by the time she was 40. We were so lucky it had been treated in time.

By the autumn, Natalya was back in London and I decided that it was time I paid attention to her ADHD. There was to be a conference about ADHD at The Royal Institute of Psychiatry in November and I bought a ticket and went. It was another enormous eye opener and yet another time when I wondered why I had done nothing about this condition earlier. I had been told that Natalya had acute ADHD when she was 12, but I had not wanted her put on Ritalin nor had I learnt anything on the subject. At the one-day conference, I heard of the thousands of ADHD children who are routinely excluded from school and of prisons full of adults with ADHD. Pathetic letters from children and adults alike, begging for help, were read aloud by Andrea Bilbow, the founder of ADDISS (Attention Deficit Disorder Information and Support Service).

At that first seminar on ADHD, I learnt that the sufferers all experienced what was termed 'executive processing difficulties'. This meant that they were incapable of 'seeing the wood for the trees'. For example, an ADHD person with a very untidy office or bedroom, and told to tidy it up, would not know where to begin. They would be instantly overloaded with all the things that had to be done. They could not order their thoughts to, in the case of a messy bedroom, first hang up all the clean clothes, second, take out all the dirty laundry, third, make the bed and so on. What would usually happen is that they would panic, do nothing all day except become more and more stressed and, at the last minute, make a feeble and very bad job of tidying up. They also repeatedly did things that annoyed others, without realising it. In the early days of my marriage, Johnnie realised almost immediately that Natalya did annoying things again and again without any malicious intent. She just didn't take it in. She would also very quickly become overloaded and, consequently, panic-stricken with instructions for homework, from school. She was hopeless at organising her belongings and would lose her school books, pens and homework, all the time. In the case of her schoolwork she would become engrossed in the minutiae and be incapable of giving the bigger picture.

Like autism, ADHD is a hidden disorder. It is also a biological disorder, and the difference between an ADHD brain and a normal brain can be quite clearly seen with an MRI scan. The Magnetic Resonance Imaging, or MRI scan, takes pictures of the brain's activity, showing in colour the areas of an ADHD brain that are functioning differently from a normal brain. Neurotransmitters in the brain are responsible for passing messages, but in the brain of someone with ADHD they are not transmitted normally and cause a problem similar to short-circuiting. Consequently, Ritalin, which is a stimulant, can be used to stimulate the brain into normal activity and, strange though it seems, this stimulant calms the person down, so that they are able to focus and concentrate. The drug Ritalin has been tested more vigorously than almost any other drug currently on the market and yet huge controversy continues to this day over whether it should be prescribed to children at all. There is also a school of thought that ADHD is only a childhood disorder and that such children grow out of it as they mature. I find this idea incredible. In my experience of ADHD, it continues throughout life, but I suspect that the reason for this thinking is that adults with ADHD gradually, and painfully, learn to cope with this disability through maturity, learning by bitter experience what they can, or cannot, manage. The lucky ones find jobs that do not require hours of paperwork, or long periods of sustained concentration, but many, if not most, are not so fortunate and find holding down a job, or a relationship, extremely difficult. Ritalin is frequently accused of 'cracking a nut with a sledge hammer', but my response to that argument is to ask the decrier to live, if only for a day, with someone who has ADHD, before making such a sweeping statement. If there is help for such people, why deny them what could mean the difference between a life of quality and fulfilment, and one of misery and failure?

The problem is not with the medication; after all, cancer patients are given morphine, a class A drug, but that the condition exists in the first place. This is nothing new. As I had learnt through my studies in autism, in very recent history autistic children were considered uneducable. Merely because the scientific world has not yet come to terms with a condition, does not mean that it does not exist. Or, as Lorna Wing says, 'No label, no condition.'

ADHD people often self-medicate, by taking alcohol or drugs to stimulate their brains. It is only then, or in a state of high excitement, that they feel really alive. It was very comforting for me to hear that there were so many people who had this disorder, albeit tragic for all concerned. Throughout Natalya's life, I had been berated and told that her behaviour was the result of my bad parenting. To be in a room full of parents who were experiencing the same difficulties was as wonderful as it had been to be with parents of autistic children. It was due to her ADHD that Natalya had been to so many schools for short periods of time. But what could be done to help her?

Sitting next to me at the conference was a specialist in ADHD called Dianne Zaccheo. Dianne is an American with thick dark hair, a lovely low, soft voice and black eyes that she focuses on you, giving her entire attention to what you are saying. We started a conversation during one of the breaks between speakers and she told me that she was starting to coach ADHD people. Her method was first to explain the biology of ADHD and make sure that that person realised that it was something they were born with and not their fault. Most ADHD people have extremely low self-esteem and feel like complete failures. Secondly she helped them, using strategies and coaching, to train themselves to be better able to cope with everyday life. I liked what I heard and took Dianne's phone number so that I could take Natalya to her for an evaluation. What I also learnt was that there was a wealth of information available on the subject and during the lunch break I bought several books with enigmatic titles, such as *You Mean I'm not Crazy, Stupid or Lazy?* My overriding comfort in not having given Natalya Ritalin, I discovered, was that it would have exacerbated her heart condition and, in her case, been positively dangerous.

At the end of the seminar, I introduced myself to Andrea, the founder of ADDISS, who had one son with Asperger syndrome and another with ADHD. Her sons were a similar age to Natalya and Olivia, and we joked about pairing them up. Andrea has ADHD herself and had set up the charity because so many people had asked for her help. She promised to send me her information sheets and told me of an annual three-day seminar that her charity holds every year at which specialists on ADHD from all over the world come to speak. Two years later, Andrea invited me to become the patron of ADDISS, which I was more than happy to accept.

By the late autumn of 1998, I felt a new sense of confidence, or control. Olivia had settled into Otford County Primary School, and had even been invited to 'friends' for tea. We had had one or two of these children to tea at our house and there was one particular boy whom Olivia really liked and he seemed fond of her too. I thought that she had taken a liking to him because he replaced Charles, whom she missed enormously now he was at prep school, and this sweet boy was certainly as kind and forgiving as her brother towards her odd behaviour. Natalya had recovered well from her heart operation and I was on the fast learning track for ADHD. I had time to phone the Helen Allison School in Kent, one of the six National Autistic Society schools, and ask if I could visit. I had met the headmistress, Jacqui Ashton Smith, at the NAS conference the year before and she welcomed me into her school one wet and windy November morning. I had never been to an autism-specific school and was really looking forward to meeting the children and finding out how they were taught. I was also hoping to pick up some ideas.

The Helen Allison School takes in a wide ability group. There were those who had to be helped to eat at mealtimes, those who were non-verbal and others who had Asperger syndrome and some who were academically very able. I was still a beginner in the world of autism and although I had already read fairly extensively on the subject, I had not yet met another autistic child. So, macabre though it may seem to the layman, I was excited to see children who were hand flapping, walking on their tiptoes and biting themselves. What I was not prepared for was the completely silent playground. It was the eeriest place on earth. I had arrived just before break time and was shown to the playground and warned about the peculiar habits of some of the children.

The whole area was surrounded with a high wire fence to stop potential runaways from escaping. As Olivia could walk off her playground at any moment, I didn't find this anything but eminently sensible. But Olivia was at an ordinary county primary school with all the usual noisy chatter, ball games, skipping ropes and cliques of intrigue, and in this playground all I could hear was the screech, screech of the rusty chains that held the swings. A couple of boys played alone with a football each and another boy rode a tricycle wearing a helmet because he had epilepsy and often fitted. About 30 per cent of autistic children develop epilepsy, something that had not happened to Olivia, yet. Epilepsy tends to appear in the teens. A teenage girl approached me and, without looking at me, began to play with my earrings. A teacher told me that she loved earrings, and so, without looking at her, so that I would not frighten her, I told her what they were made of and asked her if she would like to try them on.

I visited many of the classrooms and I noticed that there were labels on everything. When we met the IT (information technology) teacher, he introduced me to a wonderful computer programme of words and symbols, called Widget, which wrote out the word, with a simple, clear, outline picture below. As I was currently searching for a way to teach Olivia to read, this seemed like the answer. Each drawer in the classroom had labels such as 'Pencils' or 'Lego' and a picture below. I wrote down where to buy the programme and ordered it as soon as I returned home. Our house quickly resembled a schoolroom with Widget pictures and labels on everything from the grandfather clock to the bath. The teachers also suggested that I make a book for Olivia, with photographs, to help her to read. With the aid of a Polaroid camera, Karen, our nanny, made several books for Olivia. We started with a photo of Daddy, with 'Daddy' written underneath and photos of other members of the family. We then extended the second book to sentences, such as, 'Daddy is reading the newspaper'. I was also advised at the Helen

Allison School to use whatever Olivia was interested in, as a tool to help her learn. Olivia was mad about Disney films and so we made reading books for her using all the current Disney characters. She loved them and very quickly learnt to read. As I had been Montessori trained, I tried to teach her to break down words into sounds. This had no effect whatsoever because, as Mary Hampton had pointed out earlier, Olivia learnt the whole word in one go, and never learnt, or was able to learn, reading in the conventional way. I have been told that this method of 'whole word' reading is very common with autistic children. We consequently had a lot of fun with words such as 'blackboard' and 'cupboard', which we broke down into two words and analysed. Olivia loves words, and word play, and often remarked on what she found funny, which were frequently people's surnames, such as 'Onion' or 'Weatherill' and we would make jokes together, asking each other 'What is the weather today, Mr Weatherill?' This sometimes backfired, of course, if we had guests to lunch, when Olivia would burst out laughing at being introduced to some poor, unsuspecting visitor who had an unusual name, and would repeat it loudly, until she was told by me that it was rude to make fun of another's name and would say 'Sorry Mummy, do you forgive me?', which compounded an already awkward situation.

My visit to the Helen Allison School was such an education that I asked if I could spend a day or two there, helping out and making notes. Free teaching assistants are always welcome and I was allocated a place in two weeks' time, in a classroom that had children from ages five to eight, as that would be of the most use and interest to me, Olivia then being age six.

On my first morning, I was introduced to the class teachers and asked to sit next to a girl of six, the same age as Olivia, who was non-verbal. This tiny, adorable Indian girl quite stole my heart, and I was glad that Olivia could speak, although her speech was faint and rapid. We had a couple of lessons and then I was moved on to supervise two eight-year-old boys with Asperger syndrome. What a contrast! I had never come across anyone with Asperger syndrome and although they were very bright and able to do their maths, they were almost instantly involved in an old rivalry over their favourite football teams. The taunting began, then one of the boys dashed to the drawer holding the personal belongings of the other boy, took out his treasured football magazine, and deliberately tore it in front of him, laughing with cruel pleasure. Mayhem ensued. They had to be physically separated, while I tried to repair the magazine with a role of sticky tape.

Each child had his own learning station, which was a cubicle closed on three sides with nothing in it that would distract or distress him while decreasing the possibility of sensory overload from the rest of the class. This is because autistic children need a very ordered and quiet environment in which to learn, and class teaching is something that very rarely takes place in schools for autism. The morning continued with a few interruptions between my Asperger boys, until suddenly, the doors flew open and a red-faced teacher ran in and nodded to the teacher. Seconds later a large, overweight black boy of about 15 ran into the classroom, lurching forward with outstretched hands, his eyes wild, followed by three other teachers, who calmed him and withdrew him as quickly and as gently as possible from the classroom. I watched from behind the open door in amazement as the children went into a well-rehearsed routine. They all moved quickly and with very little prompting to the back of the classroom and were instantly surrounded by a wall of teachers and assistants in a tight protective circle. The big boy was removed from the class and the children returned to what they had been doing as if nothing unusual had happened. I was left shaken and bewildered, and was told that this particular boy was very aggressive and frequently burst into this classroom as he had an ongoing issue with this particular class. The children had a well-rehearsed drill, which I had just experienced and admired, and luckily, so far, there had been no accidents.

I was introduced to the term 'low arousal' that morning. This means using techniques to keep the anxiety levels of an autistic person as low as possible. Every autistic person has extremely high anxiety levels, whether one can actually see a physical manifestation of it, or not. The world is such a crazy, terrifying place for them that it is often extremely difficult for them just to maintain 'normal' behaviours. General techniques include speaking to an autistic person with a soft, slow and quiet voice, being extremely patient, even if one has to explain something several times over and using non-aggressive body language. Sitting down facing the autistic person at eye level often helps the calming process, or taking them out of the room into a quiet room with dim lights and no other sound or person, can be a good starting point. Thereafter, it depends on the individual and their particular calming strategies. Some autistic children and adults can't stand anything out of place, or they need a special toy to play with or their favourite soft toy to hold. Olivia had to close the dishwasher door, and make sure that all the kitchen cupboards and drawers were fully closed, before she could even begin to make her breakfast. These calming techniques can, of course, become obsessions in themselves, and so the parents or carers must be vigilant in addressing the possibility of an obsession before the habit has become entrenched. We had to break Olivia's various calming habits by, in the case of the kitchen cupboards, for example, leaving one cupboard door open for a few seconds, to begin with. We told her that it was all right to eat breakfast without everything in place and that sometimes things aren't perfectly ordered as she would like. It was torture for her but every day she managed a few seconds more, until, eventually she broke the habit. But she still *has* to close the cap on the washing-up liquid bottle and pull down the bread bin lid before she can make her breakfast!

To my relief, we broke for lunch shortly after the incident of the boy rushing into the classroom. Some of the children needed a great deal of help with eating and drinking. I sat opposite one boy who had to be spoon-fed by his helper, but he loved to throw hot custard over her, or whatever was served that day! She took it all with a pinch of salt, and told me that wearing old clothes and an apron was essential. By the time I left at 3.30 p.m. I was completely exhausted and deeply admiring of those exceptional, dedicated people who work with autistic children. I had also learnt many practical techniques and asked if Karen Wilcox, Olivia's nanny, could also come for a few days to learn, so that we could pool our information. With great generosity, Jacqui Ashton Smith agreed.

Meanwhile I continued to take a keen interest in media reports and books on autism. I read with horror of the misery caused by Bruno Bettelheim, an American psychoanalyst, who wrote a book in the 1960s called *The Empty Fortress: infantile autism and the birth of the self*, in which he claimed that autism was caused by 'refrigerator mothers'. These mothers had, according to Bettelheim, withheld their love for their child to such an extreme degree that many children were removed from their families and taken into care, while the poor mothers were told they must have psychiatric treatment since their child's autism was entirely their fault. I am happy to say that this theory died out a long time ago, but not before many families' lives were destroyed.

Then there was Holding Therapy, developed by Martha Welch in New York in the 1980s. Parents of autistic children were told to hold their child quite tightly for long periods of time. The idea was to produce a connection between the parent and the child, and some parents claimed that it had indeed made a difference, but this has not been proven. Olivia, like many autistic children and adults, hates to be touched, let alone held in a tight hug and it must have been agony for these poor children. I certainly wasn't going to try Holding Therapy! Next I read about the Daily Life Therapy, a Japanese practise at the Higashi Schools in Japan and in Boston in America. The idea here is that the children are given vigorous and highly regimented physical activity for much of their waking day and are not allowed to lapse into self-stimulatory behaviour for a second. Most autistic children have some kind of self-stimulatory behaviour, which calms and comforts them. This can be hand flapping, hugging a familiar beanie baby or more socially difficult behaviours, such as rhythmically rocking, hitting their heads against a wall. I watched a television documentary about the Higashi method with amazement at the use of an almost army-training-camp approach with very young children, but I could understand why parents of severely autistic children might try it. Some of the parents thought that it had benefited their children quite considerably, but Olivia's autism was not severe enough for me to contemplate such drastic measures. Daily Life Therapy is a method that is still in use today and is not one of the many methods that have disappeared with time, which alone makes me think that there is real benefit to more severely autistic children for it to continue to survive in a market abounding with mountebankery.

Another miracle 'cure' to hit the headlines around the late 1990s was the one where autistic children were taken swimming with dolphins in Florida. Many parents spent over a year fundraising, holding car boot sales and coffee mornings in order to raise the enormous amount of money it cost, as well as the cost of flying to Florida for a week, or even two, with their families, so that their autistic child could try this method. I met one mother at a conference who had tried it with her non-verbal daughter. After two weeks, she had learnt one word: 'no'. No, to any more swimming, I wondered? This method had no scientific evidence to prove it was of any value, although some parents claimed to have had remarkable results, as was the case with every alternative therapy. There was always one person for whom it had performed a miracle and it was the constant search for a miracle cure for our children that made families try each one, again and again.

Much has also been written about Facilitated Communication, which also claimed extraordinary results for non-verbal children in the 1970s. This was a method of communication by keyboard, developed in Australia. The 'facilitator' holds his hands very lightly over the hands of the autistic child's, which are placed on the keyboard. He then helps the child to press the keys that the child has apparently chosen. Books have been written about the miracle of what the child has stored inside and has been hitherto unable to express verbally. Later, there was an equal amount of bad press, in which there were allegations that the facilitators were merely guessing what the child wanted to type. This was another unscientific 'cure', which came and went with equal fanfare. Years later, many of these 'treatments' or 'cures' are viewed as tantamount to a form of abuse of these poor, autistic children.

Barry and Samahria Kauffman live in Sheffield, Massachusetts and have an autistic son, Raun, now an adult. They developed a method of reaching their son by being 'autistic' with him. They claimed that he rapidly developed skills after this change of approach, and they opened a school called the Son-Rise Program. Parents are invited, at

RIGHT: Wedding day, 5 May 1990, at the Rosslyn Hill Unitarian Church in Hampstead, London. My brother Charles, pictured, gave me away and Violet (left) and Natalya (right) were bridesmaids.

BELOW: Gathered in our drawing room for Olivia's christening in November 1992. From left: Violet, Tania, Camilla, Natalya, Olivia – aged 3 months – in my arms, Johnnie, Charles, my mother Bronda and my stepfather, the Reverend Roger Tarbuck.

LEFT: *Oliva aged 4 in our dining room on Easter Sunday, escaping the noise and family by eating before everyone else. I usually put her beside me at large family occasions which she is much more able to manage now, aged 13.*

BELOW: *All dressed up and ready to go to the State Opening of Parliament!*

BELOW: *Celebrating my mother-in-law Lady Irene Astor of Hever's 75th birthday, in the grounds of Hever Castle which was the Astor family home from 1903 to 1982. This was the weekend that Olivia (dressed in red, on Johnnie's lap) took her first steps.*

BELOW: Olivia at 9 months, looking at me and smiling naturally. She had just learnt to sit up by herself but still needed to be supported with cushions.

ABOVE: Oliva being steadied by Angela, her nanny, on her 3rd birthday in our flat in France. Although she had learnt to walk 10 months before, she was still unsteady. We didn't know then that she was very dyspraxic.

BELOW: Olivia aged 2 and ready for bedtime stories. Her love of books began early and continues to this day. Reading and words are her strength.

OPPOSITE PAGE: *Olivia, aged 5, and Charles, aged 7, on our new trampoline, taken by Natalya for her GCSE photography course. Olivia is holding 'Ghosty Whosty' who is one of her two lifelong favourite toys. Note how anxious she is. She didn't like bouncing and has a book in front of her. Charles is typically loving and protective.*

ABOVE: *Olivia having Auditory Intervention Training (AIT – see page 60) in January 1997, just before she was diagnosed with autism.*

LEFT: *Aged 7 at Disneyland, Paris. The most successful holiday so far with Olivia. She adores all things Disney and was transported, meeting the characters. (Never ask an autistic child to smile for the camera as they are usually unable to do so naturally and the result is the grimace you see on the left.)*

ABOVE: *Olivia with Johnnie, Christmas Day 2004, at Tillypronie, Scotland. Olivia had had her long hair cut a few days before. She is only relating to 'Bullseye', her alter ego, a heavily patched toy from the film* Toy Story 2.

TOP: *May 2003 in the garden at Frenchstreet, Kent. Natalya (left) just 22, Charles 12½ , and Oliva 10½ with her precious long hair. Natalya and I went to Machu Picchu that month.*

OPPOSITE PAGE, LEFT: *Natalya, aged 7, tree climbing in Vermont. This photograph captures the impulsive behaviour, energy and total lack of fear so typical of children with ADHD.*

OPPOSITE PAGE, RIGHT: *Summer 2005. Olivia, aged 13, in her bedroom, 'sorting' her toys. Most of her carpet is covered in carefully placed and sorted cards, books and beanie babies etc. This is her safety zone and extremely typical of autistic 'container play'. The toys are matched and grouped but never used in imaginative or interactive play.*

BELOW: 29 September 1999. Tania (left), myself and my brother Charles (right), freezing cold with pounding heads but thrilled to have reached the summit of Kilimanjaro in aid of the National Autistic Society. Charlie managed a smile but was suffering from bad altitude sickness so we didn't stay long.

BELOW: *Natalya and I on the Inca Trail, Peru, in May 2003. We were emotional, exhausted and filthy dirty having walked for three days to reach Machu Picchu.*

ABOVE: *About to launch myself off Canary Wharf Tower, London, 15 July 2002 in aid of the Lord Mayor of London's mental health charities. Beyond terror at this point....*

BELOW: *Looking terrible but feeling euphoric. I had completed the 2005 London Marathon in a respectable time and I never had to do it again!*

a not inconsiderable cost, to spend a minimum of a week with their child, at the Kauffman Institute, where they immerse themselves in playing with their child in his or her chosen manner. They are given stern talks about the acceptance of autism, that it is fine to be autistic and they must adjust their lives to fit in with the child's, as far as possible, of course. Some of this really made sense to me. I had been taught by Sue Brown, the first speech and language therapist we saw, to verbally describe what Olivia was doing in order to catch her attention. It had worked and I had discovered for myself that playing with Olivia, by lying or sitting on the floor next to her and very slowly taking part in her activity, did open a door of communication between us. However, I wasn't ready to down tools and fly to Massachusetts to experiment with another unproven cure, a proportion of which I had already taken on board.

It was becoming clear to me why the National Autistic Society had been unable to give me any answers to my questions about whether this or that therapy worked and was worth trying, when I had rung them 18 months before. It was impossible for them to give credence to the myriad of therapies that had no scientific basis. It would have been unprofessional and potentially dangerous to the autistic person and opened the society to the possibility of litigation. In 2004, I was invited by Simon Baron-Cohen, Professor of Developmental Psychopathology and Director of the Autism Research Centre in Cambridge, to be a patron of a new charity he was setting up called Interventions in Autism Research Trust. The research was to evaluate as many of these alternative therapies as it could and I was delighted to accept. This was just what parents urgently needed and desperately wanted. Although the research will take many years to complete and will be too late for Olivia, it is essential that alternative therapies are clinically trialled by professionals in the field of autism so that as little as possible time, money and indeed lives, are wasted.

Back in 1998, I had already decided that I wanted to help others who had an autistic child, in whatever small way I could. I rang the National Autistic Society and offered my services to the then head of fundraising, a handsome and charming Israeli called Assaf Admoni, who came to visit me at home and informed me about what the NAS were currently involved in in the field of fundraising and what the plans were for the future. We discussed my helping him with some events in the following year. Just before Christmas in 1998, we had a friend, Julie Hyde Mew, from South Africa to stay for a weekend. She arrived with her fiancé and as they were leaving, my stepdaughter, Tania, said 'See you on Kili!' I asked what she meant and she told me that Julie and her fiancé were planning to spend his 30th birthday on the top of Mount Kilimanjaro, in Tanzania. I mentioned that I had always dreamed of climbing Mount Kilimanjaro and Julie said immediately, 'Why don't you join us?' 'I'd love to,' I replied. 'But I am not going all that way without a purpose, I'll make it a fundraising trek in aid of the NAS!' And thus began my years of trekking in aid of autism. Serendipity.

CHAPTER 9

Family Trips,
Mishaps and Magic

CHRISTMAS 1998 WAS SPENT AT HOME. I had learnt to allow Olivia to open her presents in a quiet room with me alone, and she managed the family noise quite well. I sat her next to me at mealtimes and let her leave the table as soon as she had finished eating. In the new year, we had a family skiing holiday and stayed at the Hotel Flüela in Davos, Switzerland. The year before we had also been skiing in early January and, on the last day, discovered that Charles's ski instructor Carolyn was also a special needs ski instructor. We had booked Carolyn immediately for the following Christmas and so with a large family of nine in total, which included all the girls, Charles and Karen, the children's nanny, we joined the Anglo Swiss All Party Parliamentary Group and their families, for a week.

Johnnie had joined the Anglo Swiss All Party Parliamentary Group several years before we married and had taken his girls many times to Switzerland for this skiing week. The idea began about 50 years ago, when the British, who loved both skiing and the Swiss people, decided that it would be a pleasant and effective way to get together members of the British and Swiss Parliaments with their families in a relaxed atmosphere, to talk politics and make friends. The previous year, Olivia had tobogganed with Karen and I had taken a suitcase full of toys, crayons, books and games for them to play with while we skied. This year she was to have her own lessons, if I could persuade her to wear a hat and the hard, unnatural-feeling ski boots. I had done my best to prepare her and she had practised wearing the boots many times for a few minutes at home, as well as the balaclava and gloves, all of which she hated.

On the first morning I handed Olivia over to the kind and gentle Carolyn and we arranged to meet at lunchtime, in one of the lovely mountaintop restaurants. Carolyn is Swiss, married to an Australian ski instructor, Tony, and teaching skiing is their life. Carolyn and Tony spend the winter season teaching in Davos and then go to Australia to give skiing lessons during the Australian winter season. She had short dark hair and deep blue eyes full of humour. Carolyn had also helped Nina Law learn to ski when she noticed that her mother, my friend Carola, who had given me so much help and advice before Olivia was diagnosed, was struggling to keep her tall, beautiful daughter upright on skis, aged about ten. Carolyn came equipped with a tiny pair of skis and what she called an 'Edgy-Wedgy', which was a large, brightly coloured thick rubber band that held the tips of the skis together in a snowplough position. She also had reins to hold Olivia from behind so that she did not slip away from her and to keep her upright. It seemed to work and, as I skied beside Olivia, I looked down at her little face half-hidden by her balaclava and saw her smiling.

Carolyn was an angel and very inventive with her ideas of how to make it fun for Olivia. She took her to the kindergarten slope first, where she helped Olivia to very, very slowly snowplough around painted Disney characters, which Olivia seemed to enjoy. In the afternoon Karen would take Olivia back to the hotel and play games with her and also take her swimming in the hotel pool. I loved skiing and being able to ski with my family in the knowledge that Olivia was also taking part in our holiday meant so much to me. I knew that there would be times when we simply couldn't do things together. It would be unfair to make Olivia come on inappropriate holidays or to adult parties, which would be a misery for her, but as far as possible I thought it extremely important that she was included in all family activities.

Each evening we met other families in the lounge of the Hotel Flüela for drinks and conversation before dinner. Olivia seemed to be quite happy to be with us, drinking her cola and colouring in pictures in one of the books I had brought for her. One evening she got up from her armchair, walked to the next table and, without looking at anyone, picked up their bowl of crisps and brought it back to her seat and began to tuck in. There was a look of astonishment on the face of the British Ambassador to Switzerland, and his guests, from whose table Olivia had nicked the crisps. I rushed to the bar, bought another bowl and presented it to the ambassador with my profuse apologies. Johnnie admonished Olivia, who very quietly and without the slightest real feeling, said 'Sorry, Daddy.' After dinner, the Ambassador's wife, a very large Greek lady swathed in voluminous black, wearing Nana Mouskouri glasses and smoking a small dark cheroot approached Johnnie. 'Is your daughter autistic, by any chance?' she asked, her eyes twinkling. It transpired that her nephew was autistic and she had spotted Olivia long before she had stolen their crisps.

I was surprised that Olivia's autism had been so easily detected because she was perfectly normal to look at and it was only her odd behaviour that had given her away. Her speech was poor and the content bizarre, but she had not spoken to anyone at the Ambassador's table. However, it was a real pleasure to talk to someone who understood the difficulties of having an autistic child, and was relaxed and ready to laugh with me at some of the funny things these children do.

On our third day out, in glorious sunshine, we waved goodbye to Olivia and followed our instructor to the ski lift that would take us to the top of the Rinerhorn, one of the beautiful mountains that surround Davos. The weather was perfect, the sky a bright blue and the freshly bashed piste sparkled with silver glints in the morning sun. After two long runs down the mountain, we decided to take a different route towards a mountain chalet where we planned to have a coffee break. Our young and extremely handsome ski instructor set off on what appeared to be a steep, straight slope, which turned into a long, flat run ending at our chalet. We all pushed ourselves off the top of the piste as hard as we could, digging in our ski poles in order to gain enough speed to carry us to the end of the long, flat run so that we wouldn't have to walk. After the ski instructor went Camilla, followed by Tania, three others, Johnnie, me and the rest of the group.

Half-way down the slope, quite impossible to see, was a bump that made quite a sudden jump. The instructor and Camilla managed to ski over it, but after that everyone fell. By the time Johnnie came down the hill, there was no space for him to fall and he crashed into one of the fluorescent painted pine poles that mark the centre of the piste. As I skied down behind him, I could see fallen bodies everywhere and veered off to the right, where I fell too, on the soft snow at the edge of the piste. I heard yelling and crying, and tore off my skies to run across the piste to Johnnie, who was lying on his side with his leg at an awkward angle. At least, that is what I first thought, until I saw, to my horror, that he had broken his femur and the awkward angle was the break in the middle of his thigh bone. He was in shock and in agony as the ski instructor tried to work out which way to put the metallic sheet over his body to keep him warm. I grabbed it from him and wrapped it around my white and shaking husband as the ski instructor called a helicopter ambulance.

Johnnie was so brave, he just kept asking, 'When is it coming? When is it coming?' After what seemed like hours a helicopter arrived over the mountainside and out jumped several paramedics who immediately put him on a drip and asked me if he had any allergies. Within minutes they had him in the helicopter, but there was no room for me and, with trembling legs, I had no alternative but to ski to the bottom of the mountain and take a taxi back to the hotel to collect his pyjamas and a credit card en route to the hospital. Poor Camilla and Tania were distraught. They adore their father and had never seen him in pain before. They crept slowly towards the café to stop and get over the shock before they too made their way down the mountain, back to Davos.

Johnnie was lucky, in that right next to the hospital is the factory where the titanium rods, which are inserted into broken femurs, are made. Within an hour of my reaching the hospital, Johnnie had been operated on and was in his room, happily high and hilarious on the anaesthetic. He was still in cracking form in the early evening when all the children came to visit him, which was a good thing for Charles to see, as he was only eight and had been terribly upset and tearful to hear what had happened to his father, while Olivia, showing no concern for her father whatsoever, was only interested in the metal cage that supported the blankets over his bed.

The next day, it was altogether another matter. Johnnie had broken several ribs, but there was so much blood around his chest from internal bleeding, that the hospital couldn't take a clear X-ray. He was now in terrible pain and quickly became bored lying in hospital. I spent my days with him, sitting in a large armchair beside his bed, doing what I could to keep up his spirits. I was becoming used to living in hospitals, since it was only four months since I had spent a week in hospital with Natalya. The Swiss are all too familiar with broken bones and fractures, and to my amazement had Johnnie walking down the corridor within two days of his operation and would send him home with a full physiotherapy programme to follow. As well as being extremely efficient, the hospital in Davos was spotless and the food delicious. We watched in dismay at the frequency of the paramedic helicopter, which seemed to deliver another casualty from the ski slopes almost hourly, and considered ourselves lucky that this was the first skiing accident anyone in our family had had. In fact a broken femur is somewhat more than just an 'accident'. In the First World War, many soldiers died of a broken femur as it was too great a trauma for the human body to withstand. I held Johnnie's hand tightly and kissed him every time that thought crossed my mind.

Once the skiing week was over, I sent the children and nanny home and stayed on for another five days, until we could, very gingerly, take Johnnie home in a taxi to the airport with his leg up across the back seat of the car. The driver of this beautiful Mercedes drove on the icy roads as if he were in a Grand Prix, and it was with relief that we reached Zurich airport without another accident. Johnnie had just been given his first Front Bench position as Shadow Minister for Health and Social Security, and was determined not to let his broken leg stop him from attending the House of Lords. We employed a carer, called Sarah, who pushed him around Parliament in a wheelchair with his leg up in the air, and helped him to bath and dress in the morning when he was in London.

As anyone who has had the misfortune to have been wheelchair bound will know, being pushed around helpless is at best precarious and, at worst, positively dangerous. Tracy Murrell, Johnnie's wonderful PA who has worked for him for ten years, took him to lunch in the House of Lords one day, using the lift. She backed in, pulling the wheelchair as close to her as possible, but there was not enough room for the wheelchair with his leg outstretched on a narrow board, even though her back was pressed into the furthest corner of the lift. To Tracy's horror, the doors of the lift closed on the broken leg, hitting the sides of the board, sprang open again, then closed with equal speed and repetition as Johnnie yelled in pain with every jolt and Tracy tried in desperation to reach the lift buttons to hold the door open. Even more painful was when Sarah, the carer, accidentally tipped him completely out of the wheelchair and into the gutter bang outside the Peers' entrance. Maybe these two incidents made him even more determined to get up on to his feet again as quickly as he possibly could!

While Johnnie was extremely busy with his new job and trying to live normally with a broken femur, I began my first fundraising exercise for the National Autistic Society (NAS). I had given much thought to where, within the NAS, I would like my funds to go and had decided that the DISCO training, organised by Dr Lorna Wing and Dr Judith Gould, was a clear winner. Doctors Wing and Gould are also training hundreds of professionals every year to use this interview with their patients, as these doctors, child psychiatrists, speech and language therapists and so on are among the first in the medical world who are the most likely to see these children. They are also educating these professionals into what autism really is, as the official International Classification system still defines autism in a very narrow and restricted way. I owed both Judy and Lorna so much. With their continued help, advice and friendship, I was able to teach Olivia in a way that would have taken me years to discover, if ever, on my own. She had benefited enormously through their care and I wanted to help them raise the money needed to be able to get the DISCO programme published and in use.

The NAS helped in every way it could, the fundraising team and the press office working together to make the most of this opportunity to raise awareness of autism using the Astor name to attract press coverage. Together we produced a very attractive and informative leaflet in which I explained that I had an autistic daughter and was attempting a sponsored climb to the top of Mount Kilimanjaro in aid of DISCO as well as providing general information about autism. There was an adorable photograph of Olivia kissing me and an insert, which contained the sponsorship form. I was happy to be able to talk about my situation, with the thought that if it only helped one other person with an autistic child, it was worth it. Once I had received the leaflets, I raided both Johnnie's and my address books and sent leaflets out to everyone we knew, followed by everyone I thought of who might have either connections to a charitable trust, or a personal fortune and a big heart.

The results were astonishing. After several interviews in the national and local press, and particularly after a five-page spread in *Hello* magazine with my step-daughter Tania with whom I was climbing, letters began to pour in. I was amazed to be told of the surprise that 'people like me' had an autistic child, as if disability were the prerogative of the less privileged. It is true that in my grandparents' generation, people from my background would probably not have mentioned their disabled child, who would have been quietly looked after by some loving nanny, in an unfrequented wing of the house. It was only relatively recently that autistic children were considered educable, entirely due to the work of the first parents like Lorna Wing, who set up what was initially called 'The Autistic Society' in 1960 and the first school for autistic children, as there was nowhere suitable for their children to go. Until that time, most perfectly able autistic people, as well as those at the severe end of the spectrum, had spent their entire lives living quite unnecessarily in the long-term care wings of hospitals, left to rot.

I had spent some of my working life in corporate special events with an advertising agency and, when I was younger, in promotional work. However, I had been out of the loop for nine years since I married Johnnie, when I began my first personal fundraising exercise. So it was with great excitement that I opened the post each morning and watched the cheques flow in. Amounts ranging from £5 to £500 came from friends and family, mostly with notes attached, which read along the lines of, 'Rather you than me' or 'My son tried to climb Kilimanjaro in his gap year, had terrible altitude sickness and couldn't make it to the summit!'

Of course, on top of the fundraising there was the all-important physical training. I had always kept reasonably fit, but trekking up a mountain that measured 19,453 feet, or 5,895 metres, was not a walk in the park. When Charles and Olivia were small, I used to push them around the farm and down country lanes in an old-fashioned Norland nanny type of pram, loaned to me by one of Johnnie's sisters. Charles would ride backwards, facing Olivia, who sat opposite him with her back to me in case she wobbled and fell out. It was quite hard work pushing two children while trying to keep tabs on three wide ranging spaniels, but I loved it and being a fresh air fanatic, always had my babies outside as much as possible, sleeping outdoors in their prams at rest time, during the day. However, I was 49 years old, and for the past 30 years or more, summer tennis and swimming, walking the dogs and pram pushing, was the sum total of my exercise regime. I had never allowed myself to get fat, but that was more due to vanity than to exercise.

It was in the 1980s that Jane Fonda introduced us all to 'keep fit', swiftly followed by many others who sold us their videos to which we could gyrate in the privacy of our bedrooms, providing, of course, the children didn't all come in to watch this hilarious comedy show, as mine did. After Olivia was born, I was desperate to regain my 'before-two-children-after-age-40' shape and bought Rosemary Conley's *Whole Body Programme 2* on video as she promised me 'a cute butt'. Apart from occasionally entertaining Charles and Olivia with my private freak show, Johnnie and I were appalled at the very thought of the gym, or personal trainers. 'Look at Churchill,' we would declare. 'He never needed to exercise to win the Second World War. Look at his phenomenal output, all those books and paintings. Look at his phenomenal input too, all that whisky, all those cigars!' We were firmly and comfortably set in the 'Gyms, Bah! Humbug!' mode. But I knew that I would never get to the top of that mountain unless I put some effort into fitness training and so, not really knowing what to do, I simply walked the dogs for longer and swam further.

I am a poor swimmer. That is to say, I adore swimming, particularly in the sea, but I do a very bad breast stroke with my head firmly out of the water, chin pointing to the sky, neck crunched up against my shoulders, rather like my mother's generation who hated to get their backcombed, stiffly styled hair wet when they swam and wore elaborate, petal-covered rubber swimming hats in bright, tropical colours. After a few months of manic swimming, between 100 and 150 lengths up and down our own swimming pool almost every day, my back seized up in complete muscle rebellion that would not only not allow me to get out of bed one morning, but would not even allow me to turn on my side. Johnnie had to take my hand and yank me to a sitting position, where I had to stay for an hour, because he had walked off to have his breakfast and let the dogs out, without realising that I couldn't move any further.

After a trip to an osteopath, I rather gave up on the swimming. We had bought a large trampoline, really for Olivia to strengthen her legs, and so I took to bouncing like Tigger and inventing games to play on it, in order to entice Olivia to join me. I suppose it helped a bit, but playing chase round the trampoline, which is what I mostly did, probably helped very little in building up muscle tone. Tania went walking as much as she could as her training effort and spent even more time hoping for the best. She was busy in her second year at Northumbria University reading Sociology and any spare time she had was usually directed towards Newcastle's notoriously energetic night life, rather than walking the hills with a backpack. Although she claimed that hours of dancing strengthened her legs.

In the spring of 1999, Tania heard that her friend Julie Hyde Mew and her fiancé weren't going to be able to come to Tanzania in September to climb Kilimanjaro with us, after all. My brother Charles and his wife and two children, Ben and Camilla, came to visit us from their house in London one Sunday. We talked about my forthcoming challenge and I said to my brother how much fun I thought it would be if he could join us as he was clearly getting caught up in the excitement of the trip. He jumped at the idea and confirmed with me a few days later that he and Isabelle had discussed his going at length and that so long as he wasn't going to put himself at risk, she agreed that he should go. After all, she did not want to be a widow with two small children! Nor did I want to put myself at risk. Who would look after Olivia if anything happened to me? In nearly all families with a disabled child, it was the mother who was the sole carer, and we were no different. Sweet and willing to help though everyone was, Olivia's father's and sisters' lives were very busy, the girls were still young and I felt should not be burdened or curtailed by a disabled sibling. In any case it was an all-day, every-day, week-in and week-out job and they were not often at home. And even when they were, they weren't sure what to do or how to handle her tantrums and understand her difficult speech. Whereas I, more than anyone, understood this, as I had spent the past two years completely immersed in learning about autism and studying every move Olivia made and felt that I was still only scratching the surface of my understanding. I was only too aware how difficult and complex the disorder is. I decided that my motto was to be 'Death is not an option!' – certainly in terms of deliberate risk taking.

Although many people climb Mount Kilimanjaro every year, only 45 per cent successfully reach the summit; the rest failing mostly due to altitude sickness. In the early days of tourist treks up the peak many people had died and now the Tanzanian government made sure that each party had a Tanzanian guide as well as a European guide and each trip was monitored. Tania, my brother Charles and I researched altitude sickness, but it was, we discovered, totally arbitrary whom it affected. It had absolutely nothing to do with age, or one's level of fitness, but struck out of the blue. There were two precautions, both of which we opted for. One was to take acetazolamide, commonly known as Diamox, and the other was to go up slowly in order to adjust to the altitude en route. Most of the failures in reaching the summit were caused by racing up to the top as fast as possible. The human body simply couldn't cope with such a rapid change in altitude, making altitude sickness almost guaranteed. We *had* to reach the summit if at all possible;

after all, it was on the basis of this achievement that we had asked for sponsorship.

The Easter holidays came and we had planned to visit the Second World War sites in northern France with our old friends, Nigel and Françoise Percy-Davis. Johnnie had first met Nigel in Malaysia in 1966, where they were both officers in The Life Guards. Françoise was a beautiful Swiss, whose glamorous good looks were only outshone by her gentle, sweet nature. Johnnie and Charles loved to watch war films together and Charles adored listening to his father's tales of his army experiences. Johnnie's maternal grandfather was Field Marshall Earl Haig, who commanded the British Army in the First World War and set up the Royal British Legion to help ex servicemen after the war. It was also his idea to make and sell poppies in aid of the British Legion that we still buy and wear in November to commemorate all those killed or lost in action.

We drove to a lovely hotel just outside Honfleur, where we had arranged to meet Nigel and Françoise. Honfleur is a very attractive town, built around a small harbour held in by large, granite walls. From Honfleur we took day trips, visiting the American cemetery at Omaha Beach and Pegasus Bridge, returning in the evening very moved by what we had seen. I did my best to explain to Olivia that there had been two world wars and this was where some of the Second World War had taken place. I broke it down into 'goodies and baddies' but left out the Holocaust. It was difficult, at best, to know what she understood, if anything, but she was patient and did not have a single tantrum. When we left, as I tucked her into her car seat, I told her what a good girl she had been and that I thought that the whole trip had probably been rather boring for her. 'Yes, Mummy, it was VERY boring for me!' was her reply! At least she was with us I thought, and perhaps she learnt something, if only that grapes dipped in ketchup were delicious, if not true French cuisine!

On our last day, we visited Arramanches and elected to first visit the cinema to watch a film of the Normandy landings. At the end of the film we were requested to hand in our translating earphones. Johnnie, who hadn't heard the announcement, walked out of the cinema with Olivia on his tail. Charles and I replaced the earphones and when we reached the exit, I saw Johnnie standing alone, waiting for us. 'Where's Olivia?' he asked. 'She left behind you' I replied, but she was nowhere to be seen. We scanned the crowds; Arramanches was packed with tourists, and we could not see her. We ran to find Nigel and Françoise, and told them we had lost Olivia. In a panic, we divided, and Nigel, Johnnie and Charles began to check the shops, while Françoise said she would run to the beach. Arramanches is a seaside town full of tourist shops. Every shop had racks of flapping T-shirts hanging outside and carousels filled with postcards. Olivia was only six-and-a-half and could easily slip behind a T-shirt and not be seen. I ran down the main street but could not see her anywhere. After ten minutes, we regrouped. Johnnie, still recovering from his broken leg only four months beforehand, couldn't run at all so he and Charles went to get the car to drive around looking for her. Nigel met up with Françoise and they both scoured the beaches, while I ran like a woman demented further and further along the main street, asking everyone if they had seen her, to no avail.

I was beginning to despair when I came across a group of American schoolgirls. 'Have you seen a small girl holding a Disney toy?' 'Yes, we did, a little while ago. We saw a child with, what was it, one of those characters from *Toy Story*?' one of them replied. To my amazement, they went into a long discussion about which Disney toy she may have been holding, with no concern for the fact that this child was lost! I snapped at them that it didn't matter which damn toy she had, which way did she go? They looked at me, astonished at my abruptness, and pointed further down the street. I ran on, pushing people out of the way, making no apology, tears streaming down my face. After another half a mile, there was still no sign of her and I had nearly reached the edge of the town. I heard a grey-haired American talking and asked him if he had seen a small girl walking alone. He said yes, he had, and that she was following a lady and had gone up the next street, which was a long hill. My lungs were bursting as I ran up to the top of the street and, glancing in all the shop windows on my way, I finally saw her in a closed restaurant, sitting beside a lady who was using the restaurant's phone. I banged on the locked doors and yelled through the glass that that she was my daughter! A concerned waiter let me in and the lady on the phone told me that she was just reporting Olivia as a missing person to the local police and would I speak to them to verify that this was my child? Once I had stopped shaking, I thanked the lady profusely, and she told me that she and her daughter had noticed Olivia trotting along behind them, at least ten minutes after they had left the cinema. As she obviously spoke no French and didn't say who she was, or where her parents were, they took her with them until they could find somewhere to make a phone call.

I phoned Johnnie immediately on his mobile and gave him the good news. On our way back to meet him, I admonished Olivia for walking off like that. She was perfectly relaxed and utterly unconcerned. In fact she told me off for 'taking her away from her new friends and their sweet, fluffy white dog!' How easy it would be for anyone to abduct her, I mused. I felt quite sick and shaky as I realised just how vulnerable she was. There would be no need to offer *this* child sweets to entice her into a car. She, being autistic, would take everything she was told at face value, so if someone turned up at school and told her that she was going home with them that day, that Mummy was ill, for example, she would not question it, but simply get into the abductor's car. I was also shocked at how quickly and easily she had become lost even though she had been surrounded by four adults and her protective brother. What could I do about it? I couldn't risk this happening again. As soon as we returned home, I joined Medic Alert and ordered a bracelet. Medic Alert is a charity, where, for a modest annual fee, an emergency number is written on the back of a small disk attached to a necklace or bracelet. If the wearer is lost, or collapses without anyone with them, their medical details can be tracked down through their records held at Medic Alert. In Olivia's case, the information held says that she is autistic and finds speaking and understanding very difficult. There is also our home phone number and our mobile numbers. As an added precaution I also bought a lead that parents put around the wrist of their very young children, while they hold the other end, to prevent just such a thing happening again. As we had a planned trip to Disneyland in Paris in the summer holidays and I was going to take Olivia on the train, there were too many opportunities for me to lose her. I had to be sure that I was somehow physically attached to her during the whole trip, and the lead seemed to be the answer.

With her continuing passion for Disney, Olivia awaits each new Disney or Dreamworks release with months of mounting anticipation. Even though she is now 13 and boarding at school four nights a week, her telephone conversations with me are entirely taken up with when we are going to see the next film, on what day and at what time, before it has even been released. I often tease her calling her 'The Disney Queen of Kent'. This type of obsessive behaviour is extremely typical of autistic children. Many of them, Olivia included, know whole films verbatim and merrily chatter alongside the film, word perfect, while playing simultaneously with other toys and only occasionally glancing at the television screen. Olivia would choose to have wall-to-wall cartoon films all day long if we allowed it and so we curbed the viewing when she was quite young, to one film in the morning and another at teatime with nothing in between. She also adores tomato ketchup and smothers everything she eats with it, with the exception of chocolate ice-cream. On particularly heavy use days, I called her 'The Ketchup Queen of Kent', but we are gradually reducing the ketchup intake too and at school she is being allowed only one serving of ketchup with each meal as they valiantly try to encourage Olivia to taste her food without it.

At the age of six, Olivia waited to see the much-advertised Disney version of *Tarzan*. The day it came out off we went to the cinema and, to add to her joy, it was quickly released on video, which we bought at the earliest opportunity. After the first time she watched *Tarzan* at home, Olivia disappeared to the loo for a very long time. Eventually, Karen, her nanny, called me and said that I had better come and see what had happened. Olivia had covered herself in her own faeces, and as Karen and I put her in a bath and cleaned up the mess, we both felt extremely dismayed. We had read about autistic children who love to smear their own faeces over themselves or over the walls of their house and thought that this was a very bad sign of regressive behaviour.

When I tucked her up in bed that night, smelling of soap and shampoo, my heart was full of fear. The next day, she wanted to watch *Tarzan* again and as I had some mending to do, I sat with her. Not far into the film, Tarzan, feeling rejected by his adopted gorilla family, covers himself with mud from the river, to be dark in colour, like his hairy family. Olivia looked up at me and said 'Like Tarzan, Mummy!' and, with huge relief, I realised that she had just been enacting the film. And she never did that again.

Before the end of the summer term, Olivia rushed into the house one afternoon calling 'Mummy, Mummy where are you? I've missed you!' I was undone. This was the very first time in nearly seven years she had expressed any feeling for me. I spent the evening floating on air. Such everyday things in a household of normal children are taken for granted. With Olivia, as with any autistic child, every tiny step forward was a major achievement and the cause of great joy and celebration. It also gave me the stamina to continue, even when I thought that I could see no improvement for month after month, and then suddenly, a miracle like this would happen. All those hours of greeting her with love and joy, of rolling around on the floor, learning when she had taken all she could, when it was time to back off, had, it seemed, taught her to connect with me and hopefully the other close members of her family.

Olivia and I spent her seventh birthday alone at home. We had all been invited to the wedding of an old friend of Johnnie's, in San Francisco. In this case, it really was not appropriate to take Olivia, as Johnnie, the girls and Charles were to spend a week in a Dude or guest ranch afterwards, and so they departed, leaving us behind in a typically rainy, wet English summer.

At the end of a cold, wet August, we left for the much anticipated and longed-for trip to Disneyland Paris. I had asked Natalya to accompany us so that one of us could be with Olivia at all times, while leaving the other time to have a shower and so on as we were to be away for three days. Some kind parent had told me beforehand that if I had a letter from my doctor to say that Olivia was autistic, I could apply for a special needs pass at the Disneyland entrance gate and would be able to move to the front of any queue for the rides. The first morning, we stood in a long queue waiting for our pass with only one person working behind the counter, and many fractious, crying children being held in their parents' increasingly weary and impatient arms. The lady next to me held a large child of about ten years old. What was the matter with her child I inquired, after standing behind her waiting, for some time. She had cystic fibrosis, I was told. And how did that manifest itself and what was her life expectancy, I asked, as gently as I could. Her mother told me that she was becoming increasingly disabled as the days marched on and that she would probably die when she was around 40, if all went well. At that point we were both crying and the queue was still just as long. As I have more chutzpah than I have French, and even less patience, I went to the front of the queue and demanded to know just what they thought they were doing, putting these poor disabled children and their distraught parents through this intolerable wait, merely because they hadn't enough manpower to cope with the queue! Almost instantly, a couple of shamefaced Disneyland workers appeared from the back office and opened up two other booths. The queue rapidly reduced, and with cheers and thanks from my fellow parents, we finally received our passes and were able to walk into the wonderland world of Disney.

For Olivia, we had reached nirvana. Nothing was too tacky, too large or different. Each character was just like those she had been weaned on and her satisfaction seemed complete. We attempted a couple of rides, but she really didn't like them, much as Natalya and I tried our best to 'sell' them to her. Olivia has dyspraxia, another condition she was born with, which impedes all voluntary movement, making eating with a spoon, riding a bicycle, doing up shoelaces or speaking clearly, for example, extremely difficult. It also means that any movement that would twist and turn her around makes her feel sick and dizzy and she hates the sensation. She did tolerate a couple of the rides that took us through a fairyland with no sudden dips or sharp bends, but that was all. What she really liked was to get near the Disney characters and there were opportunities to meet Mickey Mouse, Pluto and the rest of the gang.

I had been told that the parade at 4 p.m. each afternoon was something really spectacular and that with our special needs pass, we could get a front-line place in the disabled section. We hurried to find that place, and when we did, we then had to wait for over half-an-hour before the parade began. But it was worth every second of the wait as the parade really was the highlight of the day. It comprised over 40 floats, beautifully decorated, each themed to a particular Disney film, fully equipped with all the characters in full costume, posing, grimacing in a menacing manner, as suitable for Captain Hook, for example, or singing sweetly like Snow White. Every ten minutes the parade would halt, and the characters from the float would descend to the pavement, take the most readily available children and dance with them, before moving on. When the parade began and Cinderella moved past us, Olivia was standing up and shaking with excitement, standing on her tiptoes, her hands flapping like mad. Her eyes were aglow, as if she had seen the Heavenly Host, and such was her obvious total joy, that I melted. My tears flowed, and I considered it worth all the queuing, junk food and the Eurostar (late) to get her here, to give her so much pure pleasure. Natalya turned around to look at me and saw me crying. 'Whatever is the matter, Mum?' she asked, anxiously. 'Nothing Darling,' I replied. 'I'm just enjoying Olivia's delight.'

Towards the end of the summer holidays, Karen, our nanny, and I took Olivia for her annual review at the assessment centre at Elliot House, where she was tested by Sue Shepherd and I gave Judy Gould an update on her skills and had the opportunity to discuss her difficulties and how to overcome them. Olivia had been hand blowing for some time. Before she could do anything she had to blow on each hand. This happened hundreds of times a day. It was rapidly becoming, or already was, an obsession or compulsion. Judy Gould told us not to worry too much, and we had been dealing with it, by saying 'Olivia, no hand blowing!' each time she did it or, at least, whenever we saw her. But it did worry me terribly, as it was one of those typically autistic behaviours that, as a parent, one never knew if it would explode into something completely uncontrollable or fade into the distance and be only a vague memory, as luckily happened in this case.

After the assessment, I was told that Olivia was doing quite well at school, despite the current hand-blowing obsession. Her greatest academic strength was undoubtedly her reading ability, which was almost up to her chronological age. I was amazed to learn that once she had reached the reading age of eight, she would be able to read a newspaper. Not a broadsheet of course, but the reading age of the tabloids is eight! Her area of greatest difficulty was, and still is, maths. Neither I nor Johnnie find maths easy, so it wasn't surprising, but for Olivia the difficulty in understanding numbers was colossal. The whole concept of number and time was so far outside her comprehension that teaching her to count and tell the time was clearly going to be a very slow process. She could rattle off numbers up to 20, but that was only rote memory with no actual understanding at all.

As I am poor at maths and am an avid reader, in some ways I considered myself lucky that my autistic child was not a maths buff. I would have had no point of contact with numbers, but I have always taken enormous pleasure in reading aloud to my children at every opportunity. When Natalya was young, I read her the whole Narnia series by C. S. Lewis and as I had only read *The Lion, the Witch and the Wardrobe* as a child, the rest were new to me too. Every evening after their bath, Charles and Olivia would get into my bed, one on either side of me, and I would read to them. This still happens with Olivia and although she can scan read faster than I can read aloud and will correct my mistakes, she continues to enjoy the ritual of 'stories in Mummy's bed'. At age 13, it is becoming quite hard to find suitable material to read to her, given her complete lack of social understanding. Most books written for teenage girls are all about relationships, boyfriends, clothes and parties, none of which interest Olivia, nor make any sense to her at all. I absolutely refuse to read any Disney or similar magazine, which she is told to read to herself, but she does love to have *Dandy* or *Beano* annuals read by Charles and Natalya, who give each character a different accent, which Olivia decides upon in advance. Desperate Dan is often Irish, rather than American, and Aunt Aggie, Welsh, and so on. Natalya being a drama student was happy to be able to practise her accents and I enjoyed hearing the gales of laughter coming from her room. I have even had to resort to The Famous Five, by Enid Blyton, through sheer lack of choice, but trying to explain phrases such as 'lashings of lemonade' or 'come on, Old Bean' to Olivia is far from easy.

The wet summer holidays of 1999 came to an end and Olivia returned to school, in her second year at Otford County Primary. She had been having swimming lessons during the holidays with James Lang, who was a wonderful teacher and excellent with autistic children. I had been recommended him by Claire Roberts, whom Mary Hampton, Olivia's first speech and language therapist, had tried to get me to meet. I had endlessly put off calling her, only because I had so much else happening in my life, but when we did finally meet at the school gate when Olivia first started at Otford, we rapidly became very good friends. Claire is French and endlessly grateful that her husband, Phil, is English, as there is almost no provision in France for autistic children and adults. She has almost black, very curly hair and dark brown eyes that are deep wells of empathy and a great sense of humour. Claire's son, Marc, has Asperger syndrome and is 18 months older than Olivia. Once I had met Claire, who is bright and very well informed about autism, I wondered why I had not phoned her years before. Heaven is having a friend who is facing the same, or similar, day-to-day predicaments. This was my first experience of having someone to talk to who understood the problems we parents with autistic children face every day, although Marc and Olivia couldn't have been more opposite. Because Marc has Asperger syndrome he is very bright and was usually at the top of his class for most subjects. He adored sport and was very competitive, which caused a great deal of stress as Marc found losing extremely difficult. Conversely, Olivia couldn't stand sport and also did not understand the point of it. In any race, she would just grind to a halt, staring around her and had to be cajoled by school staff even to complete the event. In class she struggled with understanding what was said or what was actually meant, and maths was beyond her, whereas maths was an area in which Marc shone.

But the basic approach to autism, using tactics such as low arousal, plenty of structure and planning and 'social stories' made our daily lives all too similar. Both Asperger and autistic people will have what Dr Lorna Wing calls 'the triad of impairments', whatever other differences their autism might cause. These are difficulties with imagination, communication and social interaction, and all three can be helped a great deal with time, patience and knowledgeable teaching from speech and language therapists. Autistic people generally like a highly structured day, with each moment timetabled. This makes them feel safe in what, to them, is a frightening and chaotic world. To help autistic people understand something they find difficult, the use of 'social stories' is often helpful. These are simple, three-to-four picture stories of stick people in a cause-and-effect scenario. This helps the autistic person to understand how to adapt their behaviours, or to prepare them for an unusual event, such as trip to the beach. The stories are sometimes drawn with the autistic person, sometimes prepared for them in advance, if the situation is clear and relatively easy to explain by a teacher or carer. As autistic people are already anxious *all the time*, using a gentle, low, soft voice and relaxed body language, listening first, sitting quite still and allowing them to speak, all create 'low arousal' and a calm situation. Difficult situations can cause unimaginable anxiety and loud, aggressive language from the carer is the worst possible approach to calm an already very distressed or easily upset autistic person.

But here there were two autistic children in the same school and one can see how different they are. Pity the poor teachers and LSAs who think they understand a little about autism and have to try to teach such children. It is vital to study *each child minutely* to be able to even begin to understand how he learns and thinks, before one could think of trying to teach him.

Claire was interested in every detail of my impending trip to Tanzania and promised to keep an eye on Olivia while I was away. It was not the first time that I had left Olivia and Charles. Johnnie and I try to have a holiday alone at the beginning of September for a week to ten days and we had done a certain amount of travelling without the children. Somehow Tanzania seemed different, more distant certainly, and there would be no mobile phone reception the whole time we were on the mountain, which would add to my sense of distance from home and my loved ones. On one of the trips I had taken with Johnnie, the nanny in charge thought it best not to mention me much to the children, in case it made them miss me more. This backfired terribly with Olivia, who withdrew into herself even more than usual. As there was no mention of her parents, she could have thought us dead, or gone forever! Karen and I made a timetable for my Mount Kilimanjaro trip. We were to be away ten days in total and Karen agreed to talk to the children about me and where we might be, how high up the mountain, and guess at our progress every day. Olivia would also cross off each day from the timetable Karen had made and would count how many more 'sleeps' there were until Mummy came home.

CHAPTER 10

Mount Kilimanjaro

MY BROTHER CHARLES IS ONE OF THREE HALF BROTHERS that I have, all fine men, but as he is my mother's child, I grew up with him. He is nine years younger than me, and I was ecstatic to have my own baby to play with when he was born. I adored him as a child, and I adore him now as an adult; the nine years between us seem to shrink as we age. He is tall, over 6 feet 2 inches, with long legs and he has the same hazel eyes as his father. His black hair is now mostly grey and he has skin that turns deep mahogany in the sun. In other words, he is gorgeous, a George Clooney look-alike, with an excellent brain to boot. When Johnnie and I married, my church in Hampstead was so far from our reception at the Berkeley Hotel that we didn't have, or make enough time for, the photographer. As a result, I don't have a single photograph of Johnnie and me together, but plenty of Charlie and me with my bridesmaids Violet and Natalya, and to a casual observer, it looks as if I have married my brother! He and Tania, as Johnnie's daughter, didn't really know each other as they had spent relatively little time together in the nine years since Johnnie and I had married. Tania was first at boarding school and then on her gap year when she worked in a baboon rehabilitation centre in South Africa before going on to university, so they were comparative strangers when we conferred over our shopping lists at a sports shop in Covent Garden on a hot July afternoon in 1999, trying to equip ourselves correctly for the huge temperature range we would experience on Mount Kilimanjaro.

The list we had gleaned from a variety of trekking and climbing magazines was extensive. Mount Kilimanjaro is on the Tanzanian/Kenyan border and is only 3 degrees south of the equator.

Our first day in Africa would be a rest and preparation day at a lodge near Arusha, the nearest town, and it would be hot, and so would the first day of the trek. After that, the higher we climbed, the colder it would get, and once we had reached 12,000ft, we would need hats, gloves and thermal underwear. We had been advised to buy a sleeping bag that would take us to minus 10 outside temperature and also to buy a 'thermorest', which was a light, inflatable mattress that insulated one against the cold ground and also, we hoped, the rocky terrain on which we would be sleeping. Then there were socks that would not rub or cause blisters, trekking trousers that unzip just above the knee and become shorts, and gaiters to cover the gap between the socks and the trousers so that our boots didn't fill with shale and cut our feet to ribbons. We bought foldaway pillows, water bottles and water purifying tablets that made the water taste foul, a rucksack to use as a day bag, in which we would take our sun cream, snacks, sunglasses, camera equipment, loo paper, hats, antiseptic wipes, waterproof jacket and trousers. It can rain hard on the mountain, and if you get soaked through, you are in trouble as you will quickly chill, and so is your camera equipment, which would be ruined. I also bought a note-book and pens and a short guide to Tanzania, and we each bought a torch, which was worn like a miners torch, sitting on the forehead, held in place by a thick triangular band of elastic. It gets dark very quickly on the equator and early, too. At 6 p.m. the sun sets and it is instantly black dark as there is no light pollution, the only light coming from the moon and the stars, so if we wanted to read or go behind a bush in the middle of the night, a torch was vital. Our guide would provide the tents and food, and his team of porters were to carry our bags up the mountain, preparing the camp and a fire, to be ready, waiting, for our arrival. We were asked to have light bags, carrying only what was absolutely necessary as the guides also had to carry all our food, water and kerosene to cook with, once there was no more wood to burn above the tree line.

It was really exciting preparing for our trip. We spoke almost daily on the phone discussing how much walking we had done, if any, and how much money had been raised, so far. By the time we left on 23

September, I had received over £50,000 and felt very happy. It was such a large sum and would really help setting up the DISCO interview. I had not had an adventure like this since I was in my early twenties, although we had been to Africa with the children twice beforehand.

Johnnie's first trip to Africa was in 1994, when he went as a Parliamentary Observer in the first democratic elections in South Africa. Upon arrival, he called me from his hotel room just as a bomb exploded in the street below. He returned with an appropriate T-shirt, which read 'I survived the ~~bullets~~ ballot!' and a determination to take me there, which he did, only two years later when we toured eastern South Africa on motorbikes with the All Party Parliamentary Motorcycle Group, headed by Lord Strathcarron, who was then in his mid 70s. Poor David Strathcarron had a ghastly accident on our third day, skidding his bike on loose gravel in the middle of the road and flying over his handlebars, landing like a broken rag doll on the ground. I was on the bike behind him, being driven by an expert, who managed to avoid running over him. David was taken to the local hospital in Sabi Sabi, a small town nearby, but when we visited him in the early evening, I was appalled to see him still unwashed, wearing what was left of his shredded trousers, now stiff with dried blood. I offered to clean him up, and make him comfortable, which the staff were happy for me to do, as they hadn't had time themselves. David accepted, and his son Ian said that he would gently lift his father under the arms, if I would whip off his trousers. I knelt down to do so, but realised that when I pulled off his trousers I would be an inch away from his privates. My courage failed me and I hesitated until Ian yelled, 'For God's sake, get on with it!' After that, neither David nor I cared what I saw or what he exposed. When I visited him in hospital in Johannesburg at the end of our trip, he greeted me with delight, whipped off his sheet and showed me with pride the biggest, most multi-coloured bruise I have ever seen. David is a remarkable man and within two weeks of his return to England, he was back in the House of Lords.

We had been to Zimbabwe in 1998 with the whole family, when Olivia was only six years old. She had seen the Disney film *The Lion King* and was devoted to Pumba, the warthog character, and carried a large soft toy of him everywhere. The whole family were looking forward to watching her see her first, real warthogs, but when we came across our first warthog family, she wouldn't even look up, much preferring to play with the safe, well-known, Disney variety. It was deeply disappointing for us all and made all the more noteworthy by the difference in Olivia at the age of six and Natalya, who at six years old had had her first trip to Africa and had been curious to know about everything she saw.

As we had been on two African safaris, and had brought home all the bead necklaces, engraved gourds and carved soapstone figures we could find, I asked my son Charles, who was then nearly nine, what I could bring him back from my climb. 'Bring me a rock from the very top of the mountain, would you Mum?' was his request. I just had to get there, that was all.

Tania came to stay at Frenchstreet the night before our departure. She was 21, with a gorgeous deep dimple on her right cheek that showed when she smiled, just like Charles and Olivia. She has a flawless, translucent complexion, big baby-blue eyes and blonde hair that is naturally wavy. Slightly shorter than me, she is delectably curvy in all the right places, and a complete contrast to Camilla and Violet, who are both very tall and slim with naturally dark hair. Tania, in fact looked most like Charles, as Violet looked very like Olivia, which never failed to amaze me, as they only shared one parent, their father.

Both Tania and I had done our best to keep our packing to a minimum, trying to take only the bare necessities, even in the medicine department. We had one small box with painkillers, medicines for both 'stop' and 'go', the usual disinfectant and plasters and loads of Compeed, which are cushioned plasters particularly effective for covering blisters on the feet. Our boots, we had decided, were by far the most important item of clothing and we had all three diligently worn ours in, in order to avoid 'new boot blisters'. At midnight, we were still surrounded by a sea of items and I couldn't close my bag with my boots inside. I was too tired to make a decision at this point so Tania did it for me. She took my boots and told me to wear them and pack my trainers, which I had planned to wear on the flight. By 1 a.m. we had made it to bed, only to get up three hours later for the taxi taking us to Heathrow airport. Bleary eyed and already exhausted, we met Charlie at the check-in as planned, took one look at him and burst out laughing. He was dragging behind him an enormous suitcase, the size of a school trunk, and on his back was a very heavy-looking rucksack, also full to the brim. In each hand he had plastic bags full of CDs and a portable CD player, extra snacks, extra batteries, energy bars and loads of magazines and newspapers. On his head, above his 6 o'clock shadow, he was wearing a brushed polyester deerstalker, with the flaps down. He was genuinely surprised at our laughter and warned us that if we mocked him a second longer, he would not share a single item of his goodies with us.

At 6 a.m. the gates opened and, luckily, we had three seats together on a packed KLM flight to Amsterdam, where we had only just enough time to run to the next plane that would take us to Kilimanjaro airport. At Heathrow we noticed a large group of about 40 people, all from Middlesbrough, who wore black T-shirts with white writing, which read something like 'Going up Kili for our local hospice'. There were others who looked like 'proper' climbers, with horny nails engrained with dirt, and boots that seemed to have already walked across the whole of Africa, whom we found rather intimidating. We felt like soft townies and I wished that my clothes didn't look quite so fresh-off-the-rack.

After a ten-hour flight, we arrived in the dark, at Kilimanjaro airport. Africa has a distinctive smell that assails the nostrils, the moment the plane opens its doors. It is pungent, full of the scent of flowers and rich, wet earth. Standing waiting for our luggage, we gazed outside at the vast inky blackness of the sky, packed with stars. They seemed much closer and more plentiful than I remembered. We were overjoyed to be on African soil and were looking forward to a good night's sleep at the lovely Ngare Sero Mountain Lodge where we were to spend the next day, before we began our trek, but after waiting for over an hour, there was no sign of my luggage and only one small rucksack of Tania's had arrived. How glad I was that she had made me wear my boots and that I had all my camera equipment and contact lenses in my 'day' rucksack, which I had taken on board as hand luggage! Along with about 40 other people whose luggage also did not make the rapid transfer in Amsterdam, I queued to fill in the endless forms, so beloved of most African countries.

Corbett Bishop, our American guide, had been waiting patiently to drive us to the lodge. I had found him through Hugo van Lawick, an old friend of mine, who lived most of the year in an ancient, threadbare British army tent on the Serengeti Plain and who knew everyone. Hugo was a wildlife photographer and had made many films for cinema and television, as well as writing several books on African animals. He was extremely highly regarded in this field and had won eight Oscars and an Emmy for his work. Dutch by birth, he had been brought up in England and was one of the kindest men I had ever met. I was introduced to him by two of my dearest friends, Jane and Michael May, who were endlessly scooping me up and inviting me to lunch and dinner at their house during the seven years I lived alone with Natalya. The Mays and I shared a nanny for years, our children had been to the same child minder and Jane and I travelled to work together every morning after leaving our children there. They had sold their first home to Hugo and became friends. When Natalya was six years old, Hugo invited me to join him and another couple who had a seven-year-old daughter to stay at his camp in the Serengeti for Christmas. We spent three blissful weeks in Tanzania, travelling all over that wonderful country in Hugo's antique, but mostly reliable, Land Rover, but never leaving the camp without his mechanic on board! Not long after we returned, Hugo asked me to marry him and much as I admired him, I didn't think a life in the African bush was for me, or my daughter. But I hadn't bargained on Natalya. She adored Hugo and was devastated when I turned him down. He had taken her out to tea and told her that he had asked me to marry him, but that I had said no. What, he wondered, could he possibly do to persuade me? In true six-year-old's style, Natalya said that he must 'buy me a cake and some flowers'. The following day happened to be Valentine's Day, and Hugo arrived in the afternoon with two dozen red roses and an enormous cake, covered in gooey white icing. To Natalya's further disappointment, even these delectable gifts could not persuade me and as we had only made a tiny dent in the huge cake over the weekend, I suggested that she took it into school on Monday morning and offer it to her class at break time. When I collected her at the end of the school day, I was surprised to be greeted with ribald laughter by all the teachers. What was the joke, I wanted to know? Natalya had taken the cake to every class and announced, 'This is the cake that Hugo gave my mummy to get her to marry him, but she still won't, so would you like some?' Despite my refusal we remained firm friends and Hugo was very happy for me when I eventually married Johnnie.

Ngare Sero Mountain Lodge is a lovely house, built for a German in 1912 around his coffee plantation. Michael and Gisella Leach had lived there for over 30 years running a very comfortable hotel. Both had a huge bank of knowledge about all things African – politics, agriculture, wildlife and culture – and they welcomed us with open arms that evening and told me that Hugo would be arriving from his camp the following morning.

It is rather difficult to sleep beyond the dawn chorus in Africa, even with the aid of earplugs. I lay in bed soaking up the sounds and smells of an African morning, listening to the birds, frogs croaking and a group of Colobus monkeys calling loudly to each other from tree to tree. Just behind our little house, with its six bedrooms running off a long veranda, I could hear the African staff laughing and stoking up the fire for hot water for our breakfast. It was sheer bliss to have no responsibilities. For the first time in nearly 20 years, I didn't have to get up and look after a child – nor even my darling husband! I felt quite dizzy with the sense of freedom and lack of any pressure that is always there for mothers, but particularly those with disabled children, day in day out, year after year. One accommodates and becomes used to it, but it was only when I was released from all those pressures for a while that I became aware of just how unutterably tired I was. I could have stayed in that bed listening to Africa, forever.

At 9 a.m. Corbett arrived with maps and bad news. There was still no sign of our luggage, but he would keep calling the airport all day.

We spent the morning listening to his comprehensive talk on altitude sickness, the value of Diamox, the drug that alleviates it, diet and our route up the mountain, as we sat in the beautiful lodge garden, drinking coffee. Altitude sickness is the main bugbear while climbing Mount Kilimanjaro. Corbett had been living in Tanzania for about three years and was an experienced mountain climber. Not much taller than me, he had blonde hair, a muscular body that one would expect of a mountaineer and lightly etched laughter lines around his eyes and mouth. He was fun, well informed and entertaining, with a wonderful sense of humour. A Texan with a degree in English, he was engaged to Camilla, a lovely half-English, half-Italian Kenyan, who had been born and brought up in Nairobi. He was the perfect guide; at age 28 he was a considerably experienced mountain climber and we felt safe in his hands.

By law in Tanzania, one must employ a Tanzanian guide to help generate income locally as well as any other foreign guide one might choose. Corbett had employed a team of 15 to take only three of us to the top of Mount Kilimanjaro and our local guide was called Kennedy, whom we were to discover had climbed Mount Kilimanjaro over 600 times! Kennedy was a tall, slim, ebony-skinned Tanzanian, with a quiet manner and a beautifully long-limbed, loose, easy stride that made mountain trekking look more like a waltz than a gruelling physical test. He looked about 30 but had two grown-up sons and didn't appear to notice that it took me three days to remember his name, while I struggled not to call him Winston, a name that seemed to have stuck firmly in my memory. A guide is an important man. He hires and organises the porters and cooks, negotiates their pay, quantifies the supplies of food, kerosene and water, and keeps the camp running smoothly. He answers to Corbett, but runs the camp. It takes days to prepare a trek like this.

Corbett was only able to wait one day for our luggage to turn up, and if it didn't, we would have to go without it. The reason for this urgency is that the food had already been bought and would not last in the heat, and we had planned to take it as slowly as possible, working on a leisurely four days to the summit and two days to descend. If we didn't start the next day at the latest, we would have trek up at quite a fast rate and we didn't want to risk failure through altitude sickness.

Hugo arrived mid-morning and it was heaven to see him, although I was saddened to find him in a wheelchair. A lifelong inveterate smoker, he had finally succumbed to emphysema and was in the care of his younger brother, Ghoede. We had lunch together catching up on our news and immediately after lunch Corbett drove us into Arusha to try to kit us out. My brother Charlie, by this point, was having the time of his life, deliciously smug as he generously handed out spare hats and gloves to Tania and me. Humbly, I accepted his second hat, trekking pole, socks, water bottle, jacket and so on, before we scoured the shops in Arusha for underpants, a toothbrush and toothpaste. Arusha is a very poor town, exactly half-way between Cape Town and Cairo. Because of its position, it had once been an important, beautiful, tree-lined place, but was now shabby and rundown. The minute we parked Corbett's Toyota pickup, it was surrounded by small boys asking to be paid to look after it while we went shopping. As if by radar, they appeared from nowhere, and Corbett employed his regular, a bright, cheeky ten year old, who immediately started shouting at the crowd to back off the car, with tremendous authority and self-importance. If one didn't employ a guard, Corbett explained, there wouldn't be much left of the car when we returned, and certainly nothing inside it.

All the shops were in the main street and, like many East African towns, are run by Indians. We needed toothpaste, toothbrushes and face cream, so Corbett took us to the one chemist in town. The interior was beautifully fitted out with cupboards and shelving built of dark mahogany, but all were practically empty. There were only four toothbrushes available in the whole shop and these were for children with milk teeth. We bought them. Next was underwear. We had a choice of two kinds of underpants, the first were enormous, made for an ample African derrière, in pale lemon and made in China. The others were much smaller, embossed with Superman, and Tania and I decided to go for those, but the shopkeeper was horrified, 'These are for very small boys!' he protested. We bought those, too. It was a rude reminder of how most of the world lives, outside the spoilt West.

By evening, KLM confirmed that our luggage had still not arrived and Corbett told us that we couldn't wait another day. Michael Leach dug around in his cupboards in the lodge and loaned me his sleeping bag and some trousers, and Hugo, his jumper. We spent the evening looking at Hugo's superb photographs that were to be displayed in the Serengeti museum Michael was in the process of designing.

As the mist cleared in the early morning, we could see Mount Kilimanjaro, snow capped and magnificent, between the surrounding hills. We had chosen our route, which would be to trek to Shira Plateau and reach the summit via the Western Breach. This was off the beaten track, as we did not want, if at all possible, to run into any other group. At the Londolosi Gate, we signed our names in the entry book and met our porters, one of whom carried an AK47 gun as there had been an elephant sighting on this side of the mountain. Tania, who together with her sister, Violet, had had a very nasty experience with an elephant on an island in the middle of the Zambezi River, was not pleased to hear this. Mount Kilimanjaro has five different micro climates and, having driven through the first, the cultivated lower slopes, we began to walk through the second, which was virgin tropical forest. It was African spring time and wild flowers abounded. Huge juniper trees heavily hung with pale green Spanish moss clung to the earth, which was packed with other mature trees housing birds such as the tropical booboo, a shy, black-and-white shrike whose pure flute-like notes we occasionally had the pleasure of hearing. It was breathtakingly beautiful and we felt as if we were walking through the Garden of Eden.

After a picnic lunch, we set off for our first camp, and to our dismay the pace was fast and the slope, steep and muddy. Within two hours we were shattered and wondering how on earth we could carry on like this for the next three days. By 5 p.m. we reached our first camp site, at 8,000 feet, called Mitimoja, which means 'One tree camp' set in a small clearing in the forest we had raced through. A camp fire was already burning with a pot on top to boil water for a cup of tea. I searched everywhere for my bag of loaned clothes. It was nowhere to be seen and we finally deduced that it had been left at the lodge. I was now down to what I stood up in, except for my disposable contact lenses! Corbett loaned me a fleecy top and one of the thin mats we were to sleep on and I kept warm by the fire. But sleep was intermittent as the tree hyraxes screeched and called to each other all night. Hyraxes look like a mix between a squirrel and a rabbit. Charlie had bought a rug made up of 50 hyrax skins, which stank. Somehow I couldn't visualise my beautiful sister-in-law snuggling down beneath it in their newly decorated house. Hugo was deeply unimpressed that Charlie had bought it. It only generated a need he said, and there would be more hyrax poaching as a result. Charlie was suitably chastened.

The next morning Tania told us that she had an upset tummy and had been up frequently during the night. This was bad news, as she was completely off her food and felt weak. But Tania has a strong spirit, and decided to try to ignore it as she laced up her boots and swallowed dry toast and tea. We walked up through the forest until, about midday, after a long, steep upward climb, we reached the peak of a hill and emerged from the forest at the tree line into the third climate, the heather zone. All around us were huge lichen-covered boulders, giant yellow and tangerine kniphofia thomsonii, wild gladioli and helichrysum. There had been a vast forest fire the year before, but already shoots over a foot tall of protea, the South African national flower, were emerging. We spent the afternoon walking towards a ridge in the distance. Kilimanjaro became clearer with each step, its sides frighteningly steep, its peak snow capped and icy. The path was not too difficult and conversation ranged from the latest films, great explorers, apartheid and shared secrets that I shall take to my grave!

Each afternoon, once we had eaten lunch, usually hard-boiled eggs, bread, cucumber and tomatoes, the porters, laden with our luggage, cooking pots, water, firewood, tents and food, jogged past us with bare feet, often with a 'Sportsman' cigarette hanging from their lips and a cheery 'Jambo!' (hello), to make our camp ready for the night. We were humbled. We were walking at a steady pace, only carrying our light rucksacks and had the best walking boots money could buy and yet we felt exhausted at the end of each day. The porters also passed us every morning, after they had broken camp and cleared up the breakfast, to reach the lunch spot and prepare our meal ready for our arrival. Mount Kilimanjaro is one of the most important sources of income for Tanzania and there are long daily queues of men who want to be hired as a porter, as there is little other work.

Once we had reached the ridge we had been walking towards all day, we didn't have far to walk to our next camp on the Shira Plateau, which was at 11,732 feet. It was getting cold, but when we arrived the cooks had made hot tea and freshly popped corn, which we ate looking across the vast plateau, in the fourth micro climate of mountain moorland, waiting for the clouds that surrounded Mount Kilimanjaro to clear. Just before a fuchsia pink sunset, the clouds parted and we gazed in awe at this beautiful mountain. Corbett had advised us all to take Diamox to help against altitude sickness, which, he said, would start to kick in after 12,000 feet. We had a long discussion about whether we would sleep in the crater just below the peak the night before, or whether we would sleep lower down the mountain and get up in the dark, to be on the peak at sunrise. The latter meant that the scree on the Western Breach, which was our last climb before we reached the crater, would still be frozen from the cold night air, and therefore much easier to climb. Corbett wasn't happy with our idea of sleeping in the crater. To start with, he argued, it would be bitterly cold as it was at 18,500 feet, and it can be very dangerous to sleep at such a high altitude. Another problem were the porters, who would be very unhappy as they thought the crater was full of evil spirits, and most of them would refuse to do so. There would also be the difficulty of carrying kerosene so high to cook a hot evening meal. We took Corbett's advice and decided to spend our last night at Stella Point on the edge of the Arrow Glacier, which was at 16,000 feet, and leave in daylight to climb up the Western Breach, then cross the crater floor for the last 1,000-feet climb to Uhuru Point, our destination. 'If, at any point, you feel dizzy, or hot, it is because you have altitude sickness and you MUST descend as quickly as possible. There will be no arguments, the faster you descend and the lower down the mountain you can get, the quicker your recovery.' Corbett was adamant about this and we complied.

We crossed the Shira Plateau the following morning in glorious sunshine with a sapphire blue sky. The air was crystal clear and Tania saw an augar buzzard and a rare lammergeyer vulture with long wings and a wedge tail that has the habit of carrying bones up to a great height and dropping them on rocks to crack them open. Giant heathers of 8–10 feet tall grew between the rocks but what no one had told us was that the Shira Plateau, created by a giant flow of lava, was covered in a fine, silky black dust. By mid-morning we were filthy. Every line on our face and hands was etched in black. Every pore was filled, making us look like smallpox victims. On our third day of trekking, we were already very dirty and there was no more water for washing, not even our hands. From now on we had to rely on our packets of 'Wet Ones', and getting our hands clean enough to put in contact lenses each morning was becoming increasingly difficult.

We arrived at Fisher's Camp, named by Corbett after his friend Scott Fisher, who had been part of an extreme American mountaineering group, known as Mountain Madness, who had died on an attempt to ascend Everest. Fisher's Camp was at 13,500 feet and we just had time to dive into our tents before a heavy storm broke, with strong winds and lashing rain, followed by a light flurry of snow. I was frozen, but this was the camp where we hoped to meet up with our luggage. There was a road not too far away and Corbett had radioed the lodge to ask if Tania's and my luggage could be brought up the mountain with food supplies for a large group a day ahead of us. It was impossible for the porters to carry enough food for 40 people for six days and so half-way up the mountain, at the end of a dirt road, supplies were dropped off and carried to their next camp, and our bags, we dearly hoped, would be with them.

At dusk, there were shouts and whistles from over the crest of the hill. Looking out from a small opening in my tent, I saw, to my dismay, a tall, very skinny porter bent double under the weight of Charlie's enormous suitcase, which he carried on his back, with our bows and arrows and a long hunting spear sticking out of the back of it! This was the suitcase that we had filled with our swimwear, extra clothes and presents that we had deliberately left at the lodge to await our return. How could we tell the poor man that he had carried this huge, heavy suitcase half-way up a mountain, in vain? And where were Tania's and my bags? To our tremendous relief, a second porter arrived carrying them, and within minutes we had our lovely warm sleeping bags spread out in the tent, and had put on thermal underwear. There was no point in changing my clothes, I thought, as I couldn't wash first and so I remained in the same filthy trousers and T-shirts that I had worn since we left, with my thermal underwear underneath. We were beyond caring; so long as we made it to the summit, there would be plenty of time to get clean afterwards. After some food and a rest, Corbett delicately explained the mistake to the tall, tired porter. He took the bad news well, particularly after receiving a large tip and loading up the redundant suitcase once more on his back, he set off in the dark down the mountain to try to catch the truck on its return journey to Arusha.

Tania had not been feeling well the whole trek and when we arrived at Stella Point in the late afternoon for our last night before the summit, she was quite downcast and tearful. She felt weak and was extremely worried that she would not have enough energy to take her to the top. I staggered into the camp, which was at 16,000 feet and immediately fell into a deep sleep in my tent. This made Corbett anxious. It was a bad sign, he told Tania, to sleep so deeply probably meant that I had altitude sickness already. But after two hours, I awoke feeling quite refreshed and ready to eat another spaghetti dinner on the rocky slope of the mountain. We were full of anticipation for the next day, when we hoped to reach Uhuru Point, but were made slightly anxious to see beside our three small tents, a large decompression chamber belonging to a group of noisy Americans, who were camping next to us. Typical of paranoid, litigious Americans, we scoffed! But it made the serious- ness of altitude sickness sink in and we all promised Corbett that if we felt ill, we would descend immediately.

As the sun rose, we began our climb up the Western Breach. It was very hard going, zigzagging across the mountainside on shale. Every three to four steps, we had to stop to catch our breath. We felt exhausted and our 10-pound day bags felt like houses on our backs. I had been warned that this would happen but I didn't really believe it until I found that I just couldn't walk more than a few steps at a time before I had to rest. My head began to throb and, after two hours, the shale gave way to a cliff face made up of huge rocks over which we had to climb, sometimes on all fours. I had a splitting headache and felt nauseous, and as I caught up with Charlie, he stopped and, turning to me said, 'Lizo, I feel terrible; I don't think I can go on. What shall I do?' At the same moment, Corbett, who was not far ahead of us, suddenly announced that he was going down and would leave us in the care of Kennedy. He had altitude sickness and without wasting any time, took one of the porters and began to descend, fast. Near the top of the Western Breach, Kennedy was waiting for us and, very slowly, we inched our way up the rock face towards him. Leaning over the rock wall of the Kibo crater, the porters who had already arrived called out to us that it was not much further, encouraging us to carry on.

Tania, who had been ill the whole trip, suddenly became the leader and reached the crater long before Charlie and me. We almost fell into it, gazing in awe at the snow wall over 100 feet high that surrounded it. The crater floor was staggering in its size, about 2.5 kilometres in diameter, flat and dusty, with a scattering of rocks, rather like the surface of the moon. But by this time, Charlie was rocking on all fours, and groaning. Kennedy was deeply concerned and we conferred as to what we should do. Kennedy thought that Charlie should descend immediately, but Tania was sure he could make it, since we only had just over 1,000 feet more to go and it was on a fairly gentle upward slope. What did Charlie want to do? 'Get to the top,' he mumbled, his forehead resting on the ground, and so without eating anything, we decided to set off there and then and just get the whole process over with, so that we could go down and have a bath.

Uhuru means freedom in Swahili. But it was with a feeling of triumph and great emotion that we reached the summit. Standing on the highest point of the great African continent, looking as far as one could see at the Great Plains and forests, with the peak of Mount Kenya jutting through the clouds, our tears made deep white rivulets down our dirty cheeks. We took photos and made emotional speeches for my camcorder about how much we loved our families and how proud we were to be there to raise funds and awareness for autism. I cried a lot thinking of the parents with autistic children, and the terrible stresses and anxieties autistic people have to suffer, all their lives. Finally, I remembered my promise to my son and, bending down, found a small round stone, which I assumed was a light piece of lava. Perfect, I thought, and I stowed it safely in the bottom of my rucksack.

But Charlie was looking worse and Kennedy was becoming even more concerned. After only 20 minutes at the summit we decided that we must get Charlie down as low and as fast as we could. But by now he could hardly walk, and so Tania and I took his rucksack and trekking poles, and Kennedy held him upright by taking a tight grip on the back of his jumper and steadying him, as he walked. Charlie weaved from side to side, his legs almost buckling underneath him and, as I followed behind, I prayed fervently that he would be all right. Two agonising hours followed. We stopped for something to eat, but Charlie just sat in a heap, staring in front of him. I felt sick with worry; supposing he had done irreparable damage? Would he make a full recovery? What was I going to tell Isabelle, his wife, and our mother? And why hadn't we listened to Corbett and Kennedy?

We kept walking and, by 5 p.m., we had gone down to 15,000 feet. We were completely exhausted, but had to continue downwards. We needed to get Charlie to 10,000 feet, if possible, before we felt it was safe to stop for the night. All our sense of joy at our achievement had vanished in the silent, anxious descent. We stopped to have a drink of tea at a camp, which was heaving with people. Looking around, we noticed that this was the same large group from Middlesbrough we had met at Amsterdam airport, and the same group who had to have their supplies driven half-way up the mountain. Charlie recognised one of the men and asked, jokingly, if he knew the latest football results? A lifelong Newcastle United fan, he almost shot to his feet when he was told that Newcastle had beaten Sheffield Wednesday, 8–0. It was as if he had just been plugged in and switched on, so rapidly did he spring back to life! It was too good to be true, so we pulled him to his feet and made him walk another three hours, until we reached our last camp, following the path the entire way by moonlight, only to be told that we were quite near a village that had a penchant for stealing campers' belongings and we must guard our belongings by taking everything into our small tents.

At 2 o'clock the following afternoon, we were at the exit of the Mount Kilimanjaro National Park and had received our official certificates, to prove we had reached the summit of the mountain. By 5 p.m., we were back at the Ngare Sero Lodge, soaking in the bath. I hadn't brushed my hair for six days, as my hairbrush had never made it up the mountain, and my hair had tangled into Rasta knots. Going down was far harder on my feet and knees than climbing up the mountain and the last day and a half of descent had been agony. I awoke the next morning hardly able to walk and, much as Charlie told me to stretch, I refused. I didn't know anything about stretching and exercise in those days, nor about how muscles store lactic acid after strenuous activity. So I spent the day hobbling about the beautiful garden, reading and sleeping.

Corbett, and his fiancée Camilla, joined us for dinner that evening. He told us that he had had a chest infection before he had left Arusha and that was probably why he had altitude sickness, and it was the first and only time he had ever had it. We remembered that he kept asking us if we were seeing spots in front of our eyes, which we had not, but he did. Corbett realised that it was altitude sickness, and that he had to abandon us and descend as quickly as possible. He reached around 10,000 feet before dark, and spent the night on the mountain with a group of African porters who told him ghost stories about their experiences on Mount Kilimanjaro, successfully completely spooking themselves and him! By the following morning he felt much better and could see clearly, although he continued to cough badly for days afterwards.

It was sad to leave Africa, but although we had only been away for ten days, it felt like weeks to us, as we had experienced something so entirely different to our everyday lives. I was longing to see Johnnie and my children, and anxious to know how Olivia had fared during my absence. Charles was thrilled to have me home, flinging himself into my arms, full of kisses and cuddles. Olivia showed her usual indifference, but I caught her looking at me out of the corner of her eye, several times, and smiling to herself. Charles wanted his rock from the top of the mountain and I had to explain to him that when I showed it to Michael Leach at the lodge, to ask if I were right in thinking it was a piece of lava, he told me that I had picked up someone's discarded peach stone, instead! Luckily, I had a handful of jet with me, which seemed to satisfy him.

Almost immediately upon my return, there were television and newspaper interviews. The National Autistic Society had succeeded in gaining considerable press interest and on the first day home, I was interviewed on lunchtime television. The money continued to come in, in response to the cards that I had sent out to all our sponsors, which told them that we had made it to the top of the mountain and would they please, if they had not already done so, send in their sponsorship money! On the front of the card was a photo of the three of us sitting on Uhuru Point, looking sick, but extremely pleased with ourselves (see photo section).

By mid-October, we had been back three weeks and had raised over £80,000. Philip, Johnnie's brother, gave a party to celebrate his 40th birthday and his mother's 80th, at Brooks's, a club in St James's. It was a wonderful party, and so many of the guests came to congratulate Tania and me. At about 2 a.m., Johnnie and I left to go home, on an unusually balmy evening. Suddenly Johnnie pulled me, in my long evening dress, into a rickshaw and we were pedalled all the way home. It was a very romantic ending to a perfect evening.

In November 1999, the long awaited and much debated reform of the House of Lords took place. The Labour government had initially wanted to remove all hereditary peers from every political party but a compromise was eventually agreed and 10 per cent from each party including the Cross Benches (independents) were to be allowed to remain, if they succeeded in winning enough votes from their fellow party members, who would also be fighting for one of the remaining seats. The Tories would be left with a mere 42 seats and each member, if they wished to be selected, had to write a short biography of no more than three paragraphs, while being expressly forbidden to canvass for votes. It had been an extremely tense time. Many peerages were ancient seats, which had had members in the House of Lords for hundreds of years. These seats were to be obliterated in a single day as it was felt by the Labour Government that there were too many Conservatives in the House of Lords, who often objected to bills that the Government wished to pass through Parliament. The titles would still remain, however, and would continue to be inherited, although there would be no more political power attached to the title if the peer was not elected. A further culling was planned at a date, so far, undecided.

On a misty, wet November morning, I took the train to London to listen to the results of the vote being read out. Johnnie did not know I was coming, but I wanted to both surprise and support him on such a momentous occasion. As the wife of a peer, I am able to take a seat in the Chamber in a small area reserved for family members and guests. Luckily, there was a seat available as there are only about 20, and I slunk in unnoticed in the middle of a debate about recycling waste. At the end of the debate, with no ceremony and no forewarning, a clerk stood and announced that he would now read out the results of the vote for the successful remaining hereditary peers. There was instant silence, everyone sat bolt upright and I heard a sharp intake of breath. I dug my nails into my hands and listened as the names were read. Then I heard 'Lord Astor of Hever', he had made it and was number 11! I was incredibly proud and pleased, as he had worked so hard for a long time and I knew he was extremely capable. But there was great dismay and sadness for those who had not been voted in. For some, it was an end to their lives as they had lived them for decades. A brutal end to a lifetime of service for some, as they were instructed to be out of their offices, desks emptied, within a very short period.

Yet it was a wonderful end to the year, for both Johnnie and me. I felt as if I were floating on air. I had achieved something of which I was proud, and something that would really make a difference to other people. I acknowledge that raiding Johnnie's address book and the Astor name helped enormously with fundraising, but, nonetheless, they were *my* legs that took me to the top of the mountain and *my* hours of writing letters day after day that achieved the result. It was a major turning point in my life. I was about to be 50 and I suddenly felt empowered, capable, energised. I also felt the need to cram into my life as much as I possibly could, while I was still physically able. I had enjoyed the challenge and felt hungry for more.

CHAPTER 11

Integration and Inclusion: A Misconceived Myth

AT THE END OF OLIVIA'S SECOND YEAR at Otford Primary School, and only a month before her eighth birthday, we made our annual visit to Elliot House in Bromley to visit Sue Shepherd, the educational psychologist, to extract what Olivia really understood and had learnt in the past year, as opposed to what the school thought she had learnt and understood. It was not an encouraging morning.

Christie Miller had been Olivia's learning support assistant for three years. She had been wonderful with her, doing her best to teach Olivia, but after three years, not surprisingly, I felt that they were both burnt out. When we sat at the kitchen table at Elliot House, analysing the results of the tests Sue Shepherd had carried out with Olivia that morning, it was clear that Olivia had not learnt a single thing in maths that whole school year. Maths was a closed book to Olivia and I could see from the work that Christie gave me that they had been going round and round in circles, not making any progress. It was a tough task to try to think up new and interesting ways of adding and subtracting numbers up to ten for over three years, and I doubt that I could have done any better than Christie, who had also been training for a Montessori teaching qualification. Even Olivia's reading, which was her area of greatest ability, had only improved by four months in the past year, and that was probably because I was doing so much reading with her at home. Olivia seemed distressed too, particularly if she was asked to complete a task she found difficult.

Rowena Linn, the excellent head of Otford School, had been seconded to an advisory board at the end of Olivia's first year at the school. There followed a whole school year where there was no head and I felt that the school lost its sense of direction during that time. A school needs a good head just as a ship needs a strong captain. The essence of the school emanates from the headmaster or mistress and it seemed to me that Otford was sailing blindly around the seas without a clear sense of direction. There was also a feeling of despair coming from Olivia's class teacher, who, when we met to discuss her progress at the end of the summer term, told me that she was finding it increasingly difficult to teach Olivia at all and keep her included with the rest of the class, because she was unable to write. Olivia had just had her eighth birthday and although she was developing normally physically, she was extremely dyspraxic, which is when the brain's messages to muscles are scrambled. This made handwriting almost impossible for her (see page 160), as well as affecting many other areas of her everyday life. She couldn't blow her nose, for example, so when she had a cold she was unable to clear her nostrils. She still can't, at age 13. She couldn't bath herself, wash her hair or even comb it, which made the whole hair business a long and tedious process, as she desperately wanted to grow out her fringe and have long hair. As she almost never made any request or expressed any strong feelings about her hairstyle or the clothes I bought her, it seemed mean not to allow her this one indulgence, and so we began to grow her straight dark hair into a long ponytail.

So much of the current work in class required the ability to write things down, her class teacher explained, and as Olivia was unable to write she was less and less included in class activities. I was shocked. 'Are you telling me' I inquired, 'that if Olivia had no hands, she would be incapable of learning anything?' There was a silence as the message hit home. 'Let's try another way,' I suggested. 'Perhaps if I bought a computer for her to use at school and she typed instead, wouldn't that help?'

I discussed my troubles at Otford School with Judy Gould and Sue

ABOVE: *Words may be Olivia's thing but writing is
an enormous challenge due to her dyspraxia.
This example is her 13th birthday wish list – all
Disney DVDs or toys, nothing else. At number 1
is the DVD of* Tarzan 2; *followed by* Clinton's
Really Big Movie; Bob, Zino and the Snurks;
The Magic Roundabout *and a toy of King Julian
from the film* Madagascar *at number 5.*

Shepherd. Judy was firmly of the opinion that if mainstream education were to work at all for Olivia, then she would need a specialist teacher in class with her *who understood how Olivia learnt*. But how was I to find such a person? We decided that I would request a special meeting with her caseworker from the Kent LEA (Local Education Authority), the SENCO and her class teacher, and put this problem before them. Olivia had been at school for three years and this was already her second school, and I really wanted it to be a success. If the teachers did not know how to teach her, a specialist was her only hope.

The approach taken in all mainstream schools to teach autistic children is the same as one would use to teach children who only have a learning disability. But autistic children are not 'normal people who learn the same way as everyone else, but at a slower pace' as is almost always assumed. They each think, understand and learn in their own individual ways and will make little, if any, progress, unless this is recognised. The huge chasm in understanding this basic, but essential fact is, I am sorry to say, endemic in all schools, including most 'special needs' schools. Only those few schools that are autism specific truly understand how to teach autistic children and how they are able to learn and in what type of environment. I am deeply sympathetic to teachers who are expected to be able to cope with autistic children in a large mainstream classroom, as it is an almost impossible task. Even those who are very able, called 'high functioning' autistic children, or those who have Asperger syndrome, find everything about mainstream school a nightmare. My friend Claire Roberts, whose Asperger syndrome son, Marc, now 15, attends mainstream school, says just this. He loves the classroom and learning, most probably because he is very bright, but loathes everything else about school apart from sport. Consider how much else there is in a school day that an autistic child must try to bear outside the classroom, and this includes 'special needs' schools, too. There is the daily assembly, all meal times, sport, which for most autistic children is a complicated, meaningless task, lining up for meals, lining up to move from one class to another, break time, gym, singing, changing rooms – the list is endless. And in how much of the school day is the autistic child included, let alone integrated? In a paper entitled 'Inclusion and autism', written by Barnard, Prior and Potter in 2000, it said 'Inclusive education is a process involving the restructuring of the curriculum and classroom organisation. This distinguishes it from integration which focuses on the placement of an individual or group and that individual or group having to adapt to what the school is able to offer.' Olivia was physically often in her school classroom, but working separately with her LSA at a table at the side of the room. This is not inclusion. For much of the school day she was taught in the library area, when it was free, as there were no distractions from other pupils, although there were huge distractions all around her. This was segregation, albeit for her benefit. The only integration she had was during whole class teaching, when the teacher would speak to all the children together, who often sat on a carpeted area in the classroom. But even this was of no benefit to Olivia, who did not understand that whole class teaching included everyone, her too! It had to be specifically pointed out each time that she was to look at the teacher, and listen. She was also quite capable of switching off completely, which was her main defence mechanism.

This was the academic part of school, but how did she fare socially? Even worse, although the staff and children were kind to her and very willing to help, she was treated by the children as a school pet, patted on the head, helped and talked down to, but not played with except in the role of compliant stooge, who was the patient in a hospital game and just had to lie there, or an audience. Otherwise she spent all her playtimes turning in circles, taking to herself in a safe corner of the playground. There were a couple of girls and one boy, to whom she really appealed, who had invited her home for tea. This had been a moderate success, mainly because the mothers and their children allowed Olivia to do exactly what she wanted, since they were so terrified that she might become stressed, or throw a tantrum and they would not know what to do. Nervously they took her to their homes, assured that I would be standing by the phone at all times. Going out for tea is a normal activity in the life of a school child and for a long time I wanted Olivia to do all these 'normal' things that all children do, but it was an uphill battle. Olivia is very pretty and has a sweet nature when she is not stressed or anxious, but although she occasionally agreed to have one of these children back for tea, she never enjoyed it beyond the idea. Almost as soon as they entered the house and sometimes before the parent had even left, she would ask what time they were going home. She hated them playing with – even touching – her toys, and would find it incredibly stressful. I had to make sure that whenever I invited a child to tea, I was completely free as, after only a few minutes, Olivia ran to her bedroom and I was left for the next two or three hours with a bewildered child. This happened with her cousins, too, and by the time she was nine, we had all adjusted to it and I gave up asking anyone over to 'play'. I slowly came to realise that she only liked to go to other people's houses to play with their toys, not for any social interplay at all. Olivia didn't like it and she never would. She was autistic and I could not and moreover, should not, force unnecessary 'normal' behaviour upon her.

So why had I been so keen for her to remain in mainstream education? I had visited the Helen Allison School and felt that Olivia would be better off in mainstream education rather than in an autistic school or a unit attached to a school. There were generally far more boys than girls, and as Olivia's autism was of the passive/aloof type she might be vulnerable in a school of largely big, bumptious boys. My second reason was that the world was made up of neurotypical people, or normal people who have no neurological disorder, so perhaps mainstream was the best, if far from the perfect, option. If she were to learn to cope with the ordinary, hurly-burly of daily life, protecting her in a sheltered environment might not be to her advantage. Although I was fully aware by now that autistic children *never* learn from being with other 'normal' children, or adults. That is, although surprisingly few people in the teaching profession understand this, the very essence of autism. If an autistic child could learn by inference, or by watching their peer groups, they would not be autistic. Conversely, they would also not learn any inappropriate behaviours by being with other autistic children, as had often been mooted to me as a negative reason for sending her to an autistic unit, attached to a local school.

Looking back, I was learning much about autism and how it affected

Olivia, for myself. I think that in the first few years after her diagnosis, I also hoped that by sheer will on my part and by trying every treatment available, I could alleviate much of, if not dispel, her autism. It took me many years to come to terms with her autism, but even now my husband sometimes expresses great sadness that she is so disabled by her autism and that he is unable to enjoy the type of relationship he has with his other children. Most fundamentally of all, I had learnt and *come to terms* with the fact that autism is incurable and that it therefore is a lifelong disorder. I now knew that nothing would remove her autism, no matter how much determination, research and practice of various therapies I put into it. But there is much that can be done to help an autistic child learn and generally manage to live in our complicated society with less anxiety and stress. I sometimes felt outrage at the many books I read in the first year of Olivia's diagnosis, where the children in question had been 'cured' of their autism.

Most parents who have a recently diagnosed autistic child are asked to make major decisions, such as which school they wish their child to attend, when they know nothing about autism themselves. They are often in shock and take any advice offered to them. Even with the help of an educational psychologist, wrong decisions are often made. The first LEA educational psychologist we saw recommended an entirely unsuitable school and, when I saw her a year later, she actually told me that I should start making plans for long-term residential care for Olivia when she reached age 16 and was finished in education. I was so angry that Olivia should be condemned to weaving baskets for the rest of her life at the age of only six that I burst into tears of frustration. If I had not, I might have been tempted to thump her. How could anyone, especially an educational psychologist, suggest such a future for a six-year-old child? It was outrageous to imply that her progress would be so limited that long-term care for life would be the only outcome. No one could possibly know, at that stage, what she might be capable of learning, in her own time. There was, and is, no crystal ball and even now I have no idea how she will live, in care or independently, or what she will be able to do once she reaches adulthood. I was greatly cheered when Josephine Shields, an American friend of mine, recently told me that Isabel, her daughter who has Asperger syndrome, had just begun university at the age of 25. When mother and daughter met Isabel's last high school teacher in their home town one day, the teacher expressed total amazement at this achievement. 'If you had told me when Isabel was 19 that she would get to college in six years' time, I would never have believed it!' she declared. Josephine passed this story on to me to encourage me to keep working with Olivia as she would continue to make progress and learn, at her own pace.

A meeting was held at school on 26 September, to discuss the findings from Elliot House. It was tense and unpleasant. There is a downside to having a title and on that day it was exposed in full colour. The general assumption is that one is, at best, an extremely rich, spoilt snob, with a complete lack of understanding of or compassion for how ordinary people live and, at worst, a gormless inbred. It was heavily implied, although not actually spoken, that just because I was Lady Astor of Hever, I should not expect special treatment. I was told how lucky I was to have had Christie Miller for the past three years, as she had a degree and that the average LSA was not nearly so well educated. To this I agreed, but pointed out that Christie's degree was in geography and that she was not trained in autism. Wonderful though she was and had been, Olivia clearly needed to be taught by someone who had training in teaching children with autism if she were to make progress in a mainstream placement. There were angry glances around the room, and I felt it necessary to explain that even though I did have a title, I was only trying to find the best solution for my daughter, to which she was, like any other child, entitled. I was asking for nothing more than any parent of a disabled child would ask. The meeting ended with the Kent LEA representative declaring that she had no one available and did not see that she would, in the foreseeable future. If I could find someone, good luck to me, but until then, we had reached an *impasse*.

Two weeks later, Christie handed in her notice and I had only one week to find a replacement. She had passed her Montessori exams and had found a job locally, as a nanny. I was so grateful for all she had done for Olivia for the past three years and recognised that it was time for her to move on. I wished her well in her new position, but this left me without an LSA. The school told me that they couldn't cope with Olivia in class without an LSA to look after her and that until an LSA had been placed, she was not to come to school. Not only that, but if the LSA were ill, or could not come into school for any other reason, Olivia would have to be excluded until the LSA returned. I offered my own services. After all, I knew more about Olivia than almost anyone and I was also a trained Montessori teacher. There were also plenty of other parents who helped in school with extra reading and other activities. My offer was firmly declined. No parents were allowed to work in the same class as their child, even though it meant that if Olivia were excluded because her LSA was unable to come in to school for whatever reason, I would of course be teaching her myself, at home. The message was clear. I was trouble and they didn't want me anywhere near the school.

This still left me with the problem of not having a specialist teacher for Olivia. She had effectively lost a whole term and, as Christmas was approaching, I wondered what I could do to find one, myself. I decided that I would place an advertisement in a few of the local papers and, as if by a miracle, after only a week, the perfect person answered. Her name was Diane and she had been teaching in special needs for many years. She had taught many autistic children and, to my joy, I found we instantly spoke the same language. She was in between jobs and could certainly teach Olivia for the foreseeable future. I was thrilled and invited Diane to meet Olivia and me and discuss the following term. What I was not prepared for, during the same week, was a letter from the new headmaster who wrote to tell me how my advertisement in the local papers had produced a 'very negative response amongst LSAs and teachers at Otford'. I rang him as he requested and we agreed to meet the following day. How could there be a problem, I wondered? After all, he was at the meeting where I had been told that if I could find someone myself, all well and good. And how else was I to find a specialist without advertising? He had to agree that this was the case and I offered to pay any extra salary that Diane and I would agree upon, over the usual salary earned by an LSA, which was paid by the county.

As we began the spring term, I was full of hope for Olivia. At last, we had the perfect scenario. She was in familiar surroundings, in a school to which she was accustomed and where everyone there knew her and her difficulties, and now we had someone who was experienced in teaching autistic children. But my hopes were dashed almost instantly. Diane was stonewalled. The headmaster would often ignore her 'Good morning' and make a point of looking the other way. When she asked for Olivia's file, to see what work she had been doing, it took several weeks for a folder to be produced. Even worse, when Diane asked Olivia's class teacher what she could best do to help Olivia, early one morning, in order to try to break the ice, she was told rudely and abruptly, that 'the best thing you can do for Olivia is to go home!' It was a complete nightmare, and defeated and depressed I began to make enquiries about other schools.

By February, I had visited Broomhill Bank, a special needs school in Tunbridge Wells for girls with a moderate learning disability. Mr Barnett, the headmaster, was charming and encouraging. With a full Groucho Marx moustache, glasses and a soft voice he took me around his school, of which he had been head for over 15 years. The girls were aged from nine to 19 and came from all the surrounding counties. About a third of them were fortnightly boarders, going home every other weekend. I liked it and although I set about applying for a place immediately, it was not autism specific and I knew now that that was the most important factor. I continued to look for the right school the whole of the summer term. Towards the middle of July, I had visited 12 schools between Canterbury and Somerset, and had met some very interesting people.

It is my impression that those who work in education are similar to those who work in the Church; the people you meet within these professions are either decidedly odd or utterly compelling. But why, I wondered, as I visited school after school, were people with a learning disability condemned to work in either horticulture or catering? At one particular school, I mooted this to the headmistress, who appeared to be an escapee from Bedlam, herself. All her students over 14 years old were training for those two occupations and I could see adolescent

Asperger syndrome boys roaring around the school grounds on the back of sit-on lawn mowers with their feet pressed hard on the accelerator. My daughter is not interested in the slightest in plants I said, and also hates cooking and anything that will make her hands dirty. I understood that for many, pricking out seedlings and watching plants grow and baking cakes and pies were satisfying occupations, but must they be the only two jobs on offer for people with any type of learning disability? Olivia liked books and I could easily envisage her happily sorting books in a quiet area of a bookshop, but also becoming extremely stressed if a customer messed up her neatly alphabetically lined rows!

At the end of the summer term I had found two schools that I thought were appropriate. One was in Hampshire and the other, 30 miles away, in Kent. But neither of these was perfect, either. The Hampshire school had, at that time, mostly Asperger syndrome boys, bright, loud and challenging. I didn't think that Olivia, who liked to be very quiet, and had enormous speech and language difficulties, among her other problems, would cope. The day school in Kent didn't accept her. The reason they gave was an extremely valid one. She would be the only girl, and coming up to puberty, this would be very difficult for her. She also had a greater learning difficulty than the boys, who had also been together for two to three years, and she would be isolated and lonely. I rang Mr Barnett, the headmaster of Broomhill Bank School, and asked if he would mind coming to tea at home and discussing my concerns?

We sat in the garden on a hot July afternoon and I outlined my main anxieties. Broomhill Bank School, although delightful, was not an autism-specific school and I was simply terrified of making yet another mistake, I explained. Olivia would be nine in August and this would be her third school, and I had had a very difficult and unhappy past year. Mr Barnett was extremely patient and understanding. Although many of his girls had not been diagnosed as autistic, he felt that he had many who were, nevertheless, on the spectrum. We agreed that Olivia would start in September, although I felt sure that once she reached 12 or 13, she would have to move to an autism-specific school, but that I would be delighted to entrust her to his care for the next few years. He understood my anxieties and we agreed that she would take up her place there in September and that her progress would be closely monitored.

During this period of turmoil, Karen Wilcox, who had been the children's nanny for three years, handed in her notice. We were devastated because she was so sweet and kind and the children adored her. Karen joined me only two months after Olivia had been diagnosed and had been an invaluable help in the early days of discovery. Her mother, Pat Wilcox, had worked for years with autistic children and often gave Karen suggestions, information and books to read, which helped us all.

We began the process of advertising for a replacement. It was not an easy job, especially as Olivia was so direct in what she said. The first girl who came for an interview was enormous. She sat in the middle of the playroom floor, filling it, enveloped in black linen, trying to engage Olivia, who would not be drawn in. 'She's very fat, isn't she Mummy?' Olivia said. I was trapped. If I muttered the usual sort of non-committal reply, it would only exacerbate the awkward situation as Olivia would undoubtedly respond: 'But she *is* fat, Mummy, she *is!* Why are you lying Mummy?' My only comeback, as it always has been, is to explain to Olivia that making personal comments is bad manners and could also easily hurt someone's feelings.

The second nanny arrived wearing very thick make-up. I employed her and was amazed to see that even at 7 a.m., she was covered in pancake foundation, not just for the interview, until we noticed that by 7 p.m. she had a distinct 6 o'clock shadow. She left. The third was a middle-aged talker. On her first morning, I took her with me on the school run so that she could memorise the route. She talked loudly and incessantly for the entire journey and by the time I had reached the school gates half-an-hour later, my head was ringing. She confessed to being garrulous and said that I would just have to get used to it. I suggested that it would be better still if she learned to control it. In the afternoon we went to collect Charles. Almost as soon as he had opened the car door, Olivia shouted out: 'You don't like the new nanny, do you Charles?' He was so embarrassed, but Olivia was right, with the best will in the world we couldn't stand all that talking and after only one more day, she also left. I was exhausted endlessly explaining what autism was and how it affected Olivia and so I was delighted when we found Tordi Kruger, a bright, cheerful and energetic South African, who arrived with a big smile and kept on smiling until the day she left, one year later to work in a local school for children with emotional and behavioural difficulties.

Olivia just didn't understand that she must not make personal comments, no matter how many times I explained it to her. She frequently told my mother that her face was very wrinkled and that was because she was very old. She stopped in the street one blustery March day next to an old couple, bent over their walking sticks and announced that they were very old and were going to die soon. Luckily, with the combination of the wind and their age, I don't think they heard her. She was also completely oblivious of what is commonly called 'personal space'. She would walk up to a stranger and straighten his tie, for example, or remove a loose eyelash from the lady sitting next to her on the train. We were all used to it, but as she was growing fast, and showing signs of puberty, it put her in a very vulnerable position. These odd behaviours were difficult enough in a child, but as an adult, they could get her into serious trouble. She never closed the bathroom door when she went to the loo, or had a bath, and of course when I tried to teach her about privacy, she went completely to the other extreme and locked herself in several times by mistake! Three years ago, at a National Autistic Society (NAS) international conference, I discovered that the NAS produce what look like business cards, on which is written 'This young person has autism', followed by three bullet points.

- Autism is a developmental disability that affects social and communication skills.
- People with autism tend to behave in an odd and unpredictable way as a result of their disability.
- Please help us by being understanding and showing tolerance.

At the bottom of the card are the contact details of NAS. These cards, which are blank on the reverse side, have been an enormous help to me and I show them to every parent of an autistic person that I meet. At only £2 for a pack of 50, I wish I had discovered them earlier. Each time I take Olivia to buy bras, shoes or have a haircut, I give a card to the shop assistant and their attitude changes immediately. I find most people smile and are very kind to Olivia and patient, once they understand that she is autistic.

Olivia was still having weekly occupational therapy classes with Jill Christmas and swimming lessons with James Lang, who was used to teaching autistic children to swim. Apart from an annual 'top up', we stopped going to Stuart Korth for osteopathy as he felt that after three years he had done everything he could for her. I had also largely given up feeding her vitamins, as they had made no noticeable difference at all and she ate a reasonably healthy diet. Olivia refused to eat most fruit or vegetables, but would willingly eat and enjoy raw carrots, apples and grapes. I gave her a whole carrot and an apple every day after school, which she nearly always finished, and that has kept scurvy and rickets at bay! The rest of her diet was restricted to about half-a-dozen meals that she would eat, and she could never be persuaded to try something new. Variety is not the spice of life if you are autistic. I often make three meals for four people at home as I am not keen on meat and my men hate fish.

Olivia also had quite an extensive after-school programme that I devised, which included reading aloud to me every day, time telling, trampolining, skipping, throwing and catching, and learning basic skills, such as trying to open doors by herself and pouring her own drinks. I took suggestions for homework from Jill Christmas and observed Olivia closely to understand what she was ready and able to learn at that time. I spent an hour every day following two or three activities, after she had had time to relax from school and have a snack. At the weekends, and in the school holidays, I structure each day, which generally runs as follows:

Friday

2 p.m.	Collect Olivia from school and go straight for a swimming lesson with Samantha.
4 p.m.	Home, Olivia unpacks her school bag and likes to 'sort out' her room, placing her toys in exactly the same spot each week, and generally settle in.
7.30 p.m.	Dinner.
8–10 p.m.	Bath time and reading in my bed. I always read to Olivia and this way we have read hundreds of books and have time to stop and discuss them together.

Saturday

9–10.30 a.m.	Breakfast in pyjamas and watch a video or read.
10.30–12.30	On Saturday mornings only, Maria Esteban (who works for the NAS Croydon Service) comes to give Olivia a hair washing/shower lesson, followed by table laying, time telling, reading etc.
12.30–1 p.m.	Free time.
1–2 p.m.	Lunch and free time.
2–6 p.m.	Bicycle ride/walk/trampolining or, in the summer, swimming. We break up the afternoon by making a drink and a healthy snack, such as slicing up an apple, and do any homework, play games, do puzzles or exercises on the computer, particularly in the winter.
6–7.30 p.m.	Free time.
7.30 p.m.	Dinner.
8–10 p.m.	Bathtime and reading in my bed.

Sunday

9–10 a.m.	Breakfast in pyjamas followed by a video.
10 a.m.	Get dressed and leave for church.
12.30–1 p.m.	Back home and play.
1–2 p.m.	Lunch with the family.
2–6 p.m.	As Saturday.
6–7 p.m.	Packing bag for school. Completing homework.
7–8 p.m.	Dinner.
8–10 p.m.	Bathtime and reading in my bed.

Olivia is allowed to watch a video straight after breakfast and again at 5 p.m. only, otherwise she would watch Disney all day long, or she would have done up to the age of 12 or 13, as she is growing out of wall-to-wall videos now. She learnt to ride a three-wheeled tricycle when she was 11, and so I take her for a bike ride at least once every weekend, which takes about 45 minutes, or three to four times a week during the holidays. 'Playtime' for her still means lining up books or plastic animals, but this is the way she relaxes and she is entitled to some down time, as we all are. We occasionally play games, but less and less these days as she does not enjoy them and I don't think that she can see the point of Snakes and Ladders, Jenga, Guess Who, Matching Pairs or Noughts and Crosses, but it does get her away from stimming (self-stimulatory play), such as sorting, and uses her brain. Bathtime tends to take ages, as she cannot stay on task, so I am constantly running up and down the stairs to prompt her. This means that there are pockets of the day when I can sort the laundry, answer emails, make phone calls, etc., but not many. I never have time to read the weekend papers, for example. It is during these structured times together that we really talk to each other and I learn much about what she is thinking and feeling, how she is getting on at school, what is bothering her or, worse, what she finds stressful. Olivia communicates best in a quiet one-to-one and often it is only at bathtime, as I sit beside her, prompting her, and when I read to her or we play a game that she really opens up and talks to me.

What distresses me the most is when I find her, an hour after I have left her, and all day, if she could, lining up books or doing any other kind of self-stimulatory play. I feel terrible and am riddled with guilt and panic stricken. How could I have left her to *that*? I reprimand myself and the answer that is so often given to me is that she is happy carrying out her self-stimulatory play, and I should leave her alone and not worry so much. But if I had left her alone, I doubt whether she would have walked, talked, read, learnt to swim, cycle or any of the other things she can now do, or at least do them so competently. Every evening my time is taken up looking after her, and I never have an evening with my husband or my other children, to watch a film or just be together, unless I leave her to her own devices, which I am loath to do, knowing that she will spend the time 'sorting'. My wonderful husband has not once, in 13 years, complained. I cannot imagine any other person on this planet who would be so patient and understanding. My son, daughter and stepdaughters are equally understanding and, when they are at home, they read to her at night to give me a break. But the guilt is not just confined to Olivia. Charles is only two years older and I tried extremely hard to give him my time and attention, particularly when he was younger and at day school. Comments like: 'I know you are very busy with Liv, Mum, but could you spare me half-an-hour some time today?' from either Charles or Natalya was a knife in my heart. I was acutely aware just how important it was not to focus solely on Olivia.

In order to maintain good emotional and mental health in the rest of the family, and a flourishing marriage, everyone had to feel equally loved and important. It is not uncommon in families where there is a disabled child, for the parents, especially the mother, to focus all the love and energy on that child, whose needs are often great, at the expense of the partner and the siblings, to the general detriment of the family as a whole. I had often heard about families where the parents' time was so taken up by their disabled child that they didn't notice the loneliness, despair and guilt of the other children until those children had been driven to drastic measures in order to draw their parents' attention to themselves. Equally true is that 95 per cent of the time it is the mother who looks after the disabled child or adult. I have never heard, for example, of a mother of a disabled child who can't take the strain any longer, and who abandons both the child and her husband, except of course, for a few tragic cases in which the mother, driven to despair has killed herself and her disabled child. However, I know many families where the father couldn't take living with disability and left his wife to cope alone with their autistic or disabled child. Families and marriages need constant nurturing; nothing can be taken for granted. As children hit adolescence their needs are more difficult to meet as they often appear sulkily self-sufficient and, beyond the teens, life continues to throw times of crisis to all members of a family.

Juggling the needs of everyone in any family is tricky and, if it includes a disabled child, it is a very great challenge, mostly for the mother, every day, all day, year after year. Add to that a programme of 20 hours a week of ABA therapy for example, with the attendant financial strain, and it is easy to understand how these family breakdowns occur. I did not want this to happen to my family. It was easier once Charles went to prep school when he was ten, as I could focus on Olivia during term time and felt guilt-free to concentrate on Charles in the holidays. But the only time I could indulge my husband was when we went out alone. Of course this is an exhausting way to live, but I never felt resentful. After all, I was looking after my precious child, and it was both fulfilling and rewarding. As Olivia loved books we have shared many together and this has undoubtedly increased her general knowledge and opened up her world. She particularly likes factual books and reads encyclopaedias to herself, but she has also read all the Tintin books and Asterix cartoon books. By the time she is in bed it is usually 9.30 to 10 p.m. and I am ready for bed myself!

Maddie Grout, a teacher from a nearby special school, had visited Otford to help train up the staff and show them different approaches to teaching the special needs children. Maddie was a wonderfully enthusiastic, positive person who gave me many tips to use with Olivia. It was she who suggested that I made a list of every tiny step that Olivia needed to follow in order to take a bath. I watched Olivia closely one evening and discovered that it would take 16 separate steps to complete the task! I reproduce my list here, as it may be of help for parents who want to write instructions for their children for any activity.

BATH TIME
1. Put the rubber mat in the bath and the white bath mat on the floor beside the bath.
2. Put the plug in the plughole.
3. Turn on the cold tap. **<u>Always turn on the cold tap first.</u>**
4. Turn on the hot tap and check the temperature is just right. If it is too hot, turn on the cold tap a little more. If it is too cold, turn on the hot tap a little more.

5. While the bath water is running, get undressed, put dirty clothes in the laundry basket and then go to the loo.
6. When there is enough water in the bath and it is the right temperature, turns off the taps. **Make sure you turn off the hot tap first.**
7. Tie back hair and then get into the bath.
8. With soapy hands wash:
    Face
    Neck
    Underarms and arms
    Body
    Between legs
    Legs
    Feet
9. Replace soap in the soap dish.
10. Pull out the plug.
11. Get out of the bath and dry yourself everywhere.
12. Fold towel and hang over towel rail.
13. Cream face, body, arms and legs.
14. Put on pyjamas or nightie.
15. Brush teeth.
16. Remove hair tie and brush hair.

This list was written to suit Olivia, so obviously such a list would need to be tailor-made for each child to match their ability and needs. Olivia can read and has a toilet inside her bathroom, and a laundry basket. I should have put a marker on the bath to indicate the 'fill point' and also a marker on the hot and cold taps, but by the time I wrote out the instructions, she already knew which was which, or so it seemed. Another method is to laminate the list and put removable pictures, with Velcro on the back, beside each instruction so that the child can remove each picture when that task is completed. Again, Olivia did not need this, but she could have found it useful if I had thought of it earlier. She finds it very hard to stay on task and can spend up to 15 minutes under the shower, with no idea of when to get out. This is partly because she has no concept of time at all and also because she needs reminding of the next step. We have now bought an egg timer, which gives a time limit to her shower and another, shorter timed egg timer for her to use when she cleans her teeth, which we hope will gradually negate the need for prompting.

Claire Roberts showed me a wonderful illustrated book about human reproduction, called *Let's Talk About Where Babies Come From*, by Robie H. Harris, which she had bought for her son Marc, to teach him the facts of life. It was full of cartoons featuring a bee and a bird and Olivia loved it, while learning obliquely everything she needed to know about sex and puberty. I had to prepare her for her periods; it was one of the many areas where I tried to be one step ahead, and so I took her to the chemist where we bought stick-on sanitary towels, which I tried to persuade Olivia to practise wearing, but without much success.

At the same time, she was learning about death. My beautiful mother-in-law, Irene, was suffering from cancer of the pancreas and during the long, hot summer of 2001, she quietly, and uncomplainingly, drifted towards the end. When she eventually died, on 12 August, Olivia could not understand why she was no longer in her house, which was at the end of our drive. After the funeral, Philip, Johnnie's brother, arranged a beautiful memorial service to her, at a church in Scotland, near the family estate which Philip had inherited after his father had died. In the afternoon, we took her ashes to be scattered in a lovely spot of which both Rene and her husband, Gavin, had been particularly fond, called The Laird's Seat. It had a magnificent view across the valley, over the fields golden with grain ripe for harvesting with hills covered in purple heather in the distance. While we waited for the vicar to arrive, Olivia kept asking me where Grannie was. I tried to explain that she had been cremated and what we were going to do. 'Ooooo, how scary!' she shouted, with a huge grin on her face, which made both Camilla and me laugh and weep simultaneously. Philip has created a stunning memorial to his parents, by renovating Migvie church, which is on the estate and, using local craftsmen, he has replaced the broken windows with new, stained glass windows, added carved granite seats and painted inspiring inscriptions and verse upon the walls.

The year 2001 had been extremely tough and testing. There had been so much personal anxiety and deep unhappiness, largely due in the first half of the year to the problems at Olivia's school where I had had to fight for her rights every step of the way. I had spent the summer term visiting other schools, and then agonising over whether I had made the right decision to plump for Broomhill Bank School. June, July and half of August had been taken up visiting my mother-in-law, worrying and praying for her, ending in her death. I was beginning to gain some hard-earned knowledge about autism and how to help Olivia, but I was very glad to be able to put it all behind me for ten days in September, when I went on my second fundraising trek to Inner Mongolia, in China.

CHAPTER 12

Training and Trekking

Since September 2000, Claire Roberts and I had been planning another fundraising trek in aid of the National Autistic Society (NAS). It was one of the highlights in my life during a very difficult period and I was training hard in preparation. As well as Claire, my great friend Denise Seely whom I had known since we were 12 years old would also join our group. But to where, we had not yet decided.

Claire and I had spent the winter searching the world for an interesting place to trek. To attract people, it had to be tough, but not impossible, and with a goal, such as the top of a mountain, include an interesting culture with ravishing scenery and be achievable within ten days. This was because on most treks at least half the participants were parents of autistic children and it is far from easy to find a carer for longer than ten days. Most of the trekkers also work, and we could use two weekends so they would only need to take one week's holiday. By January 2001, with the help and advice of the NAS, we had decided on a trek in Inner Mongolia, an autonomous state in China. To our knowledge, no other charity had led a trek there, and in China, there had only been treks along the Great Wall. We would trek along the banks of the Yellow River, cross semi-arid deserts and visit places where no Westerners had been before.

I had been training twice a week for the past year and was amazed at how much my body had changed. Within 6 months, I was able to wear a bikini again as my stomach muscles had tightened and my body was firming up. So much so, that when Camilla came home one weekend in August, she pointed to my biceps and pectorals and said that I was rapidly becoming too muscular and warned me to take it easy! I was extremely surprised that a 50-year-old body could respond so rapidly to a specific programme of exercise. I met many women of my age and some much younger who were gym fanatics and trained every day for an-hour-and-a-half. They were convinced that this was what was required to make a difference, but I only had to look in the mirror to realise that exercising correctly twice a week had dramatically changed my body and that building up stamina required a proper training programme. I could see that simply going at it hour after hour achieved nothing but exhaustion. My trainers were unanimous in their opinion that one hour done well was enough, per session, certainly for all over body conditioning and general fitness, which was what I was aiming for.

My first personal trainer was Adam, who gave me a weekly training session, but I very quickly realised that once a week was not enough to make any difference and so I began a second weekly session with Samantha Lucas, who has been training me ever since. After five years, Samantha never fails to surprise me by frequently coming up with new exercises for me to do. This makes the training sessions fun and interesting, essential if one is to keep up the momentum. I had to work hard, building up the muscles on my legs as well as all-over body strength and conditioning. Samantha enquired about my diet, which has always been healthy apart from a brief period in my late teens and early twenties when I was modelling, and starved myself into a spotty skeleton. I didn't drink enough water and still struggle to consume the requisite daily amount of 2 litres, as I would always so much rather have a cup of tea, which happily for me, according to the latest research, one can now count as part of one's daily water intake.

I would never have the discipline to take myself to a gym twice a week; I struggle to force myself out for a weekly run. Having someone come to my home and give me a lesson one-to-one was the only way I would make the effort. It is impossible to miss a session when they are ringing the doorbell. A personal trainer also gets to know one's body, its strengths and weaknesses, which muscles need work in particular and they make sure that the exercises are done correctly and that assisted stretching takes place at the end of the session. I have frequently been amazed at the difference when I am shown how to carry out an exercise correctly as this makes it 100 per cent more effective. Exercising incorrectly can cause much damage and I am not sure that trainers in most gyms keep a sufficient eye on their clients to prevent this happening.

Exercise is addictive; there is no doubt about it. Everyone knows that it releases the body's natural endorphins and one does feel happier, but usually only when it is over! I am too lazy to become obsessive about it and although I have a very busy life, if I were really serious, I would fit it in by getting up before dawn to run, or by training every evening after work, as some people do. I wanted to train enough to get my body as fit as I needed it to be to accomplish the trek without pain or injury and to be as healthy as possible so that my life would generally be enriched. There is nothing like catching a virus to remind one just how curtailed life becomes with ill health. I looked with admiration at all the active, elderly people I knew and decided that, as far as possible, I would emulate them. Of course, genetics are 90 per cent the controlling factor but a good diet and moderation, if not elimination, of the bad things we all love to eat and drink is the key. I ate humble pie many times my first year of training from all my friends who had been extolling the virtues of exercise for years, as I had been so vociferously resistant to it for such a long time.

Claire and I began the business of fundraising as soon as the dates and destination of the trek were confirmed. As I had written to everyone I knew to ask for sponsorship money when Charlie, Tania and I climbed Mount Kilimanjaro, I could not ask the same people again, only 18 months later. I had to cast my net further afield and I wrote hundreds of letters to wealthy people and grant-making trusts whom I hoped would be generous to my cause. Claire and I had decided that all the money raised from the China trek would be divided in equal portions to three schemes offered by the NAS and we set up a restricted fund for all the cheques we received. The Early Bird Scheme was designed to introduce parents of recently diagnosed children to other parents in the same situation in their area, to pool their knowledge and build a support system. The Helen Allison School in Kent was the second recipient, as it was in the midst of a huge fundraising programme to redevelop the school and on this trek we had several people from Kent. The third was the NAS's Advocacy Service, which is a free service for parents who need legal help gaining access to the correct school, or residential care, for their autistic children and adults when their local authority have refused them a place.

The NAS set up a website, which attracted several people who wanted to take a holiday that was different, challenging and had a feel-good factor about it, but who did not have any connection with autism. Participants were required to raise £1,500 for the charity and pay £1,200 for the cost of the trip, as well as take spending money. We were to fly to Beijing economy class and stay in mid-range hotels that were clean, if not luxurious, to keep the cost of the trip as low as possible. Because of the size of the country, in order to vary the trek, a coach would drive us at the end of each day to a different area, where we would begin the following day's trek in new surroundings. Information packs were produced by the NAS and, in March, we held an introductory meeting at the NAS headquarters in London, to meet the participants and to present a brief talk on fundraising. Samantha Lucas, my personal trainer, volunteered to come and present a fitness training programme. The NAS used a travel company called Classic Tours, who are the originators of overseas charity challenges, having started with a fund-raising bicycle ride in Israel in 1991, and who sent a representative to give us a talk and slide show on Inner Mongolia.

Once again, there was press coverage, but although it helped in raising awareness for autism, it rarely brought in any money. I didn't mind; as raising awareness was part of the objective to the treks and in some ways, I thought, the most important part. It was to raise awareness of autism that I had allowed *Hello!* magazine to interview me and take photographs of me and my children at home. The more people became aware of autism, the more empowered those with the disorder and their families would be. Greater understanding and knowledge of the disorder would create a wider recognition of the need for more and better schools, services and trained teachers and carers. Johnnie was also playing his part in raising awareness by taking on the secretaryship of the All Party Parliamentary Group on Autism (APPGA), which met regularly and invited eminent speakers to address it. As a result of becoming better informed, the group were able to bring to the attention of the Government the needs of, and lack of services for, people with autism through debate and questions in both Houses of Parliament. The APPGA is currently the most highly attended group in Parliament because there are so many constituency cases of autism, and parents seeking better provision for their children.

On 9 September 2001, we boarded the plane for Beijing. Olivia had had her first two weeks at Broomhill Bank School and was settling in well. Ideally, I would not have gone away so soon after she had started a new school, but the trek had been planned long before I had decided to change her school. On our second day of trekking we walked along the green and lush northern bank of the wide and mighty Yellow River. The opposite bank was semi-arid desert, full of steep sand dunes and tough grasses that we were to attempt to cross the following day. By late afternoon we had reached a farm and were busily trying to guess the use of a large, curved stone in the farmyard, which we discovered was an animal slaughtering block, when Callie Hollenden, one of our party of 22, took a call on her mobile. It was 12 September and this was the first news we received of the appalling attack on the World Trade Center in New York City. The message was dramatic, but jumbled. The whole group hovered around Callie, trying to understand what had happened. As soon as we reached our hotel at 8 p.m. that evening we rushed to the television, but the clip that showed the first aeroplane flying into the World Trade Center lasted only a few moments and I missed it. I rang my mother, as I had been unable to get through to Johnnie, and she sounded very distressed and asked me if we were flying back over America. 'No, over Afghanistan,' I quipped, but it fell like a lead balloon. My mother was terribly anxious about me being so far away and said that over 3,000 people had been killed. I assured her that we were safe and far from any possible target in the entire world at that moment, and then I rang my brother Charlie to check the facts. Charlie told me that so far around 150 people were known to have been killed, but that number was rising all the time.

'Osama who?' we kept asking each other. We were strangely detached; it is a very odd experience to be so out of touch when there has been a major world event. Mobile contact was intermittent and there was only one-eighth of a page in the Chinese newspapers about the tragedy the following day. Divine justice, I thought, remembering how many times I had read of a tragedy in China where hundreds of people had been killed and it had only generated one small paragraph in the British broadsheets. To this day, the enormity of the events of September 11 are somewhat diluted in my mind. I have never seen the full news coverage of the attacks and although Johnnie kept the newspapers for me to read on my return, the full impact was missing by not being in the UK at the time.

We all loved China, even though our Dutch guide, Theo, had no sense of distance and we walked far further each day than we had planned. Every afternoon, Theo's 'Just another 20 minutes' turned into another hour and that hour was followed by many more, so that by nightfall, when we did finally reach our bus, we were all exhausted. Everyone managed to keep going, however, except Rita, who had a strained ankle before she left and had had to spend two or three days reading in the coach. We walked through farms with pigs noisily grunting next to children defecating in the open, as no child wore nappies, but had a hole cut in their trousers. We saw herds of goats from whose hair all our pashmina scarves and shawls were made, in farmyards enclosed by walls made of mud bricks that looked like large loaves of wholemeal bread. We met families who lived in caves and at least one old lady who had had her tiny feet bound. Every day we picnicked on rice and meatballs, made from goat meat, or vegetable stew. There were no sandwiches, as the Chinese do not eat bread. We stayed in hotels built only for tourists; we were not allowed to stay in hotels for the Chinese. In most of these bleak buildings, there was only enough hot water for one shower and the electricity was often weak or erratic, and dangerous. In one of the hotels, the electric fire was at shoulder height in the bathroom, next to the shower, so consequently we didn't shower that night! The hotels were often filthy too, with the most odd and unappetising breakfasts I had seen since I travelled in Afghanistan 30 years earlier. Johnnie's cousin, who married a beautiful Chinese woman from Shanghai, told me that a Western breakfast is the most difficult meal for her to become accustomed to. We all found a Chinese breakfast the most different meal of the day and just as she finds it almost impossible to eat our sugary cereals, so did we find it difficult to eat rice, pickles and other dishes of an indefinable liquid matter, which the Chinese relish first thing in the morning. Luckily, there were always eggs, and delicious jasmine and green teas to drink.

The hotels we stayed in were all in new towns, which were surprisingly large. From our bedroom window we could see row upon row of new houses, resembling the terraced housing the Victorians built so prolifically in Britain in the nineteenth century. Each street had a communal toilet and a small back yard where the wood burning stove was housed, which was used for heating and cooking. We watched in amazement as hundreds of people worked well into the evening to lay cobbled pavements in the main streets and rode home on bicycles in their thousands, at the end of the day. New houses were built around enormous power stations alongside schools and shops, with no regard for the poisonous smoke belching out from the top of the concrete towers. We seemed to be watching modern China emerge before our eyes. It was, in truth, rather scary. We were so removed from the West, and we wondered if the world's major powers were really paying attention to China, whose billions of people were naturally extremely clever, goal orientated, diligent and disciplined. It was only in the countryside that we saw an occasional Mao jacket and peaked cotton cap and the bright blue paint on every tractor and lorry, to denote its state ownership. The people we met were very friendly to us, as we walked through areas where no Europeans had been before. It was an open, mutual and benign staring match, for they were as curious about us as we were about them. The north-west of Inner Mongolia is the largest coal-producing area for China. We walked by many open-cast mines and saw, to our horror, the Heath Robinson machinery in use.

No wonder there were so many accidents. The Chinese do not like to admit to disabilities either; this was not a country in which to have an accident or an autistic child.

We finished our five days of trekking at Genghis Khan's huge mausoleum, in the middle of nowhere, where a congratulatory banner and bottles of sparkling pear juice awaited us. Once again, we all dissolved in tears, remembering our beloved autistic children and the reason why we were in China. Finishing a trek is always such an emotional business. We had shared many of our deep fears and anxieties about our children together; and also many wonderful experiences. Everyone had a story to tell, and the few who were on the trek simply for the adventure learnt much about autism while we walked and talked. That evening, we ate a traditional Chinese celebratory meal in a yurt or Mongolian tent, of a whole roast goat, served on a silver platter, which I, as the trek leader, had the dubious honour of carving. We had raised over £70,000 and, as I gave my short speech of thanks to everyone, I suggested that we try to raise the figure to £100,000. By the time all the money had been collected some months later, we actually raised £115,000, £30,000 of which I had raised myself.

Our two days of sight-seeing in Beijing were the icing on the cake of the trip. After the most wonderful foot massage I have ever had, we were ready to visit the great sights of this fabulous city. We had time to visit the Forbidden City, the Summer Palace and the Temple of Heaven. What remains in Beijing after the devastations of the Cultural Revolution are the shells of buildings, most of the contents having been destroyed. The archaeology museum was curious, in that it was empty apart from a few replicas on the first floor. It was, in fact, a huge restaurant and shop. After the group left, my friend Denise Seely and I moved into a 5-star hotel for a further two nights and visited the Great Wall, the Peking Opera and took a rickshaw around what remains of the Hutong, traditional Beijing housing, most of which has been torn down in order to build huge motorways in preparation for the 2008 Olympics. The Hutong are rapidly becoming a tourist trap. Our rickshaw driver took us to visit a nursery school where, immediately upon our arrival, the children stopped what they were doing and broke into a rousing rendition of *London's Burning* to Denise's and my utter astonishment. On our last morning, before taking the plane home, we rose early to queue to visit Mao, in his mausoleum in Tiananmen Square. He is only brought out of cold storage for four hours a day and consequently the queue was very long. We were pushed at speed past his body encased in a navy suit, his skin a waxy pale yellow and the sight reconfirmed my determination to be cremated.

At the same time as I was busy fundraising for the NAS, I had also become increasingly involved with ADDISS, the charity for people who have Attention Deficit Hyperactivity Disorder and their families. Andrea Bilbow, the founder and director had asked me in 2000 if I would be patron and I was glad to accept. On my return from China, in November, I opened an ADDISS International Conference at a large hotel in Russell Square in London, where there were over 400 hundred delegates, of which half were parents and the others were professionals in this field.

Living with someone who has ADHD is really tough. But it is infinitely more difficult for the person who has ADHD, who finds it very difficult to concentrate, has extremely impulsive behaviour, an inability to organise himself and, consequently, lives with nothing but failure and low self-esteem. Over lunch one day with Jane May, my friend with whom I had shared a nanny for several years when our children were younger, I discussed Natalya's ADHD, which had always been apparent to Jane. As an example she recounted one particular day in which Natalya had been in her son's immaculate bedroom for no more than 20 minutes before I came to collect her to take her home. Within that short space of time, Natalya had pulled every single boxed game out from the cupboard and had scattered them all across the floor, mixing their contents, while she searched for one game in particular, oblivious to the mayhem she had created. This is normal behaviour for a two year old, but by then Natalya was nine years old. Stephanie Berni, whose daughter Alice was Natalya's best friend for many years, dealt with this type of problem in a very practical manner when they were young. Each time Natalya went to play with Alice, it took us ages to find all her clothes and special teddies when it was time to go home.

Natalya had a habit of shedding her clothing whenever she found it restricting or when she felt hot, so Stephie circumnavigated the problem by stripping both girls down to their underpants (Alice was also a clothes shedder) and guarding all school books and toys until the time of departure.

Natalya had tried office work, but after a few days was bored out of her mind and had left. She quickly realised that this type of work was not an option for her, as she needed to have short, varied tasks, if she were to maintain momentum.

Having an ADHD child is very hard for the parents, who are demonised, their apparent bad parenting being seen as the sole cause of their child's bad behaviour. Because Olivia was the passive/aloof type of autistic, I sometimes found Natalya's ADHD more difficult to live with. There was much more acting out, doing wild things, causing mayhem all around her. At the time of the conference, she was 21 years old and, as she had grown up, her difficulties and problems had become more serious. I had been living in a state of what I can only describe as 'crisis management' for the past 10 years, and I felt it was important to support other parents by being open and frank about this disorder.

Dianne Zaccheo, whom I had met two years earlier at my first ADDISS conference, was attending and we had lunch together. I told her that Natalya was having problems finding the type of job that would suit her and that her self-esteem was at an all-time low and that it was high time we looked into her Coaching Technique. Dianne suggested that I bring Natalya to her office, where she would explain to her, with the use of a flip chart and drawings, how the ADHD brain differed from the 'normal' brain and how her coaching programme worked. Delighted, I accepted and we made a date for the following month.

Dianne's house contains her office, but she welcomed us into her cosy living room and offered us tea. We spent considerable time discussing what Natalya found most difficult to deal with and then Dianne began to draw diagrams to show Natalya that she had a genuine disorder and this was what caused her to react in the way she did. Natalya found the explanation extremely comforting and reassuring, and then Dianne went on to explain how her theory of 'coaching' worked. People with ADHD become stuck or overwhelmed with everyday tasks that people without the disorder take in their stride. They need support with even the simplest tasks that require the use of the 'executive' side of the brain, such as tidying up a messy desk or paying bills. This method of coaching was similar to the way I had learnt to teach Olivia, by breaking down a task into small steps, before overloading set in. A coach is always available by phone, to guide, inspire, and rescue, if necessary. I took on the job of coach and was to be in daily contact with Natalya to talk her through any difficulty she might have and, hopefully, help her to keep motivated. I love my daughter and wanted to help her so that she was able to flourish, so being her coach was not a burden for me. It was, in fact, what I had been doing for years, only this time it was much more structured by Dianne, although Dianne stressed to me that this was a very unusual situation. In most cases, the parent is the last person to be a coach as the parent/child relationship has already been strained to breaking point and an independent coach is vital. It was only because our relationship was still so healthy that Dianne would even recommend something so contrary to normal coaching practice. In many ways, coaching is similar to being a sponsor for a new member of Alcoholics Anonymous from what little I understand of that delicate position. I have been told that I have ADHD myself, but fortunately for me it hasn't had a detrimental effect on my life since it does not impact my 'executive processing', an area in which, if anything, I tend to hyper focus.

Natalya loved hearing about my trek in China and had seen my long and boring home video of our climb up Mount Kilimanjaro. Several times on the China trek, I was asked 'Where are we going next, Liz?' and, after much conferring, the group came down heavily in favour of trekking to Machu Picchu in Peru, in 2003. This time, Natalya would come with me and I was thrilled to be able to experience a trek with her. Also in the group was my cousin, Mavy Burden, with whom I shared so many childhood memories. Our first school was a Roman Catholic primary in Newcastle upon Tyne, where for three years we shared a double desk. Mavy is Jewish and I was brought up a Methodist, but such is the power of the Catholic Church on one so young, that I was almost ten before I realised that I really would not go to hell if I didn't say my three Hail Marys in bed every night! My sister-in-law, Nancy Mackintosh, was also coming on the trek with a friend from Oxfordshire, where they both lived, so this trek was going to be especially good fun for me. But it was not to take place for a year and in 2002 I felt the need to do something fun to fill the gap. In March at a lunch with the Lord Mayor of London, I found just what I was looking for.

Richard Taylor is a very old friend of mine and had been my landlord when I rented my first flat in London when I was 19. He had invited me to join him at the Banqueting House in the City of London, for lunch with his friend Michael Oliver, who was the Lord Mayor of London for that year. Sally, Michael's wife, had trained with a trapeze artist for three months prior to the Lord Mayor's Parade, where she turned somersaults inside a helium balloon above the Lord Mayor's coach as it took its triumphant tour of the City. Over lunch, Richard asked Sally what she had planned to follow her grand entrance into the City of London and she replied that she was to abseil down the Canary Wharf Tower in July in aid of the Lord Mayor's charities, which were mental health projects and Bart's Cancer Centre. 'I would love to join you!' I found the words coming out of my mouth, before I had time to think. 'You would be most welcome,' Sally replied. 'The entry conditions are to raise £10,000 for the charities and take a compulsory training day with the London police force who have been trained by the Royal Marines.' Richard said that Rick Englert, his partner, would join me and casually brushed aside my questioning whether, perhaps, Richard should ask Rick first?

Two months later, Rick and I met at Bishopsgate Police Station and were greeted by a policeman of terrifying proportions. He was built like Arnold Schwarzenegger and gave us all the comfort that that actor gave his victims in the film *The Terminator*. Rick, who, like me, is slim and has a narrow build, was forced into his harness, which this monster then pulled so tight, I thought Rick would either faint or throw up. The other men had the same treatment but he didn't quite dare treat the women so roughly. The harness passes between the legs and across the chest, in all the most delicate areas for either gender and, once secured, we were led to a practice climbing wall with toe holds and a straight 100-feet drop to the ground. This was where we were to practise, but to reach it we had to cross a narrow metal bridge from one building to another. I found that hard enough and clung on to Rick's hand, which he kindly held out to me across the gap.

We had two trials each and the second was definitely less terrifying. If one relied 100 per cent on the equipment, it was easy. But as all people who hate flying or tend towards a controlling personality know, relying on equipment doesn't even begin to come into the equation. I like to be in control, but have never had a fear of flying and I hoped that this would stand me in good stead for the 622-feet drop down the side of the Canary Wharf Tower in one week's time.

Natalya said that she would come with me and bring her new boyfriend, Simon Hill, whereupon Charles asked if he could come too and bring his friend, Josh Green, who was staying with us at the time. I rather liked the idea, as long as I didn't bottle out at the last minute in front of them all, and so, in a party of five, on a warm, sunny morning on 15 July, I arrived at our meeting point below the building. We joined Rick and Richard and also Brock Bogarde, Dirk's nephew, who lived near them in Sussex and who had also been inveigled by Richard to take part. I was put in the second group and, while we waited for my turn, we watched the first group abseil down the huge building. There was a carnival atmosphere and hundreds of City workers were out in the street watching the event, drinking coffee and listening to Sally Oliver being interviewed by the press.

Natalya assures me that my face was a sickly green by the time it was my turn to take the lift to the top of the building. In fact, she said, I looked so utterly terrified that she was sure I would be taking the lift down again immediately and had gone to buy me a conciliatory cup of coffee from the stand in the square. With my group of five partic-ipants, I waited outside the building on the top floor, on a narrow ledge between the windows and a high wall that I was not tall enough to see over, which suited me fine. I was fourth in the group but by the time the first two had descended, I begged to be allowed to go next as my courage was draining out of me with such speed that I knew if I didn't go immediately, I would drop out and run to the lift. We were descending in pairs, each person accompanied by a newly trained policemen who abseiled beside them. Mine was a Geordie with a camcorder.

Without doubt, climbing to the edge of building out on to a shaky wooden platform to then push off into space was the worst part. About a third of the way down, we came to a halt for some unknown reason, and I dared to look around me. I waved tentatively to my children, tiny specks far below, and they waved back. My Geordie policeman asked me to say a few words to his grandma on the camcorder, as Hever Castle was apparently her favourite place to visit, and before I had finished we were off once more. I began to enjoy abseiling about half-way down, once I realised that all I had to do was to control the rope that lowered me and I could go as slowly or as fast (my choice) as I liked. In fact, I was actually disappointed that it came to an end so soon, although I doubt whether I would have felt so confident if I had gone after one participant who was only half-an-hour after me, and who was stuck half-way down the building, swaying in the breeze for 45 minutes while ropes were thrown over the top for two further marine escorts, who were lowered to her aid. Because she was so tiny, she had failed to be properly secured in her harness and had begun to slip out of it, but I didn't know about this incident until I read about it in the paper the following morning.

After one year, Adam, who had been my first fitness trainer left, and my brother Charlie put me in touch with his new trainer, Sonya Clark. Sonya was a New Zealander and a frequent participant in extreme sports. She would go off for days in a team of four and compete in the most manic races, running and biking over mountains, swimming across freezing lakes, carrying all the food they needed without stopping or sleeping. She was the perfect match with my other trainer Samantha and I began boxing for the first time in my life, which I loved. It is the best method of ridding oneself of pent-up aggression that I have ever come across plus it is fun, too. Samantha occasionally asked me to skip, which I hadn't done since I left the school playground, and both trainers invented circuits for me to follow. Natalya had always kept fit. She roller-bladed her way around London and often went to dance classes and attended the gym regularly. We were to go to Peru in May 2003 and, for the third time, I began fundraising. This time the sponsorship money was going towards the NAS Training Programme for adults who wanted to work with autistic people and towards Prospects, which helped autistic adults find the right type of employment for them and who would support them in it, while also educating the employer in the intricacies of autism. With the help of my fellow trekkers, we had previously raised substantial funds for children, but I felt that we should put our sponsorship money towards adult services on this trek. It is much easier to raise funds for adorable children, but autism is a life-long condition and provision for autistic adults is extremely expensive.

Olivia had her tenth birthday in August 2002. The summer had been a frightening time as she had inexplicably regressed and I did not know whether this would continue, or if she would come out of it, in her own time. At the end of the summer term, I had taken her to see Sue Shepherd at Elliot House in Bromley, for the annual appraisal of her academic and social development. The night before, I had asked Olivia to go and have her bath, which she had been doing fairly successfully for some months. That night, after about 20 minutes, I went to see how far she had progressed. Because she had no sense of time, she would sit in the bath until she was prompted to wash and get out. I found her curled up in a foetal position at the end of the bath, her legs scarlet, her face pulled in an expression of pain and bewilderment. I saw at once that she was sitting in boiling hot water and pulled her out of the bath immediately. Why had she not got out herself, called for help, or pulled the plug, I wondered? She had no answer, except she kept saying 'Sorry, Mummy' and I had to explain that I was not angry with her, just frightened and surprised.

When the assessment was completed, Judy Gould, Sue Shepherd and I met in the kitchen at Elliot House to discuss the results. Olivia was out of earshot, happily playing with toys in the consulting room upstairs. One of the tests that she had been asked to complete was to put in order two picture cards and explain what was happening. One set showed a Chinese boy covering his plate of food with a large amount of salt. The second picture was of him pulling an expression of disgust. Olivia could not put these two photos in the right order. She had absolutely no idea why he had pulled this expression. After some prompting, she mooted, 'Perhaps that was the face that Chinese people made when they were eating?' The second pair of photos were of a woman waving goodbye to a car full of people waving out of the car windows and in the second photo, she had her hand held high in a final wave, with tears rolling down her cheeks. Again, Olivia found these two photographs impossible to interpret and could only surmise that in the second photo the woman was 'Holding up her hand against the light'. I found these results profoundly disturbing. How could I even begin to imagine that she would interpret life in such a bizarre way and how could I, therefore, help to disentangle it for her? Judy told me that it was impossible. If I tried to guess what she was thinking, I would be almost sure of doing so incorrectly, only compounding the confusion. 'I would also be dead with exhaustion within a week,' I added, and Judy agreed. All I could do, she advised, was to disabuse her when I was extremely clear where she had gone wrong. I might never know what she was thinking, and although I knew that, it was depressing to realise the extent and depth of her confusion. I had tried to be her eyes, her ears, her interpreter and protector from the world, but I would have to learn to live with the fact that I would probably not know, most of the time, what was going on inside her head. As to the bath drama of the night before, she suggested that I take Olivia back several steps and begin to rebuild what she had learnt, reinforcing her lost skills.

But she regressed even more during the summer holidays. She almost gave up speaking and Johnnie and I had to live with neighing instead of speech. Olivia's favourite toy was the horse called Bullseye from the Disney film *Toy Story*. It still is and she takes him everywhere with her. He is now entirely patched with chamois leather with only a tiny space around his eyes remaining of the original material. During the summer holidays of 2002, Bullseye became Olivia's alter ego. 'He' neighed once for 'yes' and twice for 'no', and many times when Olivia was angry, while being waved closely before the eyes of whoever had annoyed her. She began to point to a plate of biscuits and say 'Hungry, hungry' instead of asking for one, which she had been quite capable of doing up until then. I had read about children who regressed, but they were all about 18 months to two years old. Could this happen at the age of ten? There were no answers and living with the terrible fear that she might continue to lose her hard-learned skills right before my eyes was agony for me. I hate uncertainty at the best of times, and all we could do was to follow Judy's suggestions and take her back several steps in each task and try to reinforce them.

When I took Olivia back to school in September, for her second year at Broomhill Bank, they were surprised to hear of our summer of despair. She had shown no signs of regression at school and, as the autumn progressed, she slowly recovered at home, too, and to my enormous relief began speaking normally again. At a charity lunch in Kent in October, I met a friend who has a daughter with Asperger syndrome and is two years older than Olivia. She asked me how our summer had been and when I told her of our summer of neighing, she laughed and said that Rosie had barked since she was four years old and, at 12, she still did!

I began to teach Olivia to tell the time and continued to prepare her for puberty. She needed to wear a bra, but I decided that I would first change her vest for a 'crop top' and then move on to a bra in a couple of months. This was easier said than done. Olivia flatly refused to give up her vests, until I told her that she could wear them until the end of the week, but on Monday morning, she was to wear a crop top. It worked! There was no protest and I could have kicked myself for not having used this approach before. *Of course* she agreed, it was a *rule*, not a discussion, and a very clear one at that. Why hadn't I thought of this before? I knew she liked the security of knowing what was to happen each day and this was just an extension of that need. From that day onwards, I have approached each change in this manner, giving her as much warning as she needs, followed by a *fait accompli*. It wasn't, and still isn't, quite so easy when she has her periods. The first took place in the loo at the departure lounge of Heathrow airport, just before Christmas. We were on our way to the island of Langkawi, in Malaysia, and I had to return to the main terminal to buy the necessary equipment. Although she had practised wearing pads, she was very unhappy about *having to,* and complained to me every five minutes of the flight. At around 3 a.m., I couldn't stand it any longer and told her to take herself to the loo, remove the pad and go to sleep in her seat. She did so and ran out of the loo delighted, shouting at the top of her voice, 'Charles, I don't have my period any more, Charles!' The poor boy was 12 years old and with a scarlet face and a scowl in her direction he pulled his airline blanket over his head and ignored her.

This lack of self-awareness is a continuing problem. Olivia will often come downstairs in the nude, to tell me that she can't do up her bra and she is utterly unaware of the inappropriateness of this behaviour. Each time I have to remind her that our bodies are private and she is always so sweet and apologetic to me, saying 'Sorry, Mummy, sorry'. And sometimes, 'I forgot' or 'Do you forgive me?' I have developed a skin like a rhino and am rarely embarrassed by her social ineptness, but sometimes wonder how I will feel when she is 30 or older. Those who do feel embarrassed, are, of course, all the poor strangers who are caught unaware when this sort of thing happens, like the builder and electrician in our flat in France, who were discussing plans with me when Olivia walked into the room stark naked, aged 11 and fully developed, to tell me that she couldn't find her pants. The poor men simply didn't know what to do or where to look, and were overcome with embarrassment. I put my arm gently around Olivia's shoulders and guided her back to her bedroom, calling over my shoulder that I would be back in a few minutes. I reminded Olivia, yet again, that walking around naked was not a good thing to do, particularly when there were strangers in the house. As usual, she apologised and said that she had forgotten, and I am sure that, one day, she will remember.

CHAPTER 13

From the Peaks of Peru to the Troughs of Despair: Coming to Terms with Autism

By May 2003, I realised that I had spent most of the past seven years almost totally immersed in the world of autism and ADHD. Olivia had finally been diagnosed as autistic in February 1996 and I had been on a mission to learn as much about the syndrome as I could ever since, together with as many alternative therapies as I happened upon along the way. There has to be a point when the mother or the child, if they could, cries 'Enough!' and although I was intrigued by such interesting therapies as Neurolinguistic Programming and Kirlian glasses, I had reached saturation point. My approach was becoming much more academic, in the sense that I studied Olivia minutely and tried to work out how I could help her learn to have a bath, write, read, set a table and to give everything else, apart from speech and language and occupational therapy, a rest. I was beginning to feel more relaxed and the more people I met who also had autistic children, the more I realised that Olivia could have been much more severely affected and how easy she was to live with compared with many others. There was much in my life to be grateful for and as long as I was able to take a trip abroad occasionally, I felt that I could manage to keep most balls up in the air. On 3 May, with a group of 35 others (including Natalya and my friend May Burden), I boarded the plane to Lima, via Madrid.

We all adored Peru. It is an extremely beautiful country of huge contrasts. The Andes Mountains hang in folds, like heavy serge drapes from a proscenium sky, the valleys and hillsides are filled with lamas and the porters who carried our food and sleeping bags wore traditional, brightly coloured woven ponchos and hats hung with fuchsia pompoms. Much of Peru is Amazon rainforest, but we only had time to visit a tiny area of the magnificent Andes Mountain range, which clings to the edge of the country before falling away dramatically into the South Pacific Ocean.

Cuzco, the capital of the Incas, stands at approximately 10,000 feet and altitude sickness affected some of us immediately. We flew in from Lima, which stands at sea level, and in the afternoon were taking a tour around the cathedral in the central square, trying to ignore our throbbing heads. Our first evening in Cuzco happened to be my birthday and Zoe Pinch, the NAS representative who came with us, had brought me a delicious bottle of Louis Latour wine in her suitcase, Peru not being renowned for its vineyards. As I shared the wine with everyone at my table, our Peruvian guide asked me what the traditional British birthday dish was. After I had given a description of a children's tea party and explained that the adults like to eat their favourite dish, whatever that may be, he told me that the Peruvian birthday delicacy is roast guinea pig, served on its back, stiff little legs up in the air, claws intact, with a ripe tomato in its mouth. Thank goodness he didn't know it was my birthday before it was too late to place an order! As Natalya had just had her 21st birthday and my mother was to be 80 during our trek, this would surely have required a feast of several families of these sweet creatures that my sisters and I had kept as pets in our childhood.

It took us three days to walk up the stone Inca path to Machu

Picchu. The incline was extremely steep and we were unlucky with the weather as it was wet and cloudy most of the time, which meant that we missed some of the spectacular views across the Andes. Mavy and I walked together, catching up on family news, stopping frequently to admire the stunning views, whenever there was a gap in the clouds. The path was lined with wild flowers. May was autumn in Peru, the home of the humble potato, of which Peru boasted over 200 hundred varieties, and the harvest was under way. There were fields of corn clinging to tiny terraced fields, in wonderful colours ranging from the palest yellow to a deep purple. Every day we stopped at more than one Inca site, where fortresses had been built and food stores were kept for those who were on their way to the great city of Machu Picchu. As we struggled with the steepness of the paths and the altitude we were in awe of the Inca relay runners who were able to deliver fresh fish from the sea to every corner of the Empire for breakfast. These elite runners also carried coded messages made of coloured threads. The Incas were remarkable people had no written language and had never discovered the wheel. History relates that they were defeated by a small Spanish army with only 12 horses and when one looks at the few remaining exquisite gold figures that the Spanish did not find, to melt down and ship back to Spain, it makes the loss of this heritage all the more tragic.

Nearly everyone went down with a stomach bug, which, when one considered the cooking facilities, was not surprising. Our cooks did a wonderful job, but enthusiasm for the next meal was not enhanced by looking inside the kitchen tent, where dirt-engrained fingers busily prepared our food. Perhaps the Black Cat wine, which came in waxed cartons, was to blame, but what was the major difficulty was where to 'go', when on one side of the trail was a 6,000-feet drop and, on the other, a steep cliff of dense vegetation. I thought I had found a perfect spot, one afternoon, just before we attempted the ascent to 'Dead Woman's Pass' at 14,000 feet, so called because the shape of the mountain looked like a woman lying on her back. I stepped off the path, on the cliff side, where there seemed to be a tiny space behind a tree, and having got as far as pulling down everything from the waist, was butted to one side by a large, black angry sow from the farm nearby! Black pigs abounded, they were the goose that laid the golden eggs for the farmers; pig meat was expensive and only eaten by the wealthy, but produced by poor farmers who ate guinea pigs, reared in pens inside their one-roomed houses, which they ate with all the emotional detachment we employ for chickens.

We spent the third night in a noisy campsite that clung to the mountainside on small, levelled shelves of land in a valley beside our path. There was an ugly concrete restaurant at the end of the valley, where, for a small price, hot showers were available. The queue was over an hour long, and Natalya, Mavy and I preferred to spend our time drinking local beer and trying to get some sleep as we were to be woken at 4 a.m. to be at the Sun Gate to see the sun rise. We were to watch the dawn light pass precisely between the arches of the gate to fall in a direct line over the ancient city of Machu Picchu. The mathematical precision that this entailed was as astonishing as midsummer solstice at Stonehenge.

That final morning's trek took us up a steep path, pathed with large, flat stones that had been laid by the Incas. It was overshadowed by a lush growth of trees and bushes, making the mossy stones slippery to walk on. After we had been walking for nearly two hours in the dark by torchlight, a thin, watery light began to trickle through the overhead leaves, and I realised that I would not get to the Sun Gate in time. It didn't matter as one lady in our party was struggling quite badly with fatigue and lack of fitness, and only made it to the top by being hauled up there by two guides. Small and tough, they took hold of her under her arms and almost carried her to the top. It had been a wet start, but as we reached the Sun Gate, the sky cleared, the sun came out and burnt off the mist that shrouded the city and we stood, staring in awe at the amazing sight of this astonishing place, as it slowly revealed itself. Machu Picchu deserves every lavish adjective used to describe its beauty and the wonder it inspires in all who visit it. Built on a small plateau on the top of a mountain in an extremely inaccessible place in the middle of the Andes, it is justifiably one of the man-made Wonders of the World. We stood in a group, hugging each other, crying with tears of joy and pain, thinking of the reason we had been driven to take part in this incredible journey. Some of our party had children who were so much more disabled by their autism than Olivia, and I was humbled by the courage of these devoted parents. When I remembered the difficult pregnancy and birth, with the three knots in the cord, I felt blessed, as Olivia could so easily have had brain damage as well as her autism.

We were very proud of our achievement and tired, and filthy dirty, we spent the day exploring this incredible ruined city, beside tourists in brand-new hiking boots and spotless trousers. There is an excellent train service that has recently been renovated, from Cuzco to Aquas Calientes, which runs beside the torrential Urubamba River to the town created around the train terminal, from which one can take a bus up the winding mountain road to the base of the site. Most people visited Machu Picchu this way, but it had taken us three days to get there, as we had taken the route that the Incas made over the mountains.

The trek had also been extremely successful in terms of fundraising. Our group of 36 had raised a total of £281,283, of which £47,410 was my contribution. The NAS press team had pulled out all the stops once more, and we had had another spread in *Hello!* magazine and extensive coverage in the national and local newspapers. Jacqui Ashton Smith, the headmistress of the Helen Allison School, one of the schools run by the National Autistic Society, and I, had been invited on to a television breakfast show to discuss autism from the perspective of both a headmistress of a school for autistic children, and a parent. The programme editors were thorough in their preparation and there were many phone calls between their research department, Jacqui and myself. We were collected by a chauffeur-driven car, which took us to the studio and I was really hoping to have time to explain what it was like living with a child with autism. However, we found that we were squeezed in between a bubbly, bouncy Bonnie Langford, who was promoting her new West End show, and a discussion about the benefits of breast-feeding! Both Jacqui and I felt severely short changed. We had put a great deal of effort and time into the preparation for the show, and were disappointed at how little airtime we had been given. After the show we met the presenters, who wanted to talk about autism as one of them strongly suspected that the son of his best friend was autistic. They promised us a whole show on autism, and they appeared to be increasingly fascinated by it the more we talked. However, we are still waiting.

After the trek to Peru, Natalya and I were invited on to *This Morning*, a television show hosted by Fern Britton and Philip Schofield, and these shows resulted in many letters asking me to be patron of various charities in aid of autism that parents had set up all around the UK. While I was happy to lend my name to these charities, I wrote each time to ask why the group had not joined the NAS and felt the need to start their own charity? It seemed to me that we would all be chasing the same slice of cake and that by pooling our resources, real achievements were possible. Often small groups had their own particular focus that was pertinent to their area and there can also be a strong feeling of disenfranchisement from a large established charity, which can work against it. Parents of newly diagnosed children look around them and all too frequently do not find what they feel they need in the first painful years. They want a cure, or at least answers to which alternative treatment would be the right one for their child, and research has not yet reached that point. I am deeply sympathetic to this view, as I had been very angry with the NAS in its inability to give me concrete answers in the early days of Olivia's diagnosis. Charities are often set up by families, but in order to grow and be successful, a charity needs to employ first-class fundraisers, chairmen and secretaries, who can command top-level salaries. Inevitably, these employees are rarely directly involved with the cause and sometimes this can generate resentment from the parents who are already struggling to cope with their son or daughter and working long hours trying to raise much-needed funds and who often feel that the results of all their hard work simply disappear into the charity's overall running costs without feeling any direct benefit themselves.

New charities are most likely to arise when there are no facilities for autistic people within their locality. Unfortunately schools, units or homes for autistic people are scattered around the country and one can easily find that one is living in an area where there are no amenities, understanding or knowledge of autism, at all. Desperate parents set up their own schools, often after years of running battles with their local authorities, which claim that these children should go to the local mainstream school and even go as far as to threaten the parents with prison for withholding their children from their local schools. If this is this case, I will do whatever I can to support the parents or the autistic adult who is looking for the right provision to which he is entitled.

Olivia seemed reasonably happy to have her photograph taken again and again for the press, but never asked why they wanted to take her picture! Nor did she show any sign of noticing that she was different in any way from the rest of the world. But to me, she was growing increasingly autistic as the years went by. I wondered when I should tell her that she was autistic, but Judy Gould assured me that I would know when the time was right, because Olivia would ask me relevant questions. She is 13 years old now and still hasn't asked me why she finds so much in her life so very difficult.

By the time Olivia was 11, she had grown so quickly that she had stretch marks down the sides of both hips. Her hair was long and she was very proud of it, although she was unable to wash and dry it herself, or tie it back into a ponytail, as she was required to do at school. I asked Jill Christmas, her occupational therapist, how we could teach her to deal with her hair. Jill suggested that Olivia practise by combing my hair and that we also buy a doll with long hair for her to practise on. Olivia has never been interested in dolls and quickly gave up combing my hair after a couple of token brushes, so her progress was minimal. I didn't have the heart to cut her hair as it was one of the few things about which she had a strong opinion and I felt it would have been mean of me to cut it short so that she could manage.

I had taught her to tell the time, which had taken about 18 months. We practised every day for a few minutes and I would frequently ask her to read the kitchen clock, to reinforce her skills. I had bought a clock especially for this purpose as our old one had Roman numerals, which was more difficult for her to read. I decided to give time telling a rest, once I felt confident that she had really learnt it, and we concentrated on other skills, such as spreading jam on bread and learning how to cycle. In the summer of 2003, when she was 11 years old, I bought her a tricycle and she surprised me by learning very quickly. It was a special tricycle, for children like Olivia who have gross and fine motor co-ordination difficulties. The charming man who sold it to me pointed out the unique features, which included backward pedalling and wheels that would not turn unless the pedals were driven. It was also possible to take it apart fairly easily so that, in two or three parts, it would fit inside the boot of car. But we have never done this, as she is so nervous about riding over the slightest bump or going down hill that we tend to stick to the same route, around our house and up and down the lane. Two years later, she has nearly grown out of it, but I don't think she would be confident to ride something larger.

After three years at Broomhill Bank School, I knew that it was time for Olivia to go to a school for autistic children. Broomhill Bank is a lovely school for girls with a moderate learning disability, but all Olivia's problems stemmed from her autism and dyspraxia, and I considered it time to move her to an environment where this was the primary disability. I was also deeply disappointed that after Olivia had only been two terms at Broomhill Bank, Kent County Council had reduced the very successful boarding facility from fortnightly boarding to weekly boarding, as the budget was insufficient to pay the staff. I had thought that Olivia might board there one day, if I were unable to move her to a more appropriate placement. It was a tragedy for the children, who had thoroughly enjoyed their weekends at school, going on outings and being together. Many of them went home and stayed alone in their bedrooms all weekend, as Olivia would if I didn't frequently pull her from it to do something other than sort and line up her books and toys.

I rang Phil Barnett, the headmaster of Broomhill Bank School, and explained that as I had surmised three years earlier, I felt that I should begin the process of applying for a place at Grateley House, a school for autistic boys and girls, in Hampshire. I had revisited Grateley in March 2004 and liked it even more than on my first visit, some years before. The school had taken more girl pupils who were fairly quiet and gentle and it had fewer of the more able bumptious boys, so I thought that Olivia would be able to cope well there. Phil was entirely understanding and was grateful for my straightforward, honest approach. Olivia was not generalising many of her skills and this was glaringly apparent when, after her third school trip to the 'Safety in Action' centre, she scored the highest points for the day, but would still walk across a road without using the Green Cross Code. She had again learnt everything by rote, but could not transfer her knowledge into an everyday skill. Sharon Wallis, one of the mothers at that school, told me that she had a blue disabled badge to use when her daughter, who also didn't understand the dangers of traffic, was in the car with her and that I would be able to apply for a badge for Olivia, too. It has been a godsend, because I am now able to park close to the shops or cinema and cut out as many dangerous road crossings as possible. But why, Sharon and I wondered, do parents have to find these things out for themselves? Why were we not informed of the many entitlements by the myriad of professionals who see these children in the course of their lives? It is always the parents who have to do most of the work, already struggling with their disabled children and adults, and it is for this reason that people like my friend, Henrietta Spink, set up charities that store vital information to help other parents to tweak out access, entitlements and allowances. I was extremely fortunate in having help at home and wanted to do whatever I could to help others less fortunate than I who found themselves in the same boat.

Perhaps it was because I had so much help at home that I didn't actually crack until Olivia was 11 years old. One morning in early March, I had decided to refresh her time-telling skills after having given it a rest for some months, confident that she had really learnt how to do it. While we sat at the kitchen table, eating our breakfast, I pointed to the clock and asked her to tell me the time. It was 8 o'clock, easy enough, I thought, but Olivia looked puzzled and after some minutes said she thought it was '12 to 8?' I was devastated, as it was glaringly apparent that she had not remembered anything at all. Why had this happened, I wondered? I surmised that because she had absolutely no idea of the concept of time, she had learnt it by rote and that as it had *no meaning for her whatsoever*, after a few weeks of not practising, she had forgotten it all. That evening, I sat, as I always did, on the loo seat as she took her bath. The list I had so painstakingly written out for her had not really worked, as she still needed constant prompting to move from one task to another. After I had reminded her to wash for the umpteenth time that evening, I suddenly saw myself, sitting in the same place in 30 years' time, Olivia aged 40, me, an 80 year old, and I broke down, weeping a backlog of tears, a dam that had finally burst its banks. There had been no particular reason for this to have happened, no extenuating circumstances that had triggered this glitch; it came like a bolt out of the blue, taking my breath away. I suppose that I had simply run out of energy and felt that I could not carry on, day after day, night after night, year after year, trying to teach her skills that she never learnt, or forgot immediately. I was mentally exhausted from trying to think ahead, planning what she needed to learn next, forever explaining to those around me what autism meant, and how it affected Olivia in particular. Perhaps I had had her under the microscope for too long, studying her every move, trying to discover *why* she did the things she did, what she was *thinking, how* she learnt, so that I could open up her world and effectively help her manage to live in it. But I wanted just *one* evening with my husband, to be able to watch a video with him, *one* evening with my other children, to be able to send her upstairs for her bath alone, like all normal children do. Forget going away for the weekend, that had never been on the agenda and I didn't really care, but I badly needed to have a single minute of the day when I was not thinking about what she was doing, worrying as she sat stimming in her bedroom, endlessly sorting or pointing a finger at a picture in a book, turning the page and pointing again, until she reached the end of the book and immediately beginning all over again, wondering just how quickly could I get my tasks done and give her time to do something constructive. I was burnt out and felt both terribly sorry for myself, extremely selfish and painfully guilty that I even had these thoughts.

I had, over the years, very gradually come to terms with her autism.

I had learnt to be extremely grateful that she was even able to walk and talk, and not worry about her wonky, jerking gait. I was grateful she could read so fluently and that we could share our love of books. I had even come to terms with her stimming, like Dr Manette, endlessly making shoes from the air in *The Tale of Two Cities*, for short periods of the day. Olivia is a darling person, with a sweet nature and gives me tremendous joy and often much laughter, with her hilarious comments and direct approach. My mother had taught me the joy of looking backwards, to consider how far she had come and to take pleasure in that. She often reminded me of the days when we thought that Olivia would never walk, let alone ride a tricycle or swim a length of our pool. I had felt as if we were joined at the hip, body and soul, and that she would be with me forever, because that was the way it was, I was her primary carer and probably always would be, and I had grown accustomed to this way of life.

When she was first diagnosed, I had taken her to a faith healer, in a vain attempt to 'cure' her. Ambrose Congreve, an elderly friend of ours, had suggested some years later that I take her to his guru in India who, he assured me, had brought at least 20 people back from the dead! Ambrose had total faith in his guru and we talked much about this man, while Ambrose ate the pills that his guru had given him that looked like a mixture of dried animal parts wrapped in elephant dung, and I ate the delicious dinner he served his guests. But, by that time, I felt comfortable with Olivia's autism. If I removed the autism from her, if such a thing were even possible, what would she be, after all? *Autism was Olivia,* and I had grown accustomed to it. We all loved her the way she was, quirky, funny, entirely different. I had reached the end of the seven stages of grief and had worked my way through the denial, anger, fear, loss, despair and hope, and had arrived, at last, at acceptance. I had settled into life with an autistic child, who would grow in her own way, entitled to be herself, as she was, accepted and loved for what she was, for whom she was. But on that cold evening in March, suddenly all this was not all right any more, and I felt acutely ashamed, and trapped.

The day after my crack-up, I arrived at my friend Claire Robert's house but I was crying so much that I missed the turning to her gate three times and was a weeping mess by the time I rang her doorbell. Through my tears I explained what had happened the night before. Claire engulfed me in her arms and told me that I was just suffering from 'carers' fatigue', that all carers came down with it occasionally and that it would pass. She was so kind and understanding, knowing just what I was going through, having been there many times herself.

We had decided that we would run in the Hasting Half Marathon in March. We had been to Inner Mongolia together and we continued to meet two or three times a year for dinner, to swap news, tips and anecdotes about our autistic children. I had begun running about six months before, training hard with Sonya, who was herself a runner, although I had never done any running in my life before. After a couple of cups of coffee, I felt sufficiently restored to run and talk all the way round her 12½-mile half marathon training route, near her house in Otford.

Having 'hit a wall' like this made me review my life and think long and hard about the future. Clearly, I could not carry on, for the rest of my life, with such a high-energy output. I was approaching 54, and although I was fit and healthy, I would not always be at such a peak. I had to think realistically; it would not do my family, least of all Olivia, any favours if I had a nervous breakdown. Luckily, I had decided to try to get Olivia a place at Grateley House school and, with this in mind, I rang a solicitor who specialised in fighting special needs tribunals, as I was fully aware that I would have to take this long, hard route if I had any chance of succeeding in winning a place for her there. A tribunal is a legal hearing conducted by three people, who listen to the evidence of both parties and make their judgement. Tribunals are booked up months in advance and therefore careful planning and gathering of as much evidence as possible in favour of one's case is vital before going to tribunal if there is to be any chance of a successful outcome. Like all educational authorities, Kent would not willingly pay the huge fees that special schools commanded without going to tribunal to hear me plead my cause and would fight every step of the way against agreeing to it. As I love my adopted county, I am sorry to say that I have found Kent to be one of the most difficult local education authorities (LEAs) and almost every year Kent has had more special needs tribunals than any other county. As the cost of these tribunals comes out of Government funds, local authorities freely spend vast sums on legal defence, while the parents have to either pay for themselves or apply for legal aid. Often the cost of going to tribunal is so large that the legal fees alone would have covered the school fees in question for several terms. In the majority of special needs tribunals the parents are the successful party, making it even more galling when one considers the strain on already stressed families, and the waste of time and money involved.

Robert Love, the specialist education solicitor I engaged, told me that the first thing I must do was to ask for a review of Olivia's Statement of Special Needs at the next annual review, which was in only three weeks' time. How lucky I was to have contacted him then, as, if I had missed the annual review date, I would have had to wait another year before I could make the request! Incredible though it seems, there was no allowance to request a review at any point during the following year. I wrote to request the review, particularly because Olivia's Statement of Special Needs did not even use the term autism. The reason for this is that she was only three when the statement was initially written and, in my ignorance at that time, I had also been determined not to use the term 'autism', and had had no cause to amend it until now. She was described as having a 'social and communication disorder, with a moderate learning disability'. There was no mention of dyspraxia either, which was a significant factor in itself in her difficulties with handwriting, feeding and personal care. The request was granted a few weeks after a meeting with the headmaster and a Kent LEA representative, and I began the long, slow process of working towards the tribunal.

During the course of the following year, Olivia was subjected to a variety of assessments, such as speech and language, occupational therapy and psychology. She took them all in her stride and did not seem to be fazed or even tired by them. The paper work that the potential tribunal generated began to pile up on my desk, which eventually finished being 4 inches high! I decided that I couldn't worry about the outcome, or what I would do if we failed in our appeal, but would take each stage as it came and forget about it in between. Life had to go on, and the running and training helped me to clear my mind or write a letter in my head, while I worked my way around the back lanes of Kent and Surrey, trying to build up stamina and strengthen my legs and feet for the Hastings Half Marathon. Sonya Clark, my extreme sports loving New Zealand trainer, trained me by taking me on a weekly two-hour run over the hills in the area surrounding our house. We also did speed work, where I had to run one minute at top speed, followed by three minutes at a jog, for about 40 minutes. But my second weekly personal trainer, Samantha Lucas, is not a natural runner, so she concentrated on all-over body strength and conditioning with me, and we used weights, boxed and did exercises using a large stability ball. It began to take effect, and my Saturday morning runs became faster and longer as the weeks went by.

Hamish Brown, the tall, handsome and charming son of old friends of mine, was also running the Hastings Half and came to Frenchstreet to spend the night before the race. We met Claire Roberts at Sevenoaks station and took the train that had been specially laid on to carry the runners to Hastings. A fierce wind met us as we emerged with a heaving crowd from the station. The start of the race is on the sea front and it was bitterly cold. I felt sick with nerves, as I knew that this was one of the toughest half marathons in the UK, as the first five miles are all uphill. I just hoped that I wasn't going to shame myself. Johnnie could not understand why I was doing it and thought I was completely mad, as did most of my family. Claire, Hamish and I huddled together in a tight little group, trying to keep warm, wishing it were all over, when we were found by Miriam Dorrity, Olivia's school gym teacher and the deputy head of Broomhill Bank School, whom I knew was taking part, but I never expected to see her among the thousands of people thronging in front of the start line. Miriam had taken up running several years before me and had already done the Hastings Half a few times. She was very optimistic for our success and warned us not to go too fast at the start, as we would burn out early. She was a few years younger than me, much smaller, with cropped hair and a very kind nature. She had sent me notes home, via Olivia, with training tips and a running programme and told us that, above all, we should enjoy the race! Her husband and sister were there to cheer her on, as was Claire's husband, who drove down later with their children, Marc and Marianne, as had Hamish's family. The atmosphere was terrific and as the race started, the loudspeakers blared out the theme tune from the film *Chariots of Fire*, and we were off. Hamish and I ran side by side until we had reached the top of the last hill, when, like a race horse at the starting gate, Hamish took off like a rocket, his long legs taking large, easy strides, which gobbled up the tarmac and left me far behind within minutes.

All along the route were crowds cheering us along, shouting out to those they knew, offering sweets, drinks and snacks, which we tried to snatch as we ran past. I was doing quite well, I thought, until I came to the last straight, which ran along the sea front. The wind had picked up even more and we were running against what felt like a gale, blowing directly at us. It was very hard work and I didn't seem to be covering any ground; it felt as if we were running just to keep us from being blown backwards. Just when I felt like giving up and walking, shouts of encouragement came from the Roberts's car, which was cruising beside me. Phil, Marc and Marianne were all leaning out of the window, yelling encouragement, and I reached the finish in 2 hours, 3 minutes and 7 seconds. Hamish finished in 1.55.57, Claire in 2.07.54 and Miriam Dorrity 2.09.24. We were all soundly beaten by Fred Mogaka, a Kenyan, who won the race, with the incredible time of 1.04.23! I didn't see Claire at the end of the race as Hamish's family were waiting for me and drove me home. I rang Claire that evening and the first thing she asked me was had I enjoyed the race? 'Absolutely hated it!' I replied. So had she, and we vowed never to do it again, except, like childbirth, I quickly forgot how much I had hated it and decided to prepare myself for next year's London Marathon.

The result of my carers' fatigue a few weeks prior to the Hastings Half Marathon made me search around for some help. I phoned Judy Gould at Elliot House and told her my problem. She advised me that the most important thing for Olivia to learn was her self-help skills.

Forget the academic work for the moment she counselled, Olivia needed to learn to look after herself and that should be my starting point. I made various phone calls to different departments of the NAS asking if they knew anyone who would like to help at weekends and as a result we found Maria Esteban, who worked in the NAS Croydon service, which is a day service for autistic adults. Maria came on Saturday mornings and we began with hair washing and shower lessons. Olivia would stand in the shower staring dreamily into the distance and needed constant prompting. Her long hair made the whole process take over an hour, but I explained to Maria that Olivia loved her long hair and that she did not want to cut it. After hair washing, combing and learning to use the hairdryer, she moved on to table setting. Olivia also hated to put skin cream on her body as she couldn't bear having her hands sticky. As she has chronically dry skin, this is an essential part of her bath routine, so with Maria's help, she began, little by little, to use the cream herself.

Knowing that Olivia was being taken care of for two hours every Saturday morning made a huge difference to my weekend. It meant that I could go for a run without feeling guilty, worrying the entire time that I was not with her and that she would be stimming in her bedroom while I was out. In the afternoon I took her for a bike ride and we played games, and by the evening I could relax if she were stimming again as I felt that she had been fairly well occupied for most of the day and needed her 'down time'. I am very fortunate in that I was born with a buoyant nature and am never down for long. I am always happier if I know what the problem is – aren't we all – so that I can tackle it, head on, or at least try to. Not knowing, or living with uncertainty, is a different matter altogether. In this case, the problem was greatly relieved just by having Maria one morning a week, and after a few weeks of feeling sorry for myself, it passed.

In March 2004 Johnnie was appointed Shadow Minister for Defence in the House of Lords, while remaining Opposition Spokesman for Foreign and Commonwealth Affairs and International Development. He was very pleased, as he has always been extremely interested in matters of security and defence. It was just before the Easter holidays and we went back to Davos with the Parliamentary group and found plenty of snow and, also, spring sunshine. This was the fourth time we had taken Olivia skiing, but although she had Carolyn Galeano for one year and then Tony, Carolyn's husband, for the following two years for individual lessons, her progress was small. Olivia was also much taller and heavier than when we started and I asked Tony on the first morning to tell me if she was really gaining anything from skiing. After a week, we weighed up the pros and cons. On the plus side were her being outside, breathing in the wonderful mountain air, taking exercise and being with her family on holiday. But Tony felt that she really did not benefit enough for these points to count. It was a struggle for her to put on all the awkward clothes, the woolly hat, which she hated, and the gloves, not to mention the unnaturally stiff ski boots. As Olivia was growing up, she was becoming more aware of her lack of stability and felt increasingly insecure on slippery surfaces or going on escalators. There were many times when I had had to belt back up the down escalator, as she didn't quite have the nerve to step on to it, and I had thought she was safely behind me, only to see her anxiously crying and flapping her hands at the top, with a large crowd building up behind her. Because of her sweet, relatively passive nature, she could just about endure the ski boots, the terror of the lifts, the speed (of a snail) going down hill, but Tony thought that these terrors outweighed any benefits she might gain from the experience. On our last day, when I told her that she didn't have to go skiing ever again, her pretty face lit up with a huge smile, her eyes shining with happiness. I wondered just how much she had endured to have such a strong sense of relief and felt really bad that we had put her through it. But it had been a useful experiment and at least she would be able to understand what we did, if we went again, leaving her behind in the safety and comfort of home.

During that summer, I was asked to become a patron of another new charity, the Centre for Autism and Related Disorders, run by the Institute of Psychiatry in King's College, London, which was to research the actual cause of autism. This research perfectly complemented that which was simultaneously being carried out at the Autism Research Centre, started by Simon Baron-Cohen, at Cambridge University, into the efficacy of the many alternative therapies for autistic children, thus completing the picture. At the opening ceremony for the Centre of Autism and Related Disorders, I gave a short speech and was approached by a couple afterwards who thanked me for my words of support for those who have the disorder. The lady of the couple told me that she had Asperger syndrome and felt comfortable with it, and was often distressed that she was not accepted for who she was, that her condition was always seen as something that should be controlled, or fixed. No one, she said, appreciated the good points of Asperger syndrome and people only wanted to normalise her. She was fed up with being treated like a freak and was angry that she was not allowed to be her autistic self. I listened to her carefully, bearing in mind the years I had spent trying to correct Olivia's behaviours. Had I accepted her as she was, or was it only on my terms? Acceptance is not a permanent state; I slip in and out of it depending on just how well she is doing, or how strong and positive I am feeling. I don't know if one ever arrives at complete acceptance. Inevitably there will be setbacks in her life as there are with all children and adults. Of course there is no such thing as an easy, problem-free life for any of us and in the case of disabled children and adults, times of difficulty should be met with the same sanguinity as we try to employ for non-disabled people, keeping a firm eye on the bigger picture.

CHAPTER 14

Planning for the Future

As the year rushed by and the date of the tribunal hurtled towards me, I tried to keep my eye on that bigger picture. I was still sure that an autism-specific school, such as Grateley House, was the right place for Olivia, although the tiny class of six she was currently in was the next best place. Just before Christmas in 2004, I received a letter from Kent LEA in which they offered Olivia a boarding place at Broomhill Bank School in January. She would start at the beginning of the term, boarding four nights a week in the unit, which had eight girls aged between 12 and 16, before they moved on to the 16+ unit, where they stayed for the last three years. Most special schools have a 16+ provision, as these children are not ready to leave school at 16 and go to college or start work. The job of the 16+ provision is to continue with their education, enabling them to have varied work experience and practise daily living skills, such as shopping and cooking. It is an invaluable time, during which the students build up their confidence and mature, and within a nurturing, supportive environment, begin to look at what type of employment or college course would suit them.

The offer of a boarding place for Olivia was totally unexpected. I had only two weeks to prepare her, and myself, for such a huge change. I was delighted to have this opportunity, as I had been worried about the prospect of her going straight from home to full boarding. This offered the perfect easing-in period to the next stage of full boarding, as she would be coming home every weekend, and the transfer to

Grateley House the following September would not be as much of a dramatic change for her as if she had gone there straight from living at home full time. I felt that everything was beginning to fall into place. I had visited the unit at Broomhill Bank, which was clean and cosy and in many ways far nicer than most of the expensive private schools I had visited over the years. She was to share her room with one other girl, who would only be there two nights a week, and was allowed to take in her own duvet, portable stereo (which she declined) and an agreed figure of no more than five beanie babies from her vast collection. Now we really *had* to address the hair issue. Olivia had only two weeks to learn to wash, disentangle, comb, dry and tie her hair into a ponytail before she was due to board, and I reminded her of that every morning and evening as she struggled with her comb. It was obvious that she was not going to be ready to care for her hair herself in time, and so I took the bull by the horns and took her to the hair-dressers, sweetening the pill by lunch at MacDonald's afterwards. We all loved the result. With one flurry of scissors she was transformed into a trendy teenager, looking much older with short hair. Even Olivia seemed quite pleased, as she was encouraged to admire her new hair-style in the mirror, although she still prefers to have long hair. She recently found a photograph of herself with a ponytail and walked around the kitchen hugging it to her face softly murmuring 'Ah, ah'.

The first evening I spent alone at home felt so unnatural it was almost surreal. Johnnie was in London three nights a week and I was surprised how much difference it made not having Olivia in the house. I would have expected that having only one child asleep upstairs would not have made any difference to having none, but it did, and the house felt lonely and empty, and also rather creepy. I spent the evening in the kitchen with Radio 4 on low, filling in my order forms for spring bulbs, the kitchen door firmly closed with our dogs at my feet. It wasn't until 9.30 p.m. that I realised that I hadn't had anything to eat, as there was no one there but myself to feed, and no structure to the evening. It was the first time in 24 years I had not had a child living at home and it was going to take a while to adjust. So this was what it was like to be an 'empty nester'. I had longed for some solitary space in my life, but now that I had it, I found I was floating adrift in a thick fog of silence. I opened the fridge door and grazed, then let the dogs out, locked up the house and went to bed. I lay wondering how Olivia had fared her first night at school and rang early the following morning for an update. She had been fine I was told and, within a couple of weeks, we had both slipped into this new routine. At any time that Olivia felt homesick she was asked by David Doe, her keyworker, or personal tutor, what she could do about it. The correct answer was to phone home, which she did, and we began to have long, regular chats about what DVD she was planning to watch at the weekend, and who played which part in the latest film she was looking forward to seeing. One Friday afternoon in her first term of boarding, when Olivia was collected from school by Kerryn Dicks, our lovely South African nanny who was with us for two years, she asked Kerryn: 'Remind me why I am boarding, again?' Kerryn told her that it was so she could be with people her own age, rather than just stay at home with her middle-aged mummy and her nanny. Olivia retorted 'No, Kerryn, it is so that I can become more independent!' When Kerryn related this story to me, I remarked that I thought Olivia's answer was the better of the two!

I began to relish my new freedom and watched in delight as Olivia became gradually more and more independent, learning to talk to her peers in the evening and shower by herself in the mornings, albeit with constant prompting. She settled in far more quickly and smoothly than either I or anyone at school had dared hope, with no visible signs of stress, such as an outbreak of eczema or new ticks. I kept in fairly close contact with the school, either by phone or via written messages in the home/school liaison book and was often regaled with amusing stories. On the first laundry day, Olivia was asked to remove her duvet cover and pillowcase and replace them with the clean set that was on her bed. Her reply was 'Oh no, I don't do that at home, my housekeeper does that for me!' Things had to change at home too; I had to carry over all the good work that she was learning at school.

Training for the London Marathon stepped up a few notches after Christmas. I had been running with Sonya for two hours every week during her training session as well as my weekly session with Samantha, where we concentrated on strength work using weights to counteract all the running. Sonya gave me a programme for my weekend run, to which I was to add ten minutes per week, building up to 20 miles by the beginning of April. At the end of February, Sonya left the UK, after training my brother Charlie and me for three years, to return to her native New Zealand. She handed us over to Georgie, a young, beautiful, red-headed race-winning rower, who promised to make me fast and strong in time for the dreaded marathon. My legs and feet needed to become accustomed to being pounded on tarmac, so I began to run on the road towards my friends Felix and Jane Posen's house, which is 11 miles away in Surrey. On Saturday mornings there is very little traffic on the country lanes in our part of Kent and in neighbouring Surrey. Occasionally a cyclist would pass, wheezing a breathy 'Good morning' and giving a nod in my direction, and I frequently overtook horses and their riders, which gave me a childish satisfaction, even though they were only walking. I loved watching spring emerge; it was a relief after weeks of running in snow showers and freezing sleet to see the trees daring to expose their tender shoots in our uncertain climate. The long, slender leaves that were the first sign of the bluebells that fill the woods between Frenchstreet and Crowhurst were poking through the earth and there was no one to complain at my singing at the top of my voice to a great mix of music that spanned from James Blunt to Frank Sinatra that my son Charles had downloaded for me on to my MP3. Olivia couldn't stand me singing and blocked her ears, complaining loudly that it spoilt her music for her. As I cannot sing in tune at all I sympathise with her, but find it difficult to control my exuberant spirit.

I decided that as a warm-up I would run in the Hastings Half Marathon again, using it as a test of my fitness and also as a warm-up to the real thing, following the example of the professionals. Claire Roberts, who had run with me the previous year, told me that I was completely mad, but nevertheless rang the following day to find out what time I made.

The second time at Hastings, I felt almost like an old hand. I had come prepared with my MP3 and had learnt that drinking four glasses of red wine the night before to calm my nerves and eating a banana minutes before the start were definite no-nos. Only, I couldn't figure out how to switch on the MP3. I approached three groups of young men, hoping that they would have the technological expertise required to tell me where the on/off switch was, but they were equally puzzled, until someone in the fourth group I approached took one look and said 'It's yer batteries, mate. They're dead.' It was far too late to do anything about it, and annoyed and feeling utterly incompetent, I set off. After running for about five miles or so, my eyes down, plodding along quite nicely, I ran up behind an instantly recognisable bottom that had dogged me the entire race the year before! There are over 3,300 people who take part in this race and the chances of coming across the same person twice would make interesting odds at a betting shop. But there was no mistaking that wedgie of navy blue rugby shorts almost, but definitely not, covering once bright red boxer shorts. The runner's identity was confirmed almost instantly by the same regular shouts and cheers from the crowd that I had heard every few yards last year. 'There's Paul!' and 'Hiya Paul, all right?' How could I bear it? Again we repeated our dance of the year before. I would belt past 'Paul', and then run out of steam 200 yards further down the road, only to watch him and his wedgie ploddingly overtake me. Throughout the entire 13.1 miles this 'Paul' was cheered and clapped by his adoring crowd. He must have been the most well-known and certainly the most popular runner there. As I never discovered his surname, I also never discovered which of the two of us made it over the finishing line first. I wondered if he were planning on running in the London Marathon.

I had been training quite hard and hoped that I would finish in 1 hour 50 minutes, but about two-thirds of the way round, I was overtaken by Miriam Dorrity, Olivia's gym teacher, who shouted encouragement as she flew past me. This was not a good sign, as I had beaten her the previous year and, indeed, I did not do very well, finishing in 2 hours and 13 seconds, soundly beaten by Miriam, who finished in 1.58.52, a full 1 minute and 21 seconds ahead of me. How on earth did I think I would complete the London Marathon, I wondered miserably to myself all the way home on the train. I had been dreading it for weeks, but after my dismal performance at Hastings, real fear and panic took over. Every night I dreamt about it, mostly fixating about running out of steam after two-and-a-half hours. Assaf Admoni, who used to be head of fundraising at the National Autistic Society before he moved to another charity, emailed me words of encouragement. He was also taking part in the London Marathon for the first time, and I begged him to bunk off with me after the start, go for a coffee, then take the underground to the finish, but he only laughed and told me to repeat his mantra 'I can do it! I can do it!' over and over again, as he assured me, it worked for him.

Each weekend the length of my run increased and I had to eat a huge breakfast to give me enough energy to last the course. I started with a bowl of organic oats with half a grated apple, blueberries and soya milk, then ate two boiled eggs with a slice of non-wheat bread, washed down with a large pot of tea. After so much food, I had to give myself at least 30 minutes to begin to digest it before I stepped outside with my water bottle strapped to my waist and my sports watch set at zero. In the last few weeks, as I approached Puddledock Hill, the last hill before home, my energy failed me. Ann Cairns, our neighbour who lives at the bottom of the hill, told me that during the First World War, the Royal Artillery used this hill to train their horses. Uniform buttons had been found scattered in the hedgerows and fields nearby. Puddledock Lane is steep and long and borders our farm. After running around Surrey for over two hours I just couldn't face it, and three times I telephoned home and asked Johnnie to come and collect me. The third time, I watched the car approach and saw Olivia's scowling face in the front seat, her expression thunderous. No cheery 'Hello' for me as I opened the car door and fell across the back seat in a trembling sweaty mess, begging for water, only Olivia's furious grumbling: 'Mummy, you *always* do this. It is *very annoying*. I was playing with my toys and you interrupted me.' Autism knows no empathy. And from my darling husband, an admonitory: 'I won't be able to rescue you on the day, you know. If it's that bad, why don't you pack it in now?' He hated the idea of my running the marathon and had even offered to take me on holiday if I relented. When I asked him why he was so against it, he replied that he couldn't think of doing anything worse! Was this a case of

Munchausen's syndrome by proxy? Natalya and her friend Simon were at home the same weekend he proposed this alternative to me as I crawled into the dining room looking like death, where they were all finishing lunch. 'We aren't running in the marathon, Johnnie!' they quickly remarked, to which he muttered, 'The offer is for your mother only!' How could I give up only a few weeks beforehand? It would be such a failure and I would have wasted all that time I had spent training. I *had* to do it, and do it as well as I could, since just completing the course would also make nonsense of the hard work I had put into the preparation. I had also asked around for sponsorship once more and had received over £10,000 and felt obliged to fulfil my side of the bargain. I would not be tempted; this was my 40 days in the wilderness.

Natalya and Charles said that they would come and support me, and on the clear, sunny April morning of the Marathon day, Sunday 17th, I found their handwritten notes of encouragement on each stair going down to the kitchen and all round the work tops and even in the fridge! I tried to eat as much as I could, but at 7 a.m., full of anxiety after a sleepless night, I wasn't hungry. My main concern had been how I would get to the start, as I didn't want to take the train all the way to London then fight for a place on a packed underground to get me to the station nearest to Blackheath. Johnnie offered to drive me, which was an enormous relief, as the start was only 30 minutes from Westerham. We left everyone asleep in bed and drove off in tense silence entirely generated by my fear, which became even more brittle when I saw that the slip road to the start was closed and police were waving us on, far from the point where I would have to walk to reach my start area. We managed to turn around further up the road and retrace our steps, and found a spot where other runners were being dropped off. The clock was ticking and I was still jogging towards my designated start point when the race had already begun. Running down the road towards Blackheath, I was greeted with hoots of laughter and cries of 'Ya goin' the wrong way, darlin'!' To which I shouted back 'See you again in a while!', just as Paula Radcliffe and the first six or seven élite runners whipped past. It was terribly exciting to see them so close to hand. There were only a handful of spectators in the first mile, so I had an uninterrupted view of the best in the world.

I had planned to meet up with Lucinda Brown (Hamish's sister), who was also running in aid of the NAS, but it was a hopeless task, trying to find her among the thousands of others queuing for the por-taloos and handing in their bags. Lucinda had been suffering from a badly damaged ankle and, against all advice, was determined still to take part in the marathon. I didn't mind running on my own as I had my MP3 full of energising music such as Eminem and P Diddy and I could go at my own pace. What I was worried about was the huge crowd of runners and whether there would be enough water and any food en route. The sun was out as I shuffled towards the start beside two rhinos running in aid of Tusk Force, and a mile further down the road I was still neck-to-neck with them. This was really disconcerting. If I couldn't run any faster than a man in a heavy, hot rubbery rhino head and torso, what hope was there of my completing the marathon in under four hours? For this was my goal; it would suffice if I finished in a split second under four hours, and by the time I had run 15 miles, I was on target. I began to look for Natalya and Charles as I had suggested to them that they should make for London Bridge first, then some-where in the Isle of Dogs, as I was dreading that part. It was a large loop in the middle of the race in a rather uninteresting area, where there were few spectators to cheer us on. The day was warming up and I was concerned that it would be too hot to run in the middle of the day, but despite the clear blue sky and sunshine, the air remained cool and fresh. My fear of running out of water was unfounded, since there were plenty of water stops and the crowds held out plates of boiled sweets and biscuits, which we grabbed at as we ran by. I was seriously flagging through lack of food after two-and-a-half hours when someone held out some unwrapped chocolate. It saved me. I could feel it go straight to my muscles and, if I had had the time, I would have stopped and thanked that person for giving me just what I needed. It was sur-prising that the people in the crowd mostly didn't think to unwrap their offerings as I found it was impossible to unwrap a sticky sweet while trying to keep up a reasonable speed. But I mustn't grumble, as the crowds were extremely cheerful, friendly and encouraging. This was

Britain at its best I thought, as I ran past a couple of beefy ladies in candyfloss pink tutus and silvery stars shaking from wire antennae attached to their hairbands.

Every mile or so, there was a different band playing. Near the Cutty Sark, I passed a Scottish pipe band dressed in full tartan, wearing kilts with sporrans. A little later I ran past a jazz band. There were at least two Jamaican steel drum bands, and even one school choir. Somewhere near the Isle of Dogs I ran past the famous London Pearly King and Queen with their silver staffs, beaming from underneath tricorn hats. People were dancing in the streets and children lined the pavements just wanting to touch the hands of the runners for luck. Everyone seemed to be running for someone. Most people had the names of their beloveds written on the back of their running shirts, with often a very moving epitaph below. Nearly everyone ran for their favourite charity, but during the entire 26.2 miles, I didn't see one other runner with an NAS T-shirt, which was remarkable, as there were over 100 of us. I had written 'Liz' on the licence plate shape on the top of my Thomas the Tank Engine running shirt that the NAS had given each of its particpants. I told Natalya and Charles that I would be running on the right-hand side of the road and all I could hear through my music was 'Go, Liz, go!' from the crowd in broad Cockney, but I couldn't see my children on London Bridge and so I rang Natalya on her mobile as I was coming up to the 20-mile mark. She told me that they were only half a mile ahead, one on each side of the road, and it was really wonderful to see their smiling faces, full of encouragement. Looking out for them had been a large factor in keeping me going and I couldn't resist stopping for a few moments and giving them both a kiss. As I had only the last six miles to run, I suggested that they belt to the grandstand at the finish in The Mall and I would meet them there. The last part, I was fully aware, was the real test. I had only ever run a maximum of 22 miles and had heard and read much about 'hitting the wall' after 20 miles. It seems that the human body is only capable of running 20 miles before relying on the breakdown of fat for energy as its glycogen stores will have been consumed. I had no idea how I would fare, but found myself going slower and slower, and conducting a private internal battle, mentally fighting to keep from slowing to a walk. All around me people began to walk, hobble on for a while and then walk again. When it was all over my brother Charlie asked me what I had thought about for over four hours. My answer was 'Nothing much', my mind went into some sort of meditative space and I hardly noticed my surroundings. Towards the end, running along the Embankment I deliberately did not look around me as I could judge just how long it was going to take me to finish and it seemed so far away that I might have just given up on the spot. I had expected that in the last three miles I would be filled with euphoria. The race would be coming to an end, and I would never have to do this again! But, curiously, this didn't happen. All I wanted for the last two miles was an ice-cold lager, so I fixated on that all the way to Buckingham Palace, because just around the corner from the Palace was the finishing post.

Euphoria hit me at the finish, as I stood holding my medal, having my photograph taken, as did each runner. I felt ecstatic, but mostly because it was over! Judging by my watch I had made a respectable time, although I was way over my four-hour goal. Every five miles we ran over an electric pad and our time was checked by the microchip we had had to attach to our shoes. When I checked my time the next day on the Internet, I had run slightly faster than my watch told me, in 4 hours, 23 minutes and 13 seconds. *Running Magazine* said that to be fit for my age, I should complete a marathon in a maximum time of 4 hours 15 minutes, so I was not too far from my other target. Assaf Admoni finished in 4 hours, 16 minutes and 15 seconds and Miriam Dorrity was thrilled that she had attained her goal in finishing under 4 and a half hours, in 4 hours, 25 minutes and 47 seconds (and I was secretly delighted that I had bettered her time!). She was as gracious as always and wrote me a charming note of congratulations.

I looked everywhere for Natalya and Charles, but they were nowhere to be seen. I rang Natalya, who was terribly upset that they hadn't been able to reach the finish in time to watch me come through. It had taken them more time on London transport than it had taken me to run the last six miles, so we agreed to meet at the Holiday Inn where the NAS were offering showers, food, drinks and a massage. The whole

London Marathon event had been beautifully organised and ran so smoothly that I had collected my rucksack with my warm clothes inside and also a goody bag, and was out in the street within ten minutes of finishing the race. But there wasn't an available taxi to be seen and as all Marathon runners were given free transport around London for the day, I hopped on a bus still in my sweat-soaked running clothes and trainers, my Marathon medallion swinging from a ribbon around my neck, to take me to the hotel in Piccadilly.

I met the children at the Holiday Inn and, against my better judgement, drank the longed-for lager, but only after lots of glasses of water and several cups of tea. There were many people from the NAS fundraising and public relations teams at the hotel, all offering their thanks and congratulations. Charles was thrilled to meet Alec Stewart, the famous cricketer, who was there to support the runners. I felt on such a high, the only comparable feeling being that after an operation when one is still full of anaesthetic. If this was the result of over four hours of endorphins, I was never going to experience that feeling again. After a wonderful massage, Natalya and Charles led me on my now tired and trembling legs to the underground from where we took the train back to Kent. As soon as I entered the house, I couldn't resist teasing Johnnie by telling him that I had loved the whole experience so much, I had signed up for following year! His face was predictably horrified so I had to quickly disabuse him, although I had to admit that it had been a wonderful day. And when the final cheque came in I had been able to give over £21,000 to the NAS, so it had certainly all been worth it.

At 9 a.m. on 9 May, less than a month after the London Marathon, Johnnie and I were sitting in a small meeting room in Precision House on New Bridge Street in London with our barrister, an educational psychologist and Maggi Rigg, one hour before our Special Educational Needs and Disability Tribunal was to begin. Maggi, who had been with the Hesley Group for 12 years, was a group principal for seven of the ten schools run by the Hesley Group, which had been specialising in residential education and care for young people and adults with an autistic spectrum disorder for the past 30 years. She was attending as the Hesley Group representative. In another room were Phil Barnett, the headmaster of Broomhill Bank School, and the Kent LEA team, together with their barrister. A huge file of papers sat in front of each of us, which contained our evidence. Nothing had been said to Olivia about the possibility of moving schools, as she was settled at Broomhill Bank, and if we didn't succeed in winning our tribunal, it would only have caused her months of unnecessary anxiety.

I had spent a year preparing for this day and had planned in my mind just what I hoped Olivia would gain from being in a school where autism was understood and how much this would benefit her. I had also begun to daydream about taking the occasional weekend away with Johnnie, something that we had not been able to do since the children were very small and we had a full-time, live-in nanny. It was extremely hard to explain autism to the uninitiated. How could the three people sitting on the tribunal begin to grasp how difficult life was for her, when she was so compliant? Only recently, Olivia had taken to watching a video of *The Muppets* and I had heard her laughing alongside the canned laughter in the programme. She had seemed to enjoy the humour, but then asked me, 'It's very funny, isn't it Mummy? Why?' The jokes were all social innuendo, something that was a blank sheet of paper for Olivia. At the end of the previous summer term, when she was nearly 12, I waited for her to go to the loo before we went home after Sports Day. She took ages and eventually I went into the toilets and knocked on her cubicle door, asking what was the matter. She told me that there was no toilet paper, and so she had become stuck, as she didn't know what do to. It would have been such a simple thing to call out for help and yet so enormously difficult, if you are autistic. She hated French lessons and sometimes became very upset, crying. Why? Because she was English, she explained, not French, and so why did she have to speak French? These were the types of daily problems we had to deal with and I was sure that Grateley House was better equipped and trained to do so than either me, or Broomhill Bank. Lovely though Broomhill Bank School was, it takes years of experience and training to understand the vagaries of autism and I didn't want Olivia to be the school guinea pig, while they changed their designation from

Moderate Learning Difficulties to Autism, which was the long-term plan for the school, while Kent shuffled its special schools and redesignated, or closed, many. The DFES (Department for Education and Skills) definition of a moderate learning disability is: 'A pupil will have attainments significantly below expected levels in most areas of the curriculum despite appropriate intervention. Their needs will not be able to be met by normal differentiation and the flexibility of the National Curriculum.' There is no mention of autism.

As soon as we arrived for the tribunal, however, our barrister told us that Kent LEA had offered a package of therapies, the papers for which had been promised for the Friday, but at 9.30 on that Monday morning they had only just arrived, and she needed time to read them and consider the contents. While she was doing this, we sat talking to Maggi and the educational psychologist, discussing how difficult it would be to explain to the tribunal the difference between those who understood autism and those who only thought they did. Maggi felt that while Olivia was very happy at Broomhill Bank, her autism was not being correctly addressed and that to do that she would have to go through a very uncomfortable time, but this was vital to her future. Olivia had, in Maggi's opinion, a 'learnt dependence', meaning that she was in the habit of asking someone else to do something for her, such as open a door, rather than try, or be encouraged to try, for herself and she had been treated too gently for her own good. At Grateley House, there would be a much tougher focus on dealing with everyday independence and all the issues that arose directly from autism, which ultimately would make her a much more able adult. But they were concerned that it would be difficult to persuade an inexpert tribunal that the benefits gained by sending Olivia to a school for autistic children warranted the significant fees that Grateley House commanded. For money was at the heart of the matter. If Olivia moved to Grateley House in Hampshire, Kent would be required to pay the Hesley Group her school fees, and Kent wanted to keep that money in the county, regardless of the benefits to, and needs of, the child. Grateley House had 36 students, many of whom had had to fight for their place through a tribunal.

Our barrister returned, having digested the offer from Kent LEA.

As Olivia's statement had been changed within the last year to autism, with dyspraxia and a moderate learning difficulty, with a requirement for both speech and language and occupational therapy on a weekly basis, Kent LEA had suddenly agreed to providing her with everything that she needed as set out in her Statement of Special Needs. Our difficulty was in persuading the tribunal that Grateley House offered a far superior placement and our barrister recommended that we seriously consider the offer on the table rather than risk losing everything at the tribunal. I felt sick and dizzy, and I must have looked ghastly, as Maggi told me that I looked deeply disappointed, which, indeed, I was. I could see that it was going to be an impossible task to persuade the tribunal and in a single moment all my hopes and dreams for Olivia going to Grateley House evaporated. A whole year of assessments, letters, consultations and, above all, hope, vanished as I felt the full weight of guiding, caring and planning for Olivia return once more on to my shoulders. Common sense should dictate that because autism is a life-long disability Olivia would need looking after when she left school at 19 for the next 50+ years. Couldn't the tribunal understand that the more they spent on the right type of education now, the less it would cost them in the long run? We broke for half-an-hour for a quick lunch and Johnnie advised me to bite the bullet, not a phrase I would use with Olivia I quipped, and take the advice of our barrister and accept the package that was offered. After all, we both liked and trusted everyone at Broomhill Bank, he reminded me, and wasn't the fact that it was close to home and that she was happy worth taking into consideration? An essentially non-confrontational man, Johnnie would always go for the softer option, which made him heaven to live with, but he still offered me his total support if I thought it was worth going to tribunal. But he was right; even though this was our daughter's future we were fighting for and we must do our best for her as we were her only hope, I knew that it would be almost impossible to persuade the tribunal of what I considered to be the outstanding benefits of Grateley House.

We returned to the stuffy meeting room and laid down our arms. Our barrister drew up an agreement with Kent LEA, which was legally bound to deliver all the necessary therapies that were outlined on Olivia's Statement of Special Needs and these were laid out before the tribunal panel and agreed. They then congratulated us all on reaching a compromise outside the tribunal. As a finishing touch, Phil Barnett told us all that only a few days ago he had asked Olivia what was her favourite thing about school. She paused for a moment, then answered 'Everything', to which the whole room cooed and chuckled with satisfaction at this conclusive proof that we had all come to the right decision. I looked down the long table at Maggi and raised my eyebrows in dismay. She returned my look with a sad, resigned smile and a shrug of her shoulders. That said it all. Anyone who knew anything about autism would realise that Olivia did not even understand the question. Certainly not in the way non-autistic people would assume to understand it. What did Mr Barnett mean? The question was huge. Did he mean the brief periods of peace and solitude she found in a locked toilet or the bright pink drawing pin on a pin board outside the hall? Or should she say she liked the way the dinner lady's glasses steamed up when she served hot food as it made her eyes disappear, or the shiny black stone in the corner of the playground? But Olivia was overwhelmed with too many suggestions that were too confusing and too difficult for her to process and articulate. She only had one option and it was the one he would like most to hear. So she said 'Everything' and hoped he wouldn't probe further. Most people understand so little of the complexities of autism that they are even unaware of how little they know. Wasn't I the perfect example? Only eight years before, I persuaded myself that Olivia was not really autistic, or if at all, only a little, because for me, in my ignorance, autism was *Rain Man* and nothing else. And I am fully aware that I am still a beginner and will certainly continue to learn about autism for the rest of my life.

We left the building at 4 p.m., and I felt completely wrung out, both mentally and emotionally. Phil Barnett was at the front of the building and I was grateful for his kindness and understanding as he offered me a lift to the station. He had warned me that once we went to tribunal we would be on opposite sides of the fence, but that although it could be awkward, it should not damage our good relations, which it has not. It had never been my intention to denigrate Broomhill Bank School, only to appeal for an autism-specific provision, for my deeply autistic daughter.

The result of the tribunal, and the build-up to it, had caused me to focus my mind on the possibilities for Olivia's future. Many autistic children have a good school placement and do well, learn to be partially, if not fully independent, then at the age of 19 leave school only to return home to live with their ageing parents, feeling isolated and depressed, particularly those who are academically able. I did not want this to happen to Olivia and not knowing how capable she may be in ten years' time, I began to look at local care homes with the possibility of her living in one after she leaves school.

I remembered my American friend, Josephine Shields, whose daughter Isabel, despite having Asperger syndrome, had at the age of 25 successfully applied for a place in college and, although it was on the opposite side of the USA to her mother, managed to live there alone. Olivia will continue to develop slowly and needs the possibility of going to some sort of further education college when she is much older than the normal teenager. She will need to be looked after by someone experienced with autism and I would like her to be able to have both the privacy of her own bedroom and bathroom while sharing a kitchen and dining room, as well as a sitting room, where the residents could watch television together, listen to music or sit and chat, if they wanted to. She will probably be able to cook simple meals and do her own washing and ironing and, perhaps, God willing, much, much more. But there is no crystal ball, and I can only look around for what I consider suitable now, hoping that she will not need the high level of care that she currently requires when she is an adult. I feel comfortable within myself that I am looking around for the best placement for her future, although some might think I am wasting my time, when I really have no idea at this stage of her future capabilities. Most placements are booked years ahead and I am conscious of that, not wanting Olivia to regress once her school days are over. And although her brother and sisters adore her, she should not become a burden to any of them if I can help it – a pleasure, yes, but not someone whose life lies heavily on theirs. With four sisters and a brother, I hope that between them they will be able to take her out shopping or to the cinema occasionally, and even sometimes have her stay with them for the weekend when I am gone and make sure that she does not spend her life shut in her bedroom alone, stimming. They are all such loving people that I feel sure that this will happen, as I trust them all implicitly. And what are families for, if not to support and help each other? What is life for, if not to ease the paths of those who cross ours?

Both Natalya and Olivia have taken me to places I never dreamed of; I have learnt much and met many people whom I would not have expected to meet in the ordinary course of my life. I have climbed mountains and crossed deserts, both real and emotional, and almost everything that has affected my life through them has been good and, some of it, even wonderful. Someone asked me at a talk I gave on autism in Newcastle upon Tyne to tell her 'one good thing about having an autistic child'. This mother had a son of about seven years old, with Asperger syndrome. I was taken by surprise, as I had never considered the pros and cons of this everlastingly intriguing condition. Two things sprang instantly to mind, however, the first being that autism was such an endlessly fascinating condition and the second that it was at the cutting edge of science and we were all learning about it together. But having been posed the question, I would now add that most autistic children like Olivia have no spite or meanness, and they are incapable of telling lies, cheating, bragging or stealing. They never argue with their siblings, because what their siblings do is simply of no interest to them, unless it directly affects them. Olivia is totally uncompetitive, although I know some autistic people who are deeply competitive. In fact, most of the more unattractive human characteristics are missing in autistic people and this must be acknowledged as a huge bonus. They say what they mean and they mean what they say, and there is no hidden agenda, no ulterior motive. Their frankness and honesty is as refreshing as it is so often funny, although they can be hurt by our laughter at what they say or do, without understanding the reason why we 'neurotypicals' or neurologically normal people, found it amusing.

Back at Broomhill Bank School with all the therapies in place, Olivia is making real progress. At the end of the summer term of 2005, aged nearly 13, she won her class prize for achievement. She is surrounded by staff and teachers who are doing their very best to teach her vital skills and who are all, without exception, kind and supportive. She spent the summer holidays at home in Kent, apart from one week on holiday in France, and this suited her. Annemieke Hare, a young mother who is also a primary school teacher, came three mornings a week so that I was free to write this book. She and Olivia did a project on fish, went shopping for stickers, learnt about money, crossing the road and many other practical and fun activities.

Left to her own devices, Olivia would choose to spend the whole day in a small corner of her bedroom, turning the pages of the *Dorling Kindersley Book of Dogs* (her latest craze), pointing to one dog on one page, and then pointing to another dog in the Disney book of *One Hundred and One Dalmatians*, lying open above it. Once she had reached the end of the book, she would start all over again, unless she was taken to another task. This is one of her most difficult behaviours for me to accept, as I find it soul destroying. And have I reached acceptance? Like happiness, it is often as elusive as the end of the rainbow. But I hope that over the years it will become more and more permanent, until one day I will realise that I am living most of my life in that state and that will be a good position from which to view the world. I think I have come to terms with her autism. Inevitably life will throw new difficulties, new dramas, that even with all the foresight and planning in the world will slip in and take me by surprise. It happens to everyone, so why not to an autistic person? In the meantime, I am preparing myself for the inevitable stab in the heart I will feel as the children of my contemporaries reach their milestones. There will be the passing of driving tests, university graduations, interesting careers, weddings, grandchildren, none of which I expect to celebrate with Olivia. It is the human condition to lurch from joy to despair, deluding ourselves that we are in control of our lives when we so clearly are not. For me, salvation lies in appreciating the periods of tranquillity fully conscious, sucking out each rejuvenating drop and living my life full of hope and fun, my two favourite words in the English language.

Olivia continues to have huge difficulties. During the course of past summer holidays, she told me that she sometimes forgets which is the hot tap and which is the cold. So I bought some red and blue sticky tape and marked the taps in the bath, bidet and basin, and I also put a line of tape at a fill point, on the side of the bath. Olivia still takes ages to have her bath, despite having 'Hair washing Maria', as we call her, to give her lessons every Saturday morning. I told her that I would buy a timer from the cook shop and give her seven minutes to have a bath, and that when the bell rang, it meant that she had to get out, or if she hadn't already, to wash first and then get out. The first night she took a bath with the new red and blue markers she was in the bath for over half-an-hour. Eventually, I went upstairs to see what was going on. I found her sitting in tepid water staring into space and when I asked her why she hadn't washed and got out, she told me that I had forgotten to turn on the timer! How long she would have sat in the rapidly cooling water, I will never know. Like all autistic people, she is a literal thinker and is unable to move on to the next step by herself. Anything outside the rules she has learnt or what she usually does will confuse her and can make her anxiety levels rocket. I hadn't mentioned the timer that evening, it wasn't even in the bathroom as I had forgotten all about it, but she had remembered and was sticking to the new rules. Olivia still won't open her bedroom window unless I insist, even in very hot weather, because, she says, she doesn't like draughts. She has also developed a new, odd movement with her left hand and some facial grimacing. She talks to herself quite a lot and has a distinctly wonky walk, but she is also beautiful and sweet and utterly precious. Each of these characteristics are what make up Olivia, every single bit of her is autistic and every single bit of her I love, just as she is. Just as I love Natalya, who wouldn't be the chaotic and charismatic person she is without her ADHD. Perhaps I have arrived at full acceptance, after all. As Bob Noble, a one-time chairman of the National Autistic Society and father of a severely autistic son, said to me, 'Liz, chief executives, caseworkers, teachers and carers all come and go, to them it is just a job. But for people like you and me, the parents, well, we're in this for life, aren't we?' And that's just fine with me.

Impasse

Since I have known you in your real persona
In all the long, dark years since we knew
That ever, and forever, you would not belong,
Not really belong, to us
But to others, unseen, so dear and safe to you,
Have I longed to reach you, to teach you, to touch your heart.

How many hours, days, year on year
Have I wondered: what can I do?
How can I help you to reach out to me
A fingertip touch to connect your world with mine?
The antithesis of God, we see you
But we know you are rarely with us.

How many long years have you denied me, tried to tell me
That even to come as close as a fingertip touch
Is too much, too much.
To leave you, let you breathe your own air.
Your space, your place on this earth
Is elsewhere, and will never be mine to share.

How you hate our noise, our confusion,
Our bright lights and amusements
Which you will never understand.
And yet days, months and years go by and still I long,
I long for you to join us.
And how patiently, how quietly, you wait for us to learn
To leave you in peace.

Liz Astor

Recommended Reading

Reference

Attwood, Tony, *Asperger's Syndrome* (Jessica Kingsley Publishers, 1998)

Baron-Cohen, Simon & Bolton, Patrick, *Autism, The Facts* (Oxford University Press, 1993)

Baron-Cohen, Simon, *Mind Blindness* (Massachusetts Institute of Technology, 1995)

Bérard, Guy, *Hearing Equals Behavior* (Keats Publishing Inc., 1993)

Beyer, Jannik & Gammeltoft, Lone, *Autism & Play* (Jessica Kingsley Publishers, 2000)

Csóti, Márianna, *Social Awareness Skills for Children* (Jessica Kingsley Publishers, 2001)

Culshaw, Chris & Waters, Deborah, *Headwork, Book 1* (Oxford University Press, 1984)

Cumine, Val; Leach, Julia & Stevenson, Gill, *Asperger Syndrome, A Practical Guide for Teachers* (David Fulton Publishers, 1998)

Faherty, Catherine, *What Does it Mean to Me?* (Future Horizons, 2000)

Frith, Uta, *Autism and Asperger Syndrome* (Cambridge University Press, 1991)

Frith, Uta, *Autism, Explaining the Enigma* (Blackwell, 1989)

Garcia Winner, Michelle, *Inside Out: What Makes a Person with Social Cognitive Deficits Tick* (Jessica Kingsley Publishers, 2002)

Gerland, Gunilla, *Finding Out About Asperger Syndrome, High Functioning Autism and PDD* (Jessica Kingsley Publishers, 2000)

Gray, Carol & Leigh White, Abbie, *My Social Stories Book* (Jessica Kingsley Publishers, 2002)

Happé, Francesca, *Autism, An Introduction to Psychological Theory* (UCL Press, 1994)

Harris, Sandra L. *Siblings of Children with Autism, A Guide for Families* (Woodbine, 1994)

Howlin, Patricia & Rutter, Michael, *Treatment of Autistic Children* (John Wiley & Sons, 1989)

Howlin, Patricia, Baron-Cohen, Simon & Hadwin, Julie, *Teaching Children with Autism to Mind-Read* (John Wiley & Sons, 1999)

Howlin, Patricia, *Children with Autism and Asperger Syndrome* (John Wiley & Sons, 1998)

Jordan, Rita & Powell, Stuart, *Understanding and Teaching Children with Autism* (John Wiley & Sons, 1995)

Lovaas, O. Ivar, *Teaching Developmentally Disabled Children: The ME Book* (Pro-ed, 1981)

Martin, Luanne, *Think it – Say it* (The Psychological Corporation, 1990)

Maurice, Catherine; Green, Gina & Luce, Stephen C., *Behavioral Intervention for Young Children with Autism* (Pro-ed, 1996)

McMlannahan, Lynn E. & Krantz, Patricia J., *Activity Schedules for Children with Autism, Teaching Independent Behavior* (Woodbine House, 1999)

Powell, Stuart & Jordan, Rita, *Autism and Learning* (David Fulton Publishers, 1997)

Ripley, Kate; Daines, Bob & Barrett, Jenny, *Dyspraxia, A Guide for Teachers* (David Fulton Publishers, 1997)

Vermeulen, Peter, *Autistic Thinking – This is the Title* (Jessica Kingsley Publishers, 2001)

Wing, Lorna, *The Autistic Spectrum* (Constable, 1996)

Autobiographies

Andron, Linda, *Our Journey Through High Functioning Autism & Asperger Syndrome* (Jessica Kingsley Publishers, 2001)

Claiborne Park, Clara, *Exiting Nirvana, A Daughter's Life with Autism* (Little, Brown and Company, 2001)

Delacato, Carl H. *The Ultimate Stranger* (Ann Arbor Publishers, 1984)

Fling, Echo R. *Eating an Artichoke, A Mother's Perspective on Asperger Syndrome* (Jessica Kingsley Publishers, 2000)

Gerland, Gunilla, *A Real Person, Life on the Outside* (Souvenir Press, 1997)

Grandin, Temple & Scariano, Margaret M. *Emergence, Labeled Autistic* (Warner Books, 1996)

Grandin, Temple, *Thinking in Pictures and Other Reports from My Life with Autism* (Doubleday, 1995)

Hall, Kenneth, *Asperger Syndrome, the Universe and Everything* (Jessica Kingsley Publishers, 2001)

Holliday Willey, Liane, *Pretending to be Normal* (Jessica Kingsley Publishers, 1999)

Jackson, Luke, *Freaks, Geeks & Asperger Syndrome, A User Guide to Adolescence* (Jessica Kingsley Publishers, 2002)

Johnson, Carol & Crowder, Julia, *Autism, From Tragedy to Triumph* (Brandon Books, 1994)

Lawson, Wendy, *Life Behind Glass, A Personal Account of Autism Spectrum Disorder* (Jessica Kingsley Publishers, 2000)

Maurice, Catherine, *Let Me Hear Your Voice, A Family's Triumph over Autism* (Robert Hale, 1994)

Moore, Charlotte, *George and Sam* (Penguin Viking, 2004)

O'Neill, Jasmine Lee, *Through the Eyes of Aliens* (Jessica Kingsley Publishers, 1999)

Rocha, Adriana & Jorde, Kristi, *A Child of Eternity, An Extraordinary Young Girl's Message From The World Beyond* (Judy Piatkus Publishers Ltd, 1995)

Sainsbury, Clare, *Martian in the Playground* (The Book Factory, 2000)

Schneider, Edgar, *Discovering My Autism, Apologia Pro Vita Sua (with Apologies to Cardinal Newman)* (Jessica Kingsley Publishers, 1999)

Spink, Henrietta, *Henrietta's Dream* (Hodder & Stoughton, 2004)

Stehli, Annabel, *The Sound of a Miracle, A Child's Triumph over Autism* (Fourth Estate Ltd, 1992)

Williams, Donna, *Nobody Nowhere* (Times Books, 1992)

Williams, Donna, *Somebody Somewhere* (Corgi Books, 1995)

ADHD

Barkley, Russell A., *Taking Charge of ADHD* (The Guildford Press, 1995)

Brooks, Robert & Goldstein, Sam, *Raising Resilient Children* (Contemporary Books, 2001)

Brown, Thomas, E., *Attention Deficit Disorder. The Unfocused Mind in Children & Adults* (Yale University Press, 2005)

Green, Christopher & Chee, Kit, *Understanding A.D.H.D.* (Vermilion, 1997)

Hallowell, Edward M. & Ratey, John J., *Driven to Distraction* (Touchstone, 1995)

Hartmann, Thom, *Healing ADD, Simple Exercises That Will Change Your Daily Life* (Underwood Books, 1998)

Phelan, Thomas W., *1-2-3 Magic, Folks, Guess What? This Works!* (PMI Parent Magic, Inc., 2003)

Kelly, Kate & Ramundo, Pegsy, *You Mean I'm not Lazy, Stupid or Crazy?* (Fireside, Simon & Schuster, 1996)

Munden, Alison & Arcelus, Jon, *The AD/HD Handbook* (Jessica Kingsley Publishers, 1999)

Murphy, Kevin R. & LeVert, Suzanne, *Out of the Fog* (Hyperion, 1995)

Solden, Sari, *Women with Attention Deficit Disorder* (Underwood Books, 1995)

Zeigler Dendy, Chris A., *Teenagers with ADD – A Parents' Guide* (Woodbine House, 1995)

Diet

Jackson, Luke, *A User Guide to the GF/CF Diet for Autism, Asperger Syndrome and AD/HD* (Jessica Kingsley Publishers, 2002)

Le Breton, Marilyn, *Diet Intervention and Autism* (Jessica Kingsley Publishers, 2001)

Journals/NAS Publications

Attwood, Tony, *Why Does Chris Do That?* (The National Autistic Society, 1993)

Leicester City Council and Leicestershire County Council, *Asperger Syndrome – Practical Strategies for the Classroom* (The National Autistic Society, 1998)

The International Journal of Research and Practice, *Autism, Volume 6, Number 4, December 2002* (Sage Publications, in association with The National Autistic Society)

Other

Alston, Jean & Taylor, Jane, *Handwriting Helpline* (Dextral Books, 1995)

Flowers, Toni, *Reaching the Child with Autism through Art* (Future Horizons, 1992)

Gilpin, R. Wayne, *Laughing & Loving with Autism* (Future Horizons, 1993)

Haddon, Mark, *The Curious Incident of the Dog in the Nighttime* (Jonathan Cape, 2003)

Harris, Robie H., *Let's Talk About Where Babies Come From* (Walker, 2002)

Kashman, Nancy & Mora, Janet, *An OT and SLP Team Approach* (Sensory Resources LLC, 2002)

Sacks, Oliver, *An Anthropologist on Mars* (Pan Books, 1995)

Sacks, Oliver, *The Man Who Mistook His Wife for a Hat* (Picador, 1986)

Sassoon, Rosemary, *Hand Writing – The Way to Teach It* (Leopard Learning, 1995)

Stuart-Hamilton, Ian, *An Asperger Dictionary of Everyday Expressions* (Jessica Kingsley Publishers, 2004)

Welton, Jude and Telford, Jane, *What Did You Say? What Do You Mean? An illustrated guide to understanding metaphors* (Jessica Kingsley Publishers, 2004)

Useful Addresses

Andrea Bilbow
Founder and Director
ADDISS
(The National Attention
Deficit Disorder Information
and Support Service)
10 Station Road
Mill Hill
London NW7 2JU
Tel: 020 8906 9068
Fax: 020 8959 0727
Web: www.addiss.co.uk

Afasic
(Charity for Speech
and Language Difficulties)
2nd Floor
60-62 Great Sutton Street
London EC1V 0DJ
Tel: 020 7490 9410
Fax: 020 7251 2834
Web: www.afasic.org.uk
Helpline: 0845 355 5577

Tracy Alderman
AIT (Auditory Integration
Training) Practitioner
38 Lavender Hill
Tonbridge
Kent TN9 2AT
Tel: 01732 365636

The Association of Speech
and Language Therapists
in Independent Practice
WWS
Coleheath Bottom
Speen
Princes Risborough
Buckinghamshire HP27 0SZ
Tel: 0870 241 3357
Web: www.helpwithtalking.com

Dr John McLaren Howard DSc FACN
Biolab Medical Unit
The Stone House
9 Weymouth Street
London W1W 6DB
Tel: 020 7636 5959
Fax: 020 7580 3910
Email: info@biolab.co.uk
Web: www.biolab.co.uk

British Association/College
of Occupational Therapists
106–114 Borough High Street
Southwark
London SE1 1LB
Tel: 020 7357 6480
Web: www.cot.co.uk

Mr P Barnett
Head Teacher
Broomhill Bank School
Broomhill Road
Rusthall
Tunbridge Wells
Kent TN3 0TB
Tel: 01892 510440
Fax: 01892 502460
Web: www.broomhill-bank.kent.sch.uk

Jill Christmas
Occupational Therapist
Christmas Children's Clinic
April Cottage
20 Manor Road
Rusthall
Tunbridge Wells
Kent TN4 8UE
Tel: 01892 510257
Fax: 01892 529614
Email: Christmas@FSBDial.co.uk

Sonya Clark
Personal Trainer
31 Forbes Street
Onehunga
Auckland
New Zealand
Tel: 00 64 211704485
Email: coolcatclark@hotmail.com
Web: www.orionadventure.com

Classic Tours Limited
Tramways House
377 Camden Road
London N7 0SH
Tel: 020 7619 0066
Fax: 020 7619 0077
Email: info@classictours.co.uk
Web: www.classictours.co.uk

Dianne Zaccheo (for ADHD)
The Coaching Centre
15 Holland Park Gardens
London W14 8DZ
Email: dianne@zaccheotraining.com
Web: www.zaccheotraining.com

Crick Computing
*(Easy to use computer software and
hardware such as rollerball to replace a
mouse)*
Crick House
Broaden Close
Moulton Park
Northampton NN3 6LF
Tel: 01604 671691
Fax: 01604 671692
Email: info@cricksoft.com
Web: www.cricksoft.com

The Dyspraxia Foundation
8 West Alley
Hitchin
Hertfordshire SG5 1EG
Tel: 01462 455016
Helpline: 01462 454986
Fax: 01462 455052
Email: dyspraxia@dyspraxiafoundation.
org.uk

The Fragile X Society
Rood End House
6 Stortford Road
Great Dunmow
Essex CM6 1DA
Tel: 01371 875100
Web: www.fragilex.org.uk

Grateley House School
Church Lane
Grateley
Andover SO41 8NE
Tel: 01264 889751

Helios Clinic
*(Brushing technique,cranio-
sacral osteopathy,homeopathy
and alternative therapies)*
97a Camden Road
Tunbridge Wells
Kent TN1 2QR
Tel: 01892 577690
Web: www.helios.co.uk

The Hesley Group
*(Provides services for people with
special needs)*
Brock House
Grigg Lane
Brockenhurst
Hampshire SO42 7RE
Tel: 01590 624484
Web: www.hesleygroup.co.uk

Georgina Hollings
Personal Trainer
Sports Massage Therapist
Tel: 07814 934554
Email: georginahollings@hotmail.com
Web: www.optius.co.uk

Robert J. Love
Specialist Education Lawyer
Langley Wellington Solicitors
Royal House
60 Bruton Way
Gloucester GL1 1EP
Tel: 01452 521286
Email: education@langleywellington.
co.uk
Web: www.langleywellington.co.uk

Samantha Lucas
Personal Trainer
Sports Massage Therapist
Tel: 07798 538334
Email: Samantha_personaltrainer@
yahoo.co.uk

Medic Alert Foundation
1 Bridge Wharf
156 Caledonian Road
London N1 9UU
Tel: 020 7833 3034
Fax: 020 7278 0647
Email: info@medicalert.org.uk
Web: www.medicalert.org.uk

The National Autistic Society
393 City Road
London EC1V 1NE
Tel: 020 7903 3563
Helpline: 020 7903 3525
Fax: 020 7833 9666
Email: nas@nas.org.uk
Web: www.nas.org.uk

Osteopathic Centre for Children
15a Woodbridge Street
London
EC1R 0ND
Tel: 020 7490 5511
Web: www.occ.uk.com

PEACH
(Parents for the Early Intervention of
Autism in Children)
The Brackens
London Road
Ascot
Berkshire SL5 8BE
Tel: 01344 882248
Fax: 01344 882391
Email: info@peach.org.uk
Web: www.peach.org.uk

Pembury Portage Service
Pembury Hospital
Tonbridge Road
Pembury
Tunbridge Wells
Kent TN2 4QJ
Tel: 01892 823535

Research Machines plc
(For PCs designed for education)
New Mill House
183 Milton Park
Abingdon
Oxon OX14 4SE
Tel: 01235 826000
Fax: 01235 826999
Web: www.rm.com

The Royal College of Speech & Language Therapists
2 White Hart Yard
London SE1 1NX
Tel: 020 7378 1200
Fax: 020 7403 7254
Email: postmaster@rcslt.org
Web: www.rcslt.org

SEMERC
(Computer software for all ages and special needs)
Granada Learning
The Chiswick Centre
414 Chiswick High Road
London W4 5LF
Tel: 020 8996 3333
Fax: 020 8742 8390
Web: www.semerc.com

Smart Kids UK Ltd
(Educational games and resources)
5 Station Road
Hungerford
Berkshire RG17 0DY
Tel: 01488 644644
Fax: 01488 644645
Email: sales@smartkids.co.uk
Web: www.smartkids.co.uk

Theraplay Ltd
(Special needs bicycles and more)
32 Welbeck Road
Darnley Industrial Estate
Glasgow
Scotland G53 7SD
Tel: 0141 876 9177
Fax: 0141 876 9039
Web: www.triad.com

Widget UK Ltd
(Symbols and words computer program)
PO BOX 349
Stevenage
SG1 9AD
Tel: 0845 055 0005
Fax: 0870 755 3305
Email: info@widget.co.uk

Australia
Autism Council of Australia
Web: www.autismaus.com.au

Autism Spectrum Australia
Tel: (02) 8977 8300
Fax: (02) 8977 8399
Web: www.aspect.org.au

New Zealand
Autism New Zealand
Tel: 0800 AUTISM (288476)
　　　+64 3 332 1038
Fax: +64 3 332 1024
Email: info@autismnz.org.nz
Web: www.autismnz.org.nz
Web: www.aspect.org.nz

South Africa
Autism South Africa
Tel: +27 11 486 3696
Fax: +27 11 486 2619
Email: autismsa@iafrica.com
Web: www.autismsouthafrica.org